John
Reynolds

John Reynolds with **Jason McClean**

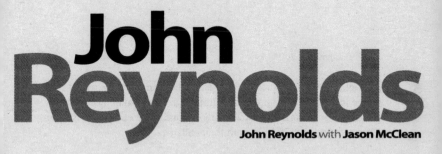

John Reynolds

John Reynolds with **Jason McClean**

THE AUTOBIOGRAPHY

Haynes Publishing

First published in hardback in September 2006
This paperback edition published in November 2008

A catalogue record for this book is available from the British Library

ISBN 978 1 84425 671 6

Library of Congress catalog card no. 2006924131

Published by Haynes Publishing,
Sparkford, Yeovil, Somerset BA22 7JJ, UK

Tel: 01963 442030 Fax: 01963 440001
Int. tel: +44 1963 442030 Int. fax: +44 1963 440001
E-mail: sales@haynes.co.uk
Website: www.haynes.co.uk

Haynes North America, Inc.,
861 Lawrence Drive, Newbury Park,
California 91320, USA

Printed and bound in England by J. H. Haynes & Co. Ltd

CONTENTS

FOREWORD

by Paul Denning

Team manager, Suzuki BSB, 1997-2004

Team manager, Suzuki Grand Prix, 2005 onwards

It's strange how things come around. I first met John Reynolds – a newly signed Suzuki factory WSB rider – in late 1995 when he came down to our Crescent Suzuki shop in Bournemouth to help launch our new showroom. Typically enough, I remember we had to almost force a pair of trick Oakley sunglasses on him as payment, John being happy to help out and seeing it as part of his job. At that time, running a race team was not even on my agenda. A lot has changed since then, and to find myself writing this foreword to JR's autobiography is a privilege and an honour.

The next time I spoke to John at any length, it cost a lot more than a pair of glasses but was the best money I've ever spent! John was the newly crowned 2001 BSB champion, and was our No 1 target to ride the prototype GSX-R1000 Superbike in 2002. As the cliché goes, the rest is history – five years on, we simply can't imagine our Suzuki BSB team without JR's partnership and influence.

The 2004 BSB season showed JR at his best, winning the championship in style, despite breaking a collarbone mid-season at Thruxton. He and I decided there and then that it wasn't going to slow us down, and that evening John travelled to Ipswich to start specialised treatment. Seven days later, heavily strapped, John won with ease in foul conditions at Brands. My job was the easy bit – to tune JR's head into believing it could be done – but only the focus, bravery and determination of a true champion was going to deliver the result.

Before I knew him, John struck me as a rather detached, serious character – maybe not a 'people' person. It's true that he was serious – serious about winning, about doing his job properly, about delivering the goods for everyone around him, on and off track. Away from work, and this has become more evident to all since his retirement, it turns out that John has a true lust for life, retains a massive passion for riding motorcycles and is fantastic company – ask anyone who has had a big night out with him! Just don't bother asking John himself as he never seems to have a clue what's happened the night before...

If it hadn't been for that horrible crash at Brands in October 2005, this book would have been delayed at least another year because, without doubt, JR would have been battling for the 2006 BSB title on our Rizla Suzuki – and possibly again in 2007. Age had no meaning to John: winning was everything. Other top riders knew how bloody good he was – world class – even if JR himself seemed to question it sometimes. John was normally modest to the point of frustration, but I do remember, at the 2003 post-season party at Donington, watching with him a re-run of the day's racing. With the help of quite a few beers, and seeing his GSX-R coming sideways out of Coppice every lap, smoke pouring off the tyre and the bike drifting inch-perfect out to the white line, JR turned to me and said, 'You know mate, if I'd started a bit younger and got the right experience on the right bikes a bit earlier, I reckon I could have been World Champion.'

John, you'd better believe it – your combination of raw ability and resolute determination to succeed is matched by very few riders. I am proud to have worked with you and even prouder to be a mate. Enjoy your new life, enjoy your family and thanks for the opportunity to have shared these thoughts with the readers of your story so far.

Paul Denning
August 2006

INTRODUCTION

The chart-topping song 'Wake Up Boo', by the Boo Radleys, reminds me of one of the happiest days of my life. It was a Sunday in August 1995 and I was in my motorhome fast asleep. My alarm radio blared into life with the Boo Radleys. It was race day at Brands Hatch World Superbikes and I was riding as a wild-card entry on a Kawasaki. I raced the best Superbike riders in the world that day – Carl Fogarty, Anthony Gobert and Troy Corser – and I gave a fair account of myself. I took fourth in the first race and third in the second.

As a wild-card at Brands Hatch on a Ducati in 2000 I took a race win – my only career WSB victory. I was very happy and spent so much time celebrating that my preparations for race two were scuppered and I ended up seventh. I didn't care though; I'd beaten the best in the world and was the happiest man alive.

Brands Hatch is my favourite circuit. It is my Mecca and if ever I lost faith or hope in racing, all I had to do was go there and ride the circuit. It has everything from flowing bends, blind crests, changes in camber and direction, to decent garages and probably the best crowd attendance of any Superbike race in the world. It always got the best out of me. I tended to finish on the podium.

And I still love it, despite the crash that not only ended my career, but nearly killed me.

After the big crash at Brands Hatch on Friday, 7 October 2005, I was terrified of my life changing. After 35 years of motorcycle racing, what was I going to do? How could I face a summer without Superbike racing? What about my friends in the paddock and the fans in the crowd? And, where was the next pay cheque going to come from? Before the crash, I'd signed a contract with Rizla Suzuki to ride the GSX-R1000 in 2006 and I'd had my mind set on winning back the British Superbike Championship for an unprecedented fourth time.

Despite the severity of my injuries – and as I began to heal – I actually started thinking that I could return to racing. But, I could see in my wife Shelley's eyes a fear for me that was deeper than my own. She had supported me every step of the way, through all the good and bad times. Without saying a word, she was telling me enough was enough, and I listened to her.

I'd crossed the finish line for the last time. But this was also the start line, and by the beginning of 2006 I'd agreed terms to work for Suzuki in a new capacity. My job was really just to be 'JR', attending British Superbike meetings as Suzuki's representative, and assisting with marketing, PR and racing plans. On top of that, businesses that had sponsored me in the past came with offers of work, and almost overnight I found myself at the start of a new career.

I was also asked to write this autobiography. To begin with I didn't think anyone would want to read it, but my family and friends thought otherwise. So this is the story of how Shelley and I chased our dreams at more than 190mph and how, by making a lot of sacrifices, we managed to beat a few of them to the chequered flag.

There are lots of people I need to thank for their support over the years and without whom my career and this book would never have happened: Mum and dad, Shelley's parents Maureen and Dave, my wife Shelley and our son Ben, David Blanchard and the Blanchard family, Vic Lamb, Barry and Chris Coxhead, Colin Wright and all the staff at Kawasaki, the Padgett family, Ben, June, Karen and Wayne Atkins, Colin Barnes, the staff at Crescent Suzuki, Paul Denning and family, Suzuki GB, the race marshals and medics, Fred Clarke and, most of all, the race fans. And to everyone else who has supported me through my career, thank you all.

Chapter 1

RIDING BEFORE WALKING

When I was growing up, football was all the rage. You couldn't walk down our street – Gloucester Avenue in Nuthall, near Nottingham – without seeing kids kicking balls against well-pounded walls, pretending they were George Best. I tried kicking a ball when I was young. I would aim straight ahead, take a run-up and boot it as hard as I could. Where it would go was anyone's guess, but you could bet your pocket money it wouldn't have gone straight. I knew from almost the first time I tried kicking a ball that I was never going to be good. But I liked football, mainly because it was a sport to be done outside, something that got me into the fresh air.

My dad, Jack, is a football fan. He was born 12 miles north of Newcastle on a farm, a child's paradise with 200 acres of land packed with animals, tractors and lots of places to find adventure. At the age of 18 months, he toddled out of the farmhouse and straight into a tank of sheep dip – the lid had been left off by a lazy farm hand. He was found face down in the dip, full of chemicals and waste from the sheep. Another minute and he would have been dead. He pulled through, though, and became a keen footballer at school. Since then he has always supported Newcastle, a team he would go and watch with his dad at every opportunity. Personally I support Nottingham Forest, my local club, but I guess my first introduction to football was through dad. After watching me kick a ball he knew as well as I did that I'd never be much good.

I was a centre back for my primary school team. The game would start and red-faced, out-of-breath teachers would scream advice at me from the sidelines: 'Go forward, go back, go to the wings.' I ended up ignoring the lot of them. The idea is to put the ball in the back of the net as far as I can tell. So that's what I tried to do. I chased the ball wherever it went and kicked it in the general direction of the opposition net whenever I got the chance. If truth be told I was lost on the pitch. I didn't know where to stand or what to do, so I did my own thing. I had no instinct for the game.

Cricket was similar. The first time I played I was out for a duck and left scratching my head about what was going on. I tried golf when I was a bit older but it bored the life out of me right from the first tee – which makes me laugh now as I'm a keen player and enjoy the game. Table tennis was all right, and I could play a decent game of chess. I even fancied rugby: the thought of jumping on people and hitting them hard appealed to my aggressive nature but was at odds with my physical stature.

For many years my mum, Win, and my dad worried that I was a bit small. Being on the slight side wasn't conducive to rugby and I got beaten up a lot – and there's only so much of that you can take. Every six months my parents would bring me into the kitchen and mark my height on the door frame. For a long time I stayed at the same height, but thankfully I grew up to be five foot six inches. That's not a towering figure by any means, but in later life it proved to be an asset. At 10-stone, fully wet, I was strong enough to muscle a Superbike or GP racer without any problems, yet small enough to minimise the rider's weight penalty on acceleration and performance.

My first experience on wheels was completely different from all the other sports I tried. Dad built me a three-wheeler, with two wheels at the front and one at the rear. I don't know when he fitted in the time to make it, but he did. He gave it to me when I was 10 months old. I sometimes think dad must have had an inkling that I would like bikes.

Mum and dad both say I took to the three-wheeler like a duck to water. I would fly around the house and, after a short period of crashing into things, I was soon able to negotiate the various tables and chairs with ease. Mum had always thought the trouble would start when I began to walk, but I was travelling around on the trike a lot faster than walking, long before I could walk!

Dad has now built a three-wheeler for my son Ben. It's almost identical to the one I had and I'm half tempted to have a go on it. I'm a bit big now, though, and if I broke it Ben might get a bit grumpy with me...

When I was about a year old, mum and dad took me to a motorcycle trial in Derbyshire. Of course the trike had to go with us, and as soon as dad had unloaded it from the van I was on it rolling down a great big quarry hill. I can't remember the incident, but spectators and marshals started running and screaming, sure I was going to kill myself. I made it down without a scratch, but mum had to be treated for shock.

For my second birthday I had a three-wheeler with pedals and brakes. Toys and board games held no interest for me. I wanted something with wheels.

When I was three my dad bought me a new three-wheeler. This one had two wheels at the back for driving and one at the front for steering. I loved that trike. It was also the first trike I was allowed to ride on the street.

Gloucester Avenue was a cul-de-sac and in the late 1960s there were fewer cars around than today, so it was pretty normal to allow your children to play in the street. The three-wheeler represented my first real freedom and I was glued to it in my spare time. I perfected riding it on two wheels and, once I got bored with that, moved on to going around the cul-de-sac, which I discovered was joined in one big circuit by the pavement. It became my race track and I'd pedal my heart out, taking the corners far faster than mum, dad or the neighbours would have liked.

Unlike my later experiences with football, cricket and rugby, there was a difference when I was riding that little three-wheeler that I recognised even at the age of four or five. I was good on it, I enjoyed it more than anything else, and I knew naturally what to do, whether it was a wheelie, riding on two wheels, braking or hitting an apex.

I can only put this down to instinct because I was too young to make objective choices. Days after being let outside and establishing my first race circuit, I'd worked out the perfect race lines. Even if I walked round the same pavement today, with a professional racer's eye, I couldn't improve on the lines I used to ride.

Mum and dad enjoyed watching motorcycle racing and would take me along to Mallory Park, which I first visited when I was six months old. I enjoyed those days and the first thing I took away from the meetings was the name Gerard's, the 120mph, 180-degree right-hander there. In my child's wisdom I named the fast left-hander in our cul-de-sac Gerard's in honour of the only circuit I knew.

After 'my' Gerard's you'd sweep uphill between a telegraph pole and water main. That was a critical corner for a good lap because you were pedalling hard and needed to hit the apex just right to carry speed up the pavement. The fact that you were so close to the pole and water main just added danger and focused your mind on the need to be inch perfect. I completed that circuit so many times that I'm surprised I didn't wear a groove in the pavement.

I had a lap record that no-one could match. All of my friends – Gary Straw, Ian Foster, Mark Smart and Peter Hanson – tried but never beat it. Even the boys a couple of years older than me couldn't touch it, and the older and stronger I grew, the faster I went.

Then one day during the summer holidays my dad told me not to ride my three-wheeler because the brakes were broken. I was nearly five and bored silly – all I wanted to do was have a crack at my lap record. If I could nail every corner as fast as possible, then I fancied I could do it. The circuit went up and down quite steeply, and on this particular day I decided that perhaps I could go faster without brakes. If I didn't use them, I thought I might be able knock a couple of seconds off my time.

My first big crash happened that day.

A critical part of the circuit was a right-hander downhill double apex. Our street started off on a steady downhill gradient but then got steeper just as you went into that corner. To go as quickly as possible you'd dab the brakes just as you entered the corner to make sure you hit the first apex, and that would set you up perfectly to hold the line for the second apex. Even on the little three-wheeler I'd be doing around 20mph on a good run, so it was important to be very precise or it could all go wrong.

I set off with fire in my belly and somewhere deep down inside I knew I couldn't take that corner without dabbing the brakes, but I was determined to try. Was it stupidity or determination? I like to think the latter, but suspect it was the former.

I always had an understanding of the trike. I knew its limits. The chassis and grip were immense compared with the engine – which was me. Basically I could pedal as hard as possible and it would remain in control. This lap without brakes was my first test of the trike's limits. It was never designed to go above 10mph, but here I was at twice that speed and on the point of being too big to ride it. I dared it to go faster than it could and had the pride to think I could save it even if things went wrong.

I tore down the hill and just at the normal braking point I realised there wasn't a hope of making the first apex – I was going to crash. People talk about moments of crisis and everything going into slow motion. For me that didn't happen then, and never has since. When I've crashed during my career, it has normally been at very high speed – and that's exactly the reason for the crash. If you're doing 140mph and something goes wrong, you don't have time to react or correct it and therefore you crash.

On my trike I had a choice: to make the corner, which would certainly have ended up planting me into a brick garden wall, or to go straight down the long, steep driveway of number 35. I chose the driveway and it gave me a couple more seconds to think as the bike gathered even more speed. At the end of the drive there was a garage and a four-foot gap to the house. Luckily the gap was open and led directly to the back garden. I aimed for it, not knowing where the journey was going to end, terrified and exhilarated all at once. I scraped through the gap and found there was a two-foot drop to the back garden, which itself was sloping downhill. I landed hard and out of control, hanging on as best as I could. Nearly three-quarters of the way down the garden, still out of control, I clocked another drop, a three-foot one this time, before the garden sloped even more steeply down to a brook. I tried to lay the bike down before reaching this drop – no mean feat on a three-wheeler – and flew off the edge, the trike going straight into the water while I bounced and tumbled after it, ending up on my backside soaking wet and stunned. I got up and found I was completely unhurt – I hadn't even scraped my knee. I picked up the trike, checked that no-one in the house had seen me, and ran out of the garden and up the driveway.

I kept playing on the trike for a while longer that day but I didn't try for the lap record again. Eventually when I'd dried out I went home, stowed the trike and pretended nothing had happened. I'd been told the brakes weren't working and knew I needed them, but I went on regardless. If I'd told mum or dad I'd have received a well-deserved rollicking.

I grew out of the trike and my parents bought me a two-wheeler from another lad on the avenue. It was a little big for me but I'd had my eye on it for ages as the next best thing I could ever own and was thrilled with it. I used stabilisers but only needed them for a couple of days, while going up and down our driveway getting used to the bigger wheels and taller gearing. For my first time on it dad set me off, the stabilisers working hard as I went down the drive. I hadn't gone very far before I buried myself into next door's wall. I didn't care, I was straight back up and trying again. I could see the potential for speed and couldn't wait to master it.

It was a proper push bike and I loved it. It represented freedom. As soon as I was able, I was flying round my street circuit setting new lap records almost on a daily basis. My friends would follow round on their bikes and we'd all race each other when we weren't playing football. No-one ever bettered me in a race round the circuit. I still hold the lap record from when I was about five years old and I don't think I could beat it today at 43.

I never liked school and on my first day I ran home and mum had to take me back on her scooter. It was a 90cc Honda and I went everywhere sitting behind her on the padded seat and loved it. She would say 'Hold tight, John' and then rev it up to full throttle. I didn't enjoy holidays much either – it was always raining or cold when we went away. One year we went to Pendine Sands in South Wales and all I wanted to do was go to an old scrapyard and pretend to drive the cars dumped there.

In rugby, football and cricket I may have been an also-ran, but on the bike I was the one everyone tried to beat. If ever anyone came close I just tried harder and beat them. I wasn't the strongest but I was the fittest and I knew how to take a corner and hold maximum speed through it. I braked later than everyone else and was already a couple of miles per hour faster on the exit without turning a pedal.

We also used to play on our bikes with the aim of knocking each other off. I was supreme at that game as well. Being on two wheels leveled the playing field for me. No longer was I smaller or weaker or slower. I learned a lot of bike-control skills playing that game and knocking other kids off their bikes. I could dart in at an impossible angle, deliver a swift boot to a backside or wheel, and be out of reach in seconds. It was great fun.

As I grew up my heroes weren't George Best or Bobby Charlton, who all my friends worshipped. My heroes were Barry Sheene and Roger de Costa. Barry was popular at the time, the fastest person on two wheels, and I idolised him. I hadn't a clue he was a good-looking lad with a hard partying attitude. All I knew was that he was the best on a bike and I wanted to be like him. Roger was the same in motocross and I fancied myself being him as well, although Barry always edged ahead in my list of favourites.

Dad had tried his hand at racing when he was younger. He left school at 14 and took an apprenticeship at a Bedford lorry agency in Morpeth. He then joined the RAF as an engine fitter and after further training worked on aircraft and high-speed air and sea rescue launches, which at that time were fitted with three aero engines and could exceed 40 knots. After spending four years working abroad, he returned to employment in a garage but left shortly afterwards to join the National Coal Board, where the pay was better.

It was at about this time that he tried sand racing before graduating to motocross and then road racing. He had just married my mum and money was tight as he got into the sport. That was when he had a crash at Cadwell Park – he bust his knee and lost two weeks' wages, ending his racing career there and then.

Bike riding is in the Reynolds family blood. Dad's younger brother, Tom, was a brilliant trials and motocross rider, winning the Scottish Championship three times riding factory Dots. Dad's pride and joy remains his 1000cc Ariel Square Four that he bought new and still rides today, with nearly 100,000 miles on the clock. He converted the undamped plunger sprung suspension to swinging arm with Girling dampers. He has been riding motorbikes since he was 14, when he and grandad used to visit the Newcastle footie matches in 'toon'.

To get to the matches, it was a mile and half walk from the farm where they lived to the Great North Road, and then a bus journey. They had a Triumph sidecar outfit, so dad hatched a plot where grandad would drive it to the bus stop and then he would ride it back to the farm. All went well until dad turned a corner and came face to face with PC Milburn, the cop from the next village. Instead of getting a clip round the ear as was the custom, dad and grandad both ended up in court with fines.

I loved my days out watching bike racing as a child but I didn't aspire to race a motorcycle even though I was completely bike crazy. Watching them fly round at 100mph was just too distant and for a seven-year-old it wasn't even on the radar as a possibility.

My mum and dad were always working. Dad was always on the night shifts, taking the extra hours when they came along. Mum was a clerical worker for as long as I can remember. She may have been part-time for a while after my birth, but otherwise she was always full-time. They wanted to own their house and worked furiously to achieve their dream. It was a good home, detached with three bedrooms, everything honestly earned and paid for. That work ethic was something that thankfully stuck with me and I'm sure it was a key to my success in years to come. I respected the ability and determination to work and the sense of achievement it brought. I understood the sacrifices required to earn something worthwhile. In my young eyes, road racing and motorbikes were beyond our means.

In no small measure I think I was a reason mum and dad worked so much. I always wanted bikes and was hard on them because I used them so much. Whether it was new tyres, brake blocks or a chain, there was always something and as I grew those appetites accelerated and cost money. They tried me on all sorts of sports and hobbies and denied me nothing. When I wanted to try football they bought me the ball, strip and boots. After that it was a cricket bat. I was an expensive child to run.

I was also a mischievous child and that was another source of expense. My sense of humour was always on the edge. I knew when I was walking a fine line with the rules and enjoyed skirting with the danger of being caught. I guess that's how I felt when I rode my trike with broken brakes even though dad told me not to.

On another occasion, practising cricket with the school team, another boy came and stood only four feet from me while I was batting. I rarely managed to hit the ball but I can remember looking at him and thinking how incredibly stupid he was to stand there.

My mischievous nature took over. It was wrong to aim at the other players but I was determined to hit him and prove just how daft he was. I deliberately aimed for him and for once I actually succeeded in putting a ball where I wanted it to go. I knocked his front teeth out. The ball smacked into his face and he fell like a sack of spuds. Very quickly I realised I'd stepped across the line and regretted it, and once I saw the blood I was genuinely sorry. All I wanted to do was prove how stupid he was, not hurt him. As it turned out, though, standing that close is part of the game of cricket and I didn't even get a telling-off. Strange game!

My luck, however, didn't hold the next time I felt up for trouble. My next-door neighbour was Peter Hanson, who was two years older than me. We were good friends and one day during holidays we were both in my driveway thoroughly bored, playfully chucking stones at each other. His parents' house had a huge eight-foot-square window and, out of nowhere, something gripped me.

'Pete, I'm going to smash that window,' I said.

There was a moment of silence and we both smiled at each other, neither of us believing I would do it. I was on the edge again and loved the feeling of risk.

'You wouldn't dare,' he said, shocked.

'Watch,' I said.

Right below the window was a wall capped with coping stone angled at 45 degrees. I took careful aim at the wall about a foot below the window. I wanted to fool him into thinking I'd dare do it but I didn't actually want to smash the glass. I needed to strike the wall close enough to make it look credible and scare him, but far enough away that there'd be no chance of breaking it.

I threw a bit harder than I meant – perhaps it was the excitement lending me strength. The rock hit the coping stone, which absorbed most of the energy but then sent it into the window and put a huge crack in the glass. We both stared at the window, mouths open. My heart was racing and I was breathing fast with excitement and a sudden sense of danger. I knew I was going to be fingered for this one, but urged Pete not to tell his parents.

I went inside and sat down in front of the telly, frantically thinking of excuses. It wasn't long before the doorbell rang. My heart was pounding as mum answered. It was Pete's mum. A minute later the door shut and mum came into the living room. All hell broke loose and for the first time I was collared properly – there was no escape. Mum and dad had to pay for that window, and it wouldn't have been cheap. I learned a lesson that day, but it wasn't that I shouldn't live on the edge of danger and excitement; it was that I mustn't ever again do anything like that so close to home or be stupid enough to get caught.

My mischievous ways continued and I might have ended up in real trouble if I hadn't found bikes. I ran through other people's back gardens with my friends, jumping fences and seeing how far we could get without being spotted. I rang doorbells and ran away. Occasionally I brawled with other kids, but being small I invariably ended up taking a beating. I even enjoyed jumping through a neighbour's conifer trees and flower beds when no-one was looking. That's all pretty bad behaviour but certainly not serious enough to be sent to borstal, which I was often threatened with by my parents, who were always fighting to keep me in check. Now I'm the grumpy man on the receiving end of children's mischief. If I ever caught any kid in our street destroying our rose bushes there'd be hell to pay.

By the time I was ten years old I had a new bicycle and was undisputed king of the race track. I was looking for new challenges and one lazy afternoon, lying in the sunshine with my mates on our driveway, I came up with an idea. I stood up and told them I needed volunteers. Peter Hanson was always game and he agreed, and then a few of the others asked what I was going to do. I told them I was going to set a world record for jumping people. Evel Knievel was a big hero of mine at about this time. He was always on the news, jumping buses and daft things, and I loved his daring. I was going to be Evel Knievel.

We rummaged in the garage and found the four-foot table we used for picnics at Mallory Park. With just two of its legs screwed in, it gave me a perfect ramp with a steep lip about 18 inches off the ground. Our driveway was on a slight downhill slope so we placed the jump at the bottom and I bombed down the drive on my bike, hit the jump and landed bang in the middle of the road. The first jump was on pure adrenalin and instantly I was addicted to the buzz. I guess I was what people would call today an 'adrenalin junkie'. A couple of my mates tried it on their bikes but no-one could touch the lengths I was reaching.

After a while we had a decent crowd trying the jumps and I declared that now was the time for the world record for jumping people. There were a few girls who agreed to lie next to the ramp and let me jump over them. I got three of them lying down and then took the bike to the top of the drive. With the excitement driving me on, I leaped further than before and easily cleared the girls. In fact, there was so much room to spare that I immediately asked for another volunteer. Four, five, six... I was flying over my friends with ease and was on top of the world. I got to 12 people lying on the ground and cleared them as well, but only just. I needed one more volunteer and Peter Hanson was the faithful friend who agreed to do it, lying down as the 13th person.

This time I rode up the driveway and took a U-turn at the top as fast as I could so that I'd be starting my run with a bit more speed. I put all of my strength into the pedals and flew off the ramp. Much to Peter's relief I cleared him with inches to spare and a great cheer went up. I was a hero that day. My mates ranked me alongside Evel Knievel and I loved the feeling. I was enjoying myself doing what was natural and was simply untouchable.

There were a couple of fields nearby where we would relax on the grass during the holidays. That summer of the jumping contest, builders started to develop part of this area and all of a sudden we had exciting new props to play with. A discarded 45-gallon drum and a long scaffold plank made a good ramp for jumps. At first we put the barrel on its side and all jumped over it, laughing. Then we stuck it on its end to make a jump that must have been nearly three feet high. That didn't daunt me though: I was the champion jumper and was determined to keep the title. I swept up the ramp, took off, seemed to be in the air for ever and landed heavily, bending the handlebars on my bike completely out of shape before falling over in the grass. I loved the exhilaration.

My natural ability in this jumping contest was coupled with my determination never to be beaten. Later in life I'm sure this combination played a big part in taking me to six British Championships.

Is talent for riding a bike something that you're born with or do you learn it? For me it was a simple case of being born with an instinctive ability to ride. Maybe I have good balance and my brain works better when things are going very fast – does that fit the definition of talent? I firmly believe we're all born with various talents, but some of them we never realise or never get to use. Sometimes I wonder what my life would have been like if I'd been born 500 years ago, when there were no bikes.

In almost every way my talent became my job, and I count myself lucky that it turned out like this. I love what I do and, despite the effort I have to invest in it, for me it isn't actually work in the sense of normal paid employment. It's doing your hobby and getting paid for it – a winner every time in my book. If you have a talent that you enjoy, then pursue it – and if you can earn a living from it then you'll be one of the happiest people alive.

One perfect summer's day, when I was seven, my mum and dad took me to a funfair at Wollaton Park, in Nottingham. When we got there I was bursting with excitement. There were rides and stalls, clowns and dodgems – everything I could have wished for. As we got out of the car, we could hear distant motorbike engines and we all caught the distinctive smell of Castrol race oil and grass dust on the breeze. To this day I love that smell – it embodies everything good about our sport and is quintessentially motorbike racing. A voice over the Tannoy said that a grass-track demonstration race was about to start so we went over to watch.

What I saw that day changed my life forever and set me on a path towards becoming a future champion. Men were climbing aboard their bikes, gunning them into life and getting ready to race in front of a decent weekend crowd. But that wasn't what changed the course of my life, as I'd seen men racing before at Mallory Park. Beyond them, however, I could see kids of my own age on mini-scramblers, fully kitted out and taking part in their own races.

My jaw dropped. As the men took off in their race, all I could do was crane my neck and watch those kids on their bikes. With mum and dad's hands in mine, I dragged them round to the scene and drank it in with my very being. It was like a button inside me had been pressed. Until now the idea of riding a motorbike had seemed impossible. All of a sudden it was possible and a whole new world unfolded in front of my eyes. I walked around the bikes and took in every detail. I watched the riders in awe and reverence.

Even before we started the drive home I was already nagging my mum and dad for a motorbike, and thereafter I'd beg daily for one. I had a very serious itch that consumed me and only a scrambler was going to scratch it. You couldn't buy an off-the-shelf kid's scrambler in those days. All of the bikes were made to measure by specialists or enthusiastic fathers with time on their hands. I was asking a lot from my parents.

One day about a year later, I was kicking a ball in the back garden when something behind the garage caught my eye. I walked over, lifted a cover and found a little petrol tank. I scooped it up and ran into the house with it, my heart beating like a pneumatic hammer. Mum and dad were in the kitchen sitting down. I looked my dad straight in the eye and he smiled. He exchanged a look with mum and that was all I needed – I knew he was building me a little scrambler and I was euphoric.

Dad is the methodical type, always planning and working things out. In later life he told me that he knew I was something special on a bike from the moment he'd seen me on my little three-wheeler. That day at Wollaton Park, both he and mum couldn't fail to notice my enthusiasm and they decided to see what they could do. In typical fashion, they said nothing as dad didn't want to promise anything in case he couldn't deliver.

Using a Honda C50 as a donor, he built me my first motorcycle, having planned everything he needed and bought parts as and when money allowed. This was the little motocross-style bike I was going to learn on. He would work on it in the afternoons, taking care not to leave any clues that I might pick up on. By the time I spotted the petrol tank, though, the project was coming to fruition. He'd had to remove the tank in order to modify the chassis and fit a lower seat so that I could reach the floor.

At the age of seven I knew exactly what I wanted to do in life – ride my motorbike and be the best. I wanted to be the next Barry Sheene.

I'm grateful to my parents for the opportunities they gave me. They're hard-working, salt-of-the-earth people who simply wanted to see their son happy. I'm sure they didn't spoil me, something that might have been easy to do as I was an only child. Instead, they recognised what I liked and encouraged me, but without putting me under any pressure. Winning wasn't important to them. Enjoyment and happiness were all that mattered. For me, though, it was very different, even at that age. Enjoyment, happiness and winning were all linked together.

All the pressure to beat my lap records and never be bettered on a bicycle came from within. I was naturally good at riding a bike but I wanted to become unbeatable – nothing else mattered. I'd have sacrificed everything to retain my lap record or jump one more person than anyone else. I could muster an instinctive determination to be best on a bike that was almost frightening to my parents and friends. In no other aspect of life was I as passionate.

Once dad had built me my first scrambler, it was only a matter of time before I left the cul-de-sac and raced against other kids, and that started a whole new chapter in my life.

Chapter 2

BECOMING BRITISH CHAMPION AND MEETING SHELLEY

The first thing I learned as a young boy who had the privilege to race motorbikes was to be careful what I said to my friends. For an enthusiastic seven-year-old that wasn't easy, but it's a maxim I've stuck to ever since.

Bikes were all the rage in the mid-1970s and Barry Sheene was coming to his peak. Every kid wanted to be a motorcycle hero. I was the lucky one in our school who got the chance because dad built me a motorbike. Other children who didn't have the same opportunities could easily have been jealous and hated me for it. I was never shy about what I enjoyed doing but I was always careful not to rub anyone's nose in it.

If I'd had a brother or sister, there's no way my working-class parents could have afforded to build me a scrambler and fuel my desire to go racing. A little sister might have been into horses or dolls' houses or – most expensive of all – boys. All that would have cost a fortune and little JR would have had to make do with his push bike. I'm not at all sure if I would ever have tried motorcycle racing. That thought sends a shiver down my spine and just makes me more thankful for the support my parents gave me.

Looking back with hindsight, I also wonder just how talented a rider I really was as a child. If only one in a thousand kids in my age group got the chance to try racing a motorcycle, then that leaves 999 who never had the opportunity. How many of them could have taken to the sport and succeeded? Would I have been a champion if these kids had been able to compete against me?

For every JR who has realised his dreams, there are probably hundreds of would-be champions who never got the opportunity to ride.

Imagine if motorcycling offered the same opportunity to take part as football. In England almost every child, boy or girl, will kick a ball early in life. Football is accessible for all classes, commands a huge following of fans, and is played in every school.

But that ease of access makes the competition much stiffer. If you're a good footballer, chances are you'll remain a good footballer and never get the chance to turn professional, despite the hundreds of scouts who attend school matches every weekend searching for talent. Just being good isn't enough – you need to be very special to get noticed. After that you need to be exceptional just to get a start in a team, and then you need to work your way up. When the pool of talent isn't one in a thousand, but open to everyone, then the competition is much hotter.

I'd love motorcycling to be as accessible as football. The standards would go sky-high and I think the sport would start to receive the following it rightly deserves. I also wonder if I would still have been a champion if I'd had to face such competition. I like to think I still would have raced and won, but I'm not proud and admit that may just be conceit.

Plenty of my friends at school thought motorbikes were cool and would have given their right arms to have the same opportunities as me. Even as a seven-year-old, I was conscious not to alienate them. I would enthuse with them but never boast or brag. I respected them and I think that kept me sane as a child. Instead of being the spoilt little kid who might receive a punch from a jealous rival, I'd be asked how I got on at the races or, if I was practising that night, could they come and watch?

When my dad had finished my little motocross-style bike, in the late summer of 1970, we took it to Annesley, between Nottingham and Mansfield. Between the coal mine and a golf course was a bit of waste land with a triangle worn in the ground where people would walk or bicycles would chew up the grass. It was only about 100 metres the whole way around, and along the middle straight was a slight dip, a step down that went along for a bit at a lower level and then up again.

It was the most exciting day of my life and I couldn't wait to get going. We unloaded the bike and dad explained that it had a three-speed gearbox with an automatic clutch. I was fine with that as it meant you could pre-select one of three gears when the bike was stationary – and besides I had enough to concentrate on just staying upright.

I toddled off for my first lap. It was shaky. Throttle control was the first thing I needed to learn. Until then I had been using pedal power and this was very different.

Wobbling from side to side, I approached the dip and took it slower than walking speed. I made it through, just, and completed my first lap to roars of laughter from the groups of kids who'd gathered around the field. I nearly died of embarrassment.

I completed a few more laps, gathering experience, confidence and speed – in that order. I was soon opening the throttle further and going round the triangle at a fair jogging pace. When I stopped, I was exhilarated and excited. Dad smiled, fiddled with something on the bike and told me to try again. I took a long drink of orange juice and leaped back on the bike.

As I pulled away again, it felt instantly faster. I approached the first corner, went through it as fast as I dared and then opened the throttle a little further than before – not much, maybe five per cent more. The bike jumped forward like it had been booted up the rear, and suddenly I was going nearly twice as fast as on previous laps. I didn't have time to react before I arrived at the little step in the circuit far faster than previously, just hanging on rather than controlling the bike. It leaped down, bottomed out its tiny amount of suspension and then ricocheted up the other step. I clung on for dear life, my legs flailing about. It took every ounce of fear-fuelled effort for me to regain some degree of control. I was catapulted towards the next corner, but managed to get my feet back on the footrests and was able to brake slightly before charging through the corner. Finally I rolled to a halt, tears in my eyes, heart beating at 10,000rpm.

Dad ran across and took the bike from me as I stopped. I went ballistic and started shouting at him, shaking with terror. What had happened? Why had it gone so fast? He'd broken it! I couldn't ride that fast! When I calmed down from my tantrum long enough to look at my dad, he was smiling. He explained that he'd switched to second gear without telling me. Five minutes later I was back on the bike, eyes dry and getting to grips with second gear, which seemed scary at the time, although it could scarcely have been more than 12-15mph.

I went home exhausted and dreaming of shifting into third gear and going faster. It wasn't many weeks later that I'd mastered third gear and could zoom round the track, taking the dip in my stride, adjusting the attitude of the bike and the throttle precisely for the fastest in-out approach. One afternoon after practising, sweating, red-faced and gulping down juice, I saw dad looking at me with his knowing smile. He said he thought I was doing really well on the bike. How would I like to go and watch a schoolboy motocross race?

A week later we visited a YMSA (Youth Motorcycle Sporting Association) event at Norwood, near Mansfield. Mum came along as well and we had a picnic. Until then I'd thought the excitement of having my own bike couldn't be beaten, but I was wrong. The racing showed me a whole new world and I wanted to be part of it.

They watched me all day at the race meeting and decided that my interest wasn't just a fad. I'd followed every race with rapture, stared at the bikes, reverently touched handlebars when owners weren't looking, and been silent as I drank in the whole experience. I wasn't faking it and they asked if I'd like dad to build me a proper race bike. While practising at Annesley he'd secretly timed me around the track and was convinced I showed promise.

I was head-over-heels happy and didn't sleep that night with excitement. I wanted the bike the next day, of course, but dad had yet to build it and that took much longer than I wanted. I kept racing my bicycle around the cul-de-sac and rode the little Honda in third gear at Annesley, pretending to myself I was in a race against a great rival and always winning at the last gasp.

I also had to go to school, of course, enduring maths and English lessons that seemed to have absolutely no bearing on what I wanted to do in life. To me, school simply wasted time. It interfered with what I really wanted to do – ride bikes. I think most kids feel the same at that age, whether it's football, computer games or just hanging around street corners with skateboards. With me though, it was close to a physical pain and I couldn't wait to get out of the classroom and back on two wheels.

Dad worked furiously to build my first racer during the winter of 1970-71. He took a Suzuki 80cc two-stroke road bike, lowered the seat, binned the road tyres and fitted off-road knobblies. To reduce weight and do away with the original tank, he cut the beam frame into three parts, inserted plates and welded everything up, forming a 1-litre compartment for petrol. It was a massive commitment from my parents to buy and build this bike, but as dad was in the garage, mum was happily looking forward to days at tracks watching her son race.

My first race bike was ready for me to try on my eighth birthday – 27th June 1971. We took it to Annesley and dad taught me how to use the clutch and gears. As the bike was much faster, we needed more space and found a field nearby. We made our own circuit and it included a steep six-foot climb that peaked and then dropped away, forming a natural table-top jump.

For weeks I practised while dad kept the stopwatch on me and mentally logged my progress. All the hopes he'd harboured about me becoming a professional footballer were now transferring to motorcycling. Because of his own motorcycling experience, he knew I was showing more than just determination and enjoyment – he could see talent coming through.

The table-top on that course used to confound me. I'd race up to it and then come off the throttle and roll over the top, both wheels firmly planted on the ground. I could sense the bike had the ability to go much faster and jump, but I was frightened as I'd never jumped a motorcycle before. One day I decided I was going to bite the bullet and go for it. My courage was growing just as fast as my bike skills. I roared up to the ramp as fast as I dared – my front wheel lifted a couple of inches while the rear stayed planted. I flew back to dad demanding to know if he'd seen my jump and he laughed and told me to do it again. It wasn't long before both wheels were airborne and I was practising a new skill on my bike.

The knobbly motocross tyres gave plenty of grip on the loose mud surface, and as I completed hundreds of laps I started to register where I was entering a corner, hitting the apex and getting on the power again as I exited. The tyres would mark the ground and I started to push myself to find the perfect corner entry and apex while daring myself to get on the gas earlier.

Dad was impressed with my decreasing lap times and it wasn't long before he felt I was ready to enter my first local schoolboy motocross race.

Looking back, I realise I was incredibly lucky to be able to practise on open wasteland in the way I did. It saddens me that it's nearly impossible for kids today to do the same. Strictly it was illegal, of course, but sometimes the local police constable would come along, watch with interest, give a couple of words of encouragement and then be on his way. There were days when hooligans tore up the 18th green of the nearby golf course on their Lambrettas and police would arrive to chase them away, and to be consistent they'd say there'd also been a complaint about dad and me and ask us to move on. However, they recognised we weren't troublemakers and gave us slack – I feel that slack would be difficult to find today.

Society has changed since then. Now, if you so much as feel insulted by someone, never mind anything more serious, you can sue them. If you're stressed or trip over the pavement, it's someone else's fault. There's now a dreadful culture where people claim for everything. I'll make no bones here. I've worked hard for everything in life and appreciated my breaks. I've no time for serial claimants who expect the world to be given to them on a plate. My attitude was the same when I was practising on my little 'crosser: if I crashed and fell off, it was my fault – not the owner of the field. If people only took responsibility for their own actions, then the whole claim culture would die down and we could all get on with our lives more easily.

The current situation means that if someone wants to practise on a motocross bike they must go to an organised venue, and from a safety point of view that's pretty sensible and I agree with it. However, the way farmers are now required to vindicate the use of their land and claim subsidies usually means it no longer pays to open a field for a motocross weekend once a month as they'll be out of pocket. They're especially out of pocket when you consider the insurances they must put in place to run an event to begin with, as they need public liability cover for millions of pounds.

Don't get me wrong. I'd hate to hear scramblers on the fields near my house all the time, but I'd be happy for there to be an evening a week or a weekend a month for kids to practise under supervision. I'd go along with my son Ben and let him take part if he wanted, or just give advice to anyone who would listen. I love bikes, racing and our sport, and I'm happy to be counted in the crowd as an enthusiast. Try keeping me away!

Councils need to provide for kids today. If every community had a practice field and kids were encouraged to take part in motocross, I'm sure it would be a success. This is a cool sport and most children aspire to it. Instead of the roguish behaviour you read about in the papers, they'd be doing something constructive and enjoyable.

My first race meeting took place at Kniveton in Derbyshire. It was a glorious spring morning, cold and damp, with the track wet throughout and drying very slowly. We arrived as a family and even though I had hardly slept the night before I was wide awake and more excited than ever before. The smell of Castrol and grass wafted to meet me and I smiled.

Dad unpacked the bike while mum got to work on volunteer duties. All parents were employed in one way or another at schoolboy motocross meetings, as marshals, lap-scorers or scrutineers. Mum even went on a first-aid course so she could help out at the races. Once the bike was ready dad said we should walk the track so that I'd know my way round. This was a trick he'd learned from his racing days and one I kept doing right to the end of my career: tracks change, and walking them – examining the corners, surfaces, new potholes and standing puddles – is important. Dressed in my racing clobber, I walked on air round the circuit as other kids started arriving.

I'd desperately wanted my own leathers for the races but we couldn't afford any. Mum came to the rescue and made me mock-leather jeans out of the PVC used to cover motorcycle seats. They were pretty uncomfortable so I wore pyjamas underneath. The rest of my kit consisted of horse-riding boots, gardening gloves and cycling goggles. I had a proper helmet, though, complete with a peak. I thought I looked like a superstar…

This was a huge adventure into the unknown. I went out in practice and got faster with every lap, pushing my little Suzuki to its limits alongside the other boys. Soon we were called in and it was time to start my first race. There would be five races on the day, all short affairs but nonetheless gripping. I rode to the start line and sat waiting for the rest of the 30 or so competitors to line up alongside me. I could see mum watching intently just down from the grid.

I wet myself before the race started. I was that excited I just couldn't hold it in. It meant riding the first race in damp pyjamas, the moisture locked in by the warm PVC suit. That sounds uncomfortable but I didn't give it a second thought.

The start was an elastic gate. Two bands of elastic met in a post and were held together by a pin in the centre of the grid. They would snap back to signal the start of the race. All thoughts of victory were banished as I stared at the post holding the elastic together. All I wanted to do was experience the race and see if I could keep up with any of the other boys.

A man raised his flag and all the engines roared. I looked at him and then at the pole holding the elastic. It snapped open and we all flew off the start line and up the hill. I got a good start and was well up the pack going into the first corner. I overtook the riders in front of me in the next couple of laps and was up to second place and living life like I'd never experienced it before. I was determined to catch the leader and win my first race. I was pushing hard and came to a short, narrow bog section that was drying out. I hit it much harder than on previous laps and went off line by a couple of inches. My front wheel stopped dead and I flew over the bars, landing on my back staring at the sky.

A marshal hauled me to my feet, looked me in the eyes and asked if I was OK. I nodded and looked at my bike, neatly parked, axle deep in mud, other racers streaming past it. He made me wait a moment until the track was clear and then in one powerful movement he pulled the bike out of the mud and held it up for me to remount. I got back on and finished the race mid-pack and slightly bemused from the crash. That was my first motorcycle crash and it happened far too quickly for me to do anything about it. I learned a lesson, though, and in the next four races I was just as quick through that section but made sure I didn't come off again.

It wasn't a dream start, but I did quite well on the day, far exceeding my own and my parents' expectations. After five races, all the points were totted up and I was third overall. I was on the podium at my first day of motorcycle racing and received a cheap plastic trophy that I wouldn't have traded for the world. I still have it, and it means a lot to me.

On the way home I was utterly elated and couldn't stop talking and asking when we could race again. Dad kept his emotions in check and said the following weekend. Mum was happy as she'd had a great day with her family. She smiled and told me I'd done awfully well, but then said that maybe I'd done so well because the other boys took pity on me as I was new to the sport. This idea of mum's that other riders felt sorry for me stretched a long way into my career, and towards the end, after winning three British Superbike Championships, I asked her if she still thought it was the reason I'd won races. She laughed and said: 'Oh, John, don't be silly, I was only joking.' It took me 34 years of racing to find that out...

The next day at school I was stiff from my exertions but exultant. That was when I learned not to rub other people's noses in my success. My real friends were happy for me and asked about the races, while there were some children who just stared at me with envy. I found out then that not everyone was into bikes the way I was, and I guess that's when I started making choices about who my friends were. It was a clear decision for me. I picked racing motorcycles above anything else. Friends, school, other activities, staying up late, eating sweets – all were secondary to my need to race a motorcycle. Along with that focus came one of the happiest periods of my childhood.

Every weekend the Reynolds family would go racing, and the days in between couldn't pass quickly enough. I had my mum, my dad and my motorcycle. I needed and wanted nothing else. My friends rarely came to watch. They liked bikes and thought they were cool, but they had their own sports and interests. We stayed mates and sometimes I wondered what they were up to, but I never dwelt on those thoughts for long. I was doing exactly what I wanted and wouldn't have traded places with anyone – except maybe Barry Sheene.

It became apparent pretty quickly that I had an aptitude for racing a motocross bike. I was rarely off the podium but thanks to Gary Dutton it took quite a time to win my first race. He was a bit older than me, and my first real rival. He was smooth, fast and precise on a bike, and watching him was a masterclass in riding. I knew the lines and wanted to take them, but sometimes missed – he didn't.

One race I got my trademark good start and trailed Gary from the off. I was in a zone, concentrating on what I was doing and flowing around the track. Going into the last lap I was right behind him – something I'd never achieved before. At the final corner he was only a bike's length ahead and I got on the throttle a fraction faster. I might have overtaken him by the finish line because of that, but not necessarily. Instead, as we rode up the hill towards the finish he rolled off the throttle to celebrate winning and I flew past him to take my maiden victory.

He was as shocked as I was and it sparked fierce racing between us. I'd beaten him and went home with new self-belief. I never looked back. After that he fought hard and pushed me all the way, but generally I came out on top. After months of seconds and thirds, all of a sudden I was winning.

Dad was delighted. Telephone calls to Uncle Tom were made and I was lifted on a wave of family support and sentiment. Maybe I could be as good as my uncle one day – that was what I dreamed for a long time.

Winning my first race also introduced me to a new fear that would continue to haunt me and become a defining aspect of my career. After winning, I was terrorised by thoughts of losing. The pressure to win was much less than the pressure not to lose. Until the moment I crashed at Brands Hatch and ended my career, I spent all of the intervening years battling with a fear of losing. I'm sure this is something all winners feel, and in my case it nurtured, drove and motivated me.

If I'm not competitive then I don't enjoy racing. I need to have a chance to win or else it removes all the pleasure. In 2005, my final year of racing, I broke my leg very badly in five places during a pre-season test at Valencia. At the start of the season I wasn't in the running for race wins and it was extremely hard work to keep riding. The fear of losing became a reality. As the season progressed, I became more competitive and started to enjoy the racing again and was able to fight the fear of losing, countering it with podiums and good results.

For the following year, 1972, I was in the junior motocross category and I won regularly. I was in a whole new world of jumping, going sideways and flying through the air. Eventually Gary disappeared and the competition for me became about how many wins I could achieve.

I loved riding and racing and all other interests were now firmly relegated to the days when I couldn't get on two wheels. But some of those non-racing days were good fun. In the fields at the back of Gloucester Avenue we would congregate, ride our bicycles, kick balls and play on swings. We used to make little fires and do what we called 'live primitive', cooking cans of beans and eating our hearts out.

One day a good friend called 'Fruit Bat' – on account of his enormous ears – brought along a little NSU Quickly. We didn't know how he got it and none of us thought to ask. We flogged this motorbike to bits and eventually the throttle cable snapped. We thought that was that, but Fruit Bat had different ideas. He strapped the throttle cable to his leg. If he stuck his knee out, the bike accelerated. Off he went round the field and almost immediately the throttle stuck open, sending him at full bore into nettles and brambles. He disappeared from view and we all watched, mouths agape. There were various banging noises, crunches and snaps, and then the bike appeared, coming at us without a rider. An instant later Fruit Bat appeared, being dragged on the ground, his leg still attached to the cable. It sounds cruel, but that was one of the funniest things I've ever witnessed. After we'd all finished rolling around with laughter, we helped him up and applied plenty of dock leaves to his stings. He hurt for a day or two.

When I turned nine I needed a new bike. The little 80cc bike just wasn't cutting the mustard any more, so dad got to work in his spare time and built me a new racer using a Suzuki A100 motor. That kept me on a par with the other competitors and I started to win on a regular basis around the Nottingham scene. After a while

I began to wonder how good I really was. I was beating the same competitors week in and week out and needed a new challenge.

That was when mum and dad decided to start taking me further afield to race. We packed the tent and bike into the car one Saturday morning and set off for Wales. Later that evening, as I was walking the course with dad, two fathers of competitors approached us.

'What class are you racing in?' asked one.

'Juniors,' said dad.

'You might as well pack up and go home now,' he replied. 'There's a local lad who's unbeatable here, a real star for the future.'

I believed him and was excited at the prospect of racing someone that good. The track had some great sections and I learned something about my mentality that day. Give me an impossible challenge and it just builds the determination in me to do my best. In other words, I focus on winning and beating the other guys out of sight. That's when I race at my best.

I beat that local lad fair and square in the races and left with the trophy. That was the start of us as a family making regular weekend camping trips to motocross meetings all around the country. The amount of money mum and dad invested in me and my sport was a lot, but what means even more to me is the amount of time they put in. As a family we all enjoyed those weekends. If I was happy, mum and dad were as well. We all remember them as very happy times.

When I was 12 it was time to move into the Intermediate class. Immediately it was obvious my home-made bike was not up to the job. Suzuki had brought out a little 100cc schoolboy racer and it was leagues ahead of anything else. The suspension was superb, the wheels bigger, and the motor was stronger and better suited to off-road racing than anything dad could build himself. It was apparent that if I wanted to win I'd need a Suzuki TM100 as the podium places were filled with them.

Dad located the last one still for sale in the country at Vale Onslow in Birmingham. It cost £600 and we picked it up together.

When we returned home I wanted to start the bike straight away, but dad told me to leave it until he'd checked it over. Being thrilled to own it, I spent hours just looking at it and sitting on it. That's when I had my first crash. I lost my balance while sitting on it and my wonderful new bike fell over. It smashed against a bench and when I picked it up there was a dent in the tank. I was inconsolable and very embarrassed. Dad said nothing – he knew I'd suffered punishment enough.

I raced that bike all round the country and Kelvin Tatum, who later became a great speedway racer, was the lad to beat in my class. We had some great battles that year and I entered the British Schoolboy Motocross Championship for the first time – it's so long ago that I now can't remember where it was held. The night before, after walking the track with dad, I asked him if he believed I could win the British Championship. He said he thought I could, but it would need to be my best effort yet as there were good riders out there. He'd pushed the right buttons and I started the race as determined as ever to do my best. There was no fear of losing, just pure determination.

I won my first British Championship that day and was presented with a huge trophy that was mine to keep for a year.

Although lessons were as dull as ever for me, it was thanks to school that I met Shelley Brown. I was 12 and in my second year, while Shelley was 11 and in the first year. One of her friends came up to me and said she fancied me. I looked over at her and thought she was nice.

In all honesty I wasn't into girls or anything other than motocross at this stage in my life. I thought I fancied her but wasn't sure what to do next. Did she have a kick-start? How did you control her throttle? What happened if she went into a tank slapper? She looked at me and smiled. I smiled back.

We talked with each other a little while and then the next day we kissed behind the bike sheds. I was a little lost on what to do next and in any case I was busy all the time on my bike, so things fizzled out after that. We would always say 'hello' and were friendly, but I had too much going on with bikes. Little did I know at the time that I'd met my future wife. She was the first girl I kissed and right from the first glance there was a spark between us.

Shelley's brother, Tony, was a year above me in school, and quite by chance we became best friends. Physically very strong, he was a no-nonsense character who didn't take hassle from anyone. Once friends with Tony, I was a protected person. Some might say he was trouble, and I guess his record of being expelled hints at that, but he wasn't trouble – he was a fun-loving guy who stood up for himself.

Tony Brown was also into bikes and had a Suzuki AP50 while at school. I can remember walking home from a party a few years later with another friend at one o'clock in the morning when we heard a horn and Tony came charging past us on his moped. At the roundabout just ahead he started doing laps and performing wheelies, standing on his seat and acting the hoon. We laughed and then he buzzed past us again on the wrong side of the road, horn blaring. No sooner had we stopped laughing than a copper on a bike pulled up and demanded to know who was on the moped. We said we didn't know. I thought Tony had got away with it, but he'd decided to do one more ride past on the wrong side of the road. As he approached, he obviously noticed the policeman with us because he cut his lights and went by with both his feet hanging over the back to obscure the number plate. There was silence for a moment.

'Brownie,' said the copper – and Tony was nailed again. He had no real harm in him, but he was unfortunate enough to keep attracting attention and getting caught.

When I was 19 I had a girlfriend I'd been going out with for three years. She was the only girl I'd dated since that first kiss with Shelley all those years before. For me it was a comfortable relationship as there was no pressure and I was still dreaming about racing bikes, but in my heart I knew it was going nowhere.

As it happened, a colleague at the signwriting company where I worked was dating Shelley, and he asked if we'd like to go out as a foursome. I agreed, more out of boredom than anything else.

Soon I found myself looking forward to these outings because I'd meet Shelley again. One night she confided in me after an argument with her boyfriend. I listened and found myself questioning my own relationship. After I split with my girlfriend I telephoned the Brown family home, and Shelley answered.

'I'll get Tony for you,' she said. I told her not to, and said I'd called to let her know I was single. She sympathised with me and I said I'd see her later. We didn't force anything. She split up with her boyfriend shortly after that and we started going out. That was when I realised there was more to life than just bikes and someone could have meaning to me outside my direct family.

Shelley was no ordinary girl. She was interested in horses as a child and found out after a few gymkhanas that she wasn't the competitive sort. She turned out to be the exact opposite to me in that respect. I can't abide losing, but she didn't care. She was a great balance to me. By this age she was also interested in bikes. She was to become a key figure and support to me and, without her, I'm sure I wouldn't have achieved what I did. I'd found someone I could communicate with, understood me and was my new best friend as well as my girlfriend.

Apart from meeting Shelley, my teenage years were when I realised I was never going to be a World Champion motocross racer and I turned my back on two-wheel motorsport.

Chapter 3

REALISING MY LIMITS

When I was 14 my mum and dad were called to school to see my form master, Mr Grundy. He told them I should stop racing motorcycles as I'd never make a living at it and my school work was suffering as a result. Dad never came to school for parent-teacher meetings. He was embarrassed by my lack of academic achievement, so he turned a blind eye to it. Mum, on the other hand, had high hopes for me being a scholar or a doctor, and was eternally optimistic that I would excel at school.

Both came to see Mr Grundy that day and I sat in the room in silence as he told them his thoughts on racing and how it was no good for me. I respected Mr Grundy more than any other teacher. He was a solid man who never took a day off work for any reason.

When he said I should pack in racing to concentrate on academic studies, there was no doubt in my mind. He was right but I wasn't going to do it – no-one was going to tell me to give up motorcycle racing.

Dad didn't say much to me after the meeting and mum just looked at me with disappointment. For some kids this might have motivated them to work harder to try to please their parents. Not me. I went out on my pushbike to the fields and played with my friends – I didn't give it a second thought.

In fact I did OK at school and at 16 left with all my exams, albeit with mediocre results. My best subjects were the ones where you use your hands, like metalwork and woodwork. I knew I was never going to be a genius and had accepted that fact long before my teachers or my mother.

Hindsight is a wonderful thing and now I can look back with a very different perspective. I would be a star pupil if I were at school now. Over the past few years I've taken my rotary and fixed-wing pilot licences. When I was 40, starting from scratch, I read through text books which, when piled together, came nearly to match my height of 5ft 6in. I had to learn the intricacies of navigation, the maths and science of flying. It was hard, but I applied myself religiously and got through, first time, what are acknowledged to be some of the most difficult exams you could ever take. With flying there's no room for error. Make mistakes in an exam and you might risk failure. Make a mistake in a helicopter and the repercussions are rather more serious.

This has awakened a thirst for learning in me that I didn't know I had. I'd love to go through school all over again. The knowledge I missed fascinates me.

As a teenager, I had no other interests apart from bikes. Girls were a distant distraction but one I never allowed to come too close. The only other activity I took part in was the school choir. My mates and I joined because you'd be excused from class 20 minutes before lunch and inevitably got to the head of the queue before the other classes were let out. You'd get the prime choice of lunch and that was always worth a little bit of crooning practice in my book.

We were rehearsing for *Joseph and the Technicolor Dreamcoat*, but it never occurred to me I might have to perform in front of an audience. Then I was told the date of the performance. I hadn't applied myself to learning the songs or trying very hard, and didn't have time to make amends. As one of only four boys in the choir I was placed in the front row facing nearly 200 proud parents and two mortified ones (my own). I mumbled my way through the night and it was crystal clear to everyone I didn't have a clue. It wasn't an uplifting play – it ended up being a tragedy of Shakespearian proportions.

That ended my career in the choir and I got back to riding my bikes and messing with my mates.

After I'd won the British Schoolboy Motocross Championship at the age of 12, Kawasaki gave me my first taste of sponsorship by supplying a bike with some spares – which was fantastic. I went up to the 125cc Championship and poured all my energy into that. I kept getting on the podium and finishing with good results, but the wins were further apart and much harder to achieve. I was struggling with the size of the 125cc Kawasaki: I was still a fair bit smaller than most of my peers and, while I had the technical ability, I just didn't have the sheer muscle to match my competitors. I kept at it, though, and mum and dad came to every race meeting – we continued to enjoy ourselves as a family.

A kid called Dave Thorpe was coming through the ranks at the same time as me, and I got to race him when I was about 14. He was in a completely different league from me and just disappeared out of sight. He went on to become a great British World Champion and I'm proud to have taken to the start gate alongside him. What that did, though, was show a young JR that his chances of ever being brilliant in motocross were severely limited. That was my first rap with a reality stick and it hurt.

Dad had witnessed the difference between Dave Thorpe and me. Many years later I learned that he told mum at this time that I was too small for motocross, but would make a superb road racer. When mum and dad were younger they'd enjoyed watching bike racing together. The TT legend Bob McIntyre was a big hero, and they were at Oulton Park the day he was killed – that tragedy turned mum off road racing. She told dad never to say anything to me about road racing or encourage me to do it, otherwise she'd leave him. So dad kept encouraging me at motocross and never did speak a word about road racing.

By this time my friends had changed a bit, although Tony Brown, Shelley's brother, was still around. Woody – Kevin Wood – was a wiry little guy not much bigger than me. Woody's sport was boxing and I used to spend far too much time trying to get him into fights because he was always a wonder to behold. I can remember one night a bouncer took exception to us and Woody knocked him out with a single punch. Then Woody met his girlfriend and they got married. She was instantly pregnant and we'd laugh that he'd become a dad on his first attempt. He's a lovely bloke, though, and still married to the same girl.

Bob 'O' Levers was the other friend, and the four of us were inseparable, with the same interests. Bob was as daft as a brush but today he's the glue that keeps us together. He's a long-distance European coach driver and whenever he comes back home he gets on the blower and rounds us up for a night of debauchery in town. We meet up maybe twice a year and there's always a fair amount of beer consumed. These are great nights out with the best of friends, salt-of-the-earth characters I had real pleasure in knowing as I grew up. I was a very happy kid.

We used to spend hours at the local tip and were lucky that the head of the council depot, Mr Syson, turned a blind eye to our activities. He'd see us tearing around on our bikes, cooking our beans on the fire and chucking stones at the sky, but he was a gem about it all. More than once he'd sit with us and ask us about school, racing or girls. He was on our side. He was the one and only person in a council position that I found positive about bikes, but more recently – through my work with the police, THINK!, Bikesafe and Shiny Side Up – I've encountered many more forward thinkers in councils all round the country. But I still wish there were even more like Mr Syson.

As I approached 16 I had to make the choice between racing in the Auto Cycle Union (ACU) or the Amateur Moto Cross Association (AMCA). I chose the AMCA as there were more local meetings and you could join when you were only 15. It was also time to step up to the 250cc bikes. For the next two years I put everything into trying to win the British Championship again. I finished second in 1981 and that was as close as I was going to get. Every time I came up against the likes of Dave Thorpe I was made to feel pretty ordinary, which grated. I won very few races and realised that I wasn't going to be a champion.

I left school just before my 16th birthday and was now faced with finding a job. As it happened, Tony Brown's parents were having a new kitchen put in, and the builder doing it was my friend Woody's dad. I offered to help, thinking that if I made myself indispensable I might get a full-time job – and being a builder sounded good to me.

After enjoying running errands for two weeks, the job finished and Woody's dad said he couldn't afford to employ me. But he did say that a friend of his in Kimberley owned a signwriting business and he'd put in a good word for me as I was a hard worker. It turned out that Phillips Signs needed a driver's mate and the owner, Phill, gave me the job. I was too young to drive but I was able to help the driver when we got to our destination. Our job was to erect and pull down 'For Sale' boards. It wasn't very glamorous and when you had 50 sites to visit in a day it was damned hard work – but I loved it. Driving around in a van all day laughing with my workmates was great fun and I thrived. Socially I'd made a big leap from sitting at the tip. All my mates had jobs as well and when we met up we'd play Space Invaders or just shoot the breeze about girls.

It was about this time when I met my first proper girlfriend. Since kissing Shelley when I was 12, I'd had no interest in girls or time for them, but at 16 your hormones make you sit up and take notice – if you know what I mean. My new girlfriend was a real looker and we stayed together until I was 19. We didn't have a lot in common, but she'd come to the odd motocross meeting and we enjoyed each other's company. I'm convinced her dad always disliked me and thought she could do a lot better than a simple sign erector. He probably hated me all the more after he caught us in bed one Sunday evening when we thought we were alone in the house...

A week before my 16th birthday I got my mitts on my first road bike. It was a secondhand Suzuki AP50 moped previously owned by a friend in Kimberley. He'd kept it in immaculate condition and I'd always hankered after it. Mum and dad bought it for my birthday – I was the happiest kid alive. I'd sat in school dreaming of the day I'd own that moped and be able to ride around with my mates. It was a true halcyon image in my mind and it consumed me. When I actually owned the moped, it was even better than the dream.

Not only did the moped give me a whole new level of freedom but it also meant I could ride to Phillips Signs. I could run the bike for £1 a week – pretty good when I was earning £23 a week. As Tony also had a moped, I was now able to join him tearing up and down the roads, sometimes playing a game where one of us would lead and have to try to lose the other. I'd be riding down the street close behind Tony and all of a sudden he'd dart left down an alley, leaving me sailing past, desperately trying to stop and turn. Driveways, pavements, fields, car parks – we'd ride over, through or round anything, whether or not we were allowed to.

Although I'd just left school, my mates and I used the hard-surface tennis courts there as a race track. In effect this was my first road race circuit, and I'd fly round as fast as I could. I wore through the soles of my Doc Martens going through corners with my footrests on the floor. Tony was a terrific rider and pushed me all the way: he could pick the right lines and had natural ability on a par with mine. We'd race each other, neither giving an inch, while Woody and Bob 'O' would simply watch, wondering why we were so competitive.

Tony fancied racing and bought a motocross bike when he was about 16. He came along to races and he was good, but there was a simple difference between Tony and me. If he was beaten or fell off, it didn't matter to him. He shrugged, laughed, brushed himself down and went on to the next thing. For me, though, racing a bike was a defining part of me – I hated being beaten.

I desperately wanted to learn to drive and put a lot of effort into it. Before I was 17, the driver I worked with secretly allowed me to drive the van whenever we were out in the countryside, so I already knew the basics before I started to learn officially. I passed the test easily at the first attempt – it was the first time in my life I'd passed anything with distinction.

Now that I could drive, Phill offered me a van of my own and I jumped at the chance. At the same time he asked if I'd like to train to become a signwriter. I'd watched the lads signwriting and knew it was a highly skilled and admirable trade, but I was having far too much fun driving around in a van putting up signs, so I said 'no thanks'. Phill was disappointed as he thought he could see more potential in me, but I didn't care – I had a job, I had wheels and I was happy.

Erecting signs was my job for the next couple of years. I didn't regret a minute of that time, and it got better still when Phill asked if I knew anyone else who could join the firm. In short measure I had Tony and Bob 'O' working alongside me. It was pure carnage when we got together…

On one occasion Tony and I were driving to a job and passed Donington Park race circuit. In those days the Melbourne Loop was open to the public almost all the time. You could camp there, drive round, pretty much do what you liked. We made our way to the entrance in our Toyota pick-up, complete with triple extension ladders tied from the rear shelf to above the cab, and 30 signs and boxes of tools in the back. There was no-one else in sight, apart from a farmer in a tractor a field away.

We screeched round for a few laps, the Toyota hanging out precariously on the corners with its engine revving harder than it was ever meant to. In between the Tarmac sections we found some loose gravel and I started pulling handbrake turns back onto the circuit. On our last run I flew along the gravel faster than before, yanked on the handbrake and flicked the rear out. The Toyota glided across the gravel, turning naturally so that we'd be pointing in the right direction when we hit the grippy track surface. We came off the gravel and the outside tyres gripped hard, pitching the truck onto two wheels. I caught it on the steering and applied opposite-lock immediately. We drove along on two wheels for a bit, teetering on the edge of balance, and then the vehicle slammed down incredibly hard onto its four wheels.

We rolled to a halt and Tony just looked at me. We burst into laughter. When we'd finally stopped laughing we found that the bonnet and cab roof had both caved in with the impact. I felt sure it would mean big trouble when Phill found out, but Tony came to the rescue. He slammed his huge ham-fist into the underside of the cab roof and it popped out with a snap. He did the same with the bonnet. We checked the ladders, signs and tools – everything was intact. We'd got away with it. The tractor driver came over just before we left and said he was sure the van should have rolled. It was with a sigh of relief that we considered how we might have had to 'phone Phill to break the news to him.

'Phill, it's John, we've had an accident.'

'Where?'

'Donington Park.'

'Where exactly?'

'Do you know the Melbourne Loop?'

That was my first go on the Donington circuit. Little did I know that I'd be back to compete for real one day.

I lived a fairly normal teenage life from 16 to 19. I worked hard through the day erecting boards and then I played hard in the evenings with my mates. Most evenings I'd either tear around on my moped or, later, my first car.

Just before I passed my driving test, I'd found a Ford Escort Mk1 that was owned by an Indian family and had set my heart on it. Dad took one look at it, proclaimed it scrap, and said 'no'. Then I hounded mum so much that she eventually went with me to look at it, and bought it for me, much to dad's disgust. He knew it was going to take a lot of effort to put it right, and had been hoping to avoid the long hours in the garage.

Legally, of course, you're not allowed to drink alcohol in a pub until you're 18, but back in my day, as now, the reality was quite different. We were in pubs from the age of 16 and it wasn't until

I was 17 that we were first rumbled. It was late on a Friday night when Tony, Bob 'O', Woody and I had rushed back from the Ilkeston Fair to the 'Nelson & Railway' for last orders. We ordered two pints each and had just put the first credits into the Space Invaders machine when the coppers walked in.

They made a beeline for me and asked if I was 18. I certainly didn't look the legal age thanks to my small build (and still didn't look it a couple of years later), but I said 'yes' anyway. One of the coppers gave me an evil stare and asked if I was sure. I respected the police and after a moment's pause I replied that I wasn't sure. He kicked all four of us out of the pub after only a mouthful of beer each – eight pints wasted. I wasn't the most popular lad that night and all I could think of was the policeman sipping the drinks we'd paid for and going for the high score on Space Invaders while we hung around the street corner contemplating our bad luck.

During those years I missed many evenings out with my friends thanks to my pursuit of motocross. I'd be travelling on a Friday or Saturday night, or in bed early ready for a race the next day. As time wore on, listening to my friends on a Monday and laughing as they recounted stories of their weekend exploits, I began to wonder if the racing was worth it.

At the time I was racing a KTM 250cc machine supplied by Stuart Hicken, who went on become a Superbike team boss and at the time of writing manages the Hawk Kawasaki squad. In 1981 I raced in the European Championship, and mum and dad travelled with me. We were given expenses by the organisers, but the money barely covered our fuel. We stayed in second-rate hotels, hostels and school dormitories, but we enjoyed the experience, not knowing what the next accommodation might be.

I finished third in the European Championship, and this was also the year I took second place in the British Championship. But despite these encouraging results, I couldn't help but wonder what I was missing in normal life. I'd was with Shelley by then and was enjoying spending time with her as well as my friends.

I approached Phill and reminded him of our conversation a few years earlier about me becoming a signwriter. I'd been enjoying my job erecting signs and bombing around, but I was starting to get bored and wanted to stretch myself a bit more. I knew there was something better in me, a person who wanted to achieve more in life. Becoming a qualified signwriter seemed to be a good way of unlocking that potential. But Phill told me he didn't need anyone. I was gutted and I guess he read that in my face because he threw me a lifeline. He said that if I wanted to stay after normal working hours he'd teach me the basics in my own time. Two years earlier I'd have been paid to train into the role, and now I was being asked to train for free. But I said 'yes' straight away – I didn't want the opportunity to pass me by again. For the next couple of months I'd work my normal eight or ten hours a day, and then stay behind for another hour or two every evening, soaking up the techniques and putting my whole heart into it. Eventually I qualified as a signwriter and my wages improved.

Just as my wages went up, dad told me that it was high time I financed my racing habit. Until then he'd funded my efforts in combination with some sponsorship when we could find it. I'd turned 20 and for six months I raced and paid for it myself. My pay rise vanished, as did all of my spare cash. Not only was I wondering what I was missing when my mates went out, but when I was free to join them I couldn't afford it.

During that six-month period I learned just how expensive motorsport is. I was having to pay for diesel, petrol, entry fees, breakages, motorway food, overnight stays, new riding kit – you name it and it cost money. I was just thankful I had the bike to start with and access to a van for travelling.

One day late in 1982 I went with mum and dad to a local motocross meeting at Warsop, near Mansfield, and was squarely beaten by someone who shouldn't have finished on the same lap as me. I got off the bike and slumped in a chair while dad packed the bike away. All around me were lads my own age who were racing motocross for pure pleasure. They were never going to be champions but they didn't care. And one of them had just given me a thrashing. I can't remember what my mates were doing that day but I'm sure I was half wishing I could be with them instead.

I was coming to a pretty hard decision in my life. I'd realised for years, ever since I first raced against Dave Thorpe when I was 14, that I was never going to be a World Champion at motocross. I'd given it my best shot in 1981 in the British and European Championships, and that year I couldn't have sacrificed any more or put in any additional effort. I knew I'd reached my level and would find it difficult to progress any further.

I'd known this for a while and had fought it every step of the way. It was my dream to become a champion at a sport I loved and had been good at ever since I was a little boy. Motocross was my escape from reality and what made me different from all my friends and people who lived in my street.

It was like a switch flicked in my head. 'Dad, I'm not enjoying this any more,' I said. I weighed up what I was sacrificing and what it was costing me trying to be a winner in a class where it didn't count and in which I was never going to make a living. Sure, I'd win some trophies, but so would a lot of the social racers I faced that day. That would make them happy, but it would never satisfy me.

Dad had been smart when he made me fund my own racing. Until then it had been rose-tinted for me, as I'd rarely had to put my hand in my own pocket. Now it was costing me, it was a different matter. I was learning a hard lesson in life.

That day at Warsop I gave up on racing and went home a changed man. My childhood dream was in tatters. I had to adjust to the fact I was going to live an 'ordinary' life. I was happy as a signwriter and would put all my effort into that, and John Reynolds would be proud to earn money doing an honest day's work with his hands.

Road racing still hadn't entered my head as a possibility. If I couldn't afford to race in motocross then there was no chance of being able to fund road racing, and I didn't think I had the bottle to do it anyway. Barry Sheene and Ron Haslam were in their heyday and short-circuit racing was on television. I can remember clearly watching a British Championship race on ITV from Mallory Park. Roger Burnett, Roger Marshall, Paul Lewis, Wayne Gardner and the Rothmans Hondas were racing, and it was fantastic to behold. The riders were bashing fairings at 100mph out of the corners and I was in awe of their skills.

The danger was immense. Circuits were not as safe as they are today and it wasn't uncommon for racers to be killed during events, whether at Cadwell Park or the Isle of Man TT. These were the fearless hard men of motorcycling who were at a level above us mere mortals.

I idolised the road racers. One day as I was being taken by a friend for a pillion ride on a new Honda CBX, we scorched up the dual-carriageway and came to a stop at traffic lights. Ron Haslam was in a new Simca car waiting at the lights. At the time the CBX was new to the UK and he looked it up and down and then smiled at my mate and me before pulling away. We were both thrilled just to have caught a glimpse of such a hero – it made our day.

Although I might have said to people that I'd love to road race, deep down I was scared by the prospect. But that was OK because I couldn't afford to try it, so I'd never have my bluff called.

Two years later I was sitting with Shelley in 'The Royal Oak' chatting over a pint. She knew me better than anyone. On an impulse I grabbed her hand and said: 'I'm going to try road racing.'

I was calling my own bluff.

Chapter 4

FINDING ROAD RACING

When I gave up motocross it was final. The bike was taken out of the van, parked in the garage and went straight into the paper for sale. I never rode it again.

I thrived as a normal person, just another one of the lads. I had a wonderful girlfriend, a solid family and a fledgling career as a signwriter that I thoroughly enjoyed. Working with my hands was rewarding and the fact that I could also release my artistic side was a bonus. Phillips Signs was a very good place to work for a 21-year-old who needed something to focus upon. Despite being offered lots of overtime, I was never keen on staying late. Without motocross to interfere, I had a very active social life. I was also living in two places: after work I'd go home to mum and dad's for dinner and then go over to Shelley's and stay the night. Her mum and dad were more like friends than my girlfriend's parents, and when Tony, Shelley's brother, was at home I'd have my best friend and girlfriend with me at the same time.

By this stage I was a proper biker. I'd bought a Honda CB900 for the road after selling my moped and Tony had bought one at the same time. I got the CB900 before I had my big bike licence and it was a huge carrot to pass the test, which I did, first time, using my old 100cc motocross training bike that I'd converted for road use. Along with a dozen or so other riders, we used to go on ride-outs at the weekends to biker pubs at places like Langley Mill and Matlock. Despite no longer racing, I loved my motorcycle and couldn't ride it enough during the summer. It represented pure enjoyment, freedom and, more often than not, lots of laughs.

One of our crew, who was a touch arrogant, had a sparkling 650cc Kawasaki that was stunning to look at. Parked alongside it, my Honda would look very average indeed. He maintained his bike religiously and it was his pride and joy, but he also loved the attention and at times he was insufferable. On one occasion at Matlock a typically large crowd had gathered around it and he was relishing the interest. The rest of us just watched, praying that he'd soon get his comeuppance – and he got it almost immediately. Nonchalantly he jumped on his bike, started it up, pulled out into the road, opened the throttle – and turned round with a look of pure horror on his face. He'd left his steering locked and gracelessly flicked over the side of the bike when he tried to straighten up. His gorgeous Kawasaki crashed into the Tarmac and slid to a halt. There were cheers and roars of laughter. I must admit I smiled once I saw he was OK.

If I was out with Tony, we would invariably end up racing each other home. We would max our bikes and laugh about it afterwards, enthusing about the speed we went round a corner or down a straight. But we weren't outrageous riders. I never have been and never will be on the road. I respect the dangers far too much. I've always ridden with plenty of safety margin. With a blind corner, I'd go into it knowing I could pull up and stop on my side of the road if something was parked out of sight. Through an open corner, I'd make sure I was always a couple of feet away from the kerb or the apex. I always had plenty in hand and was in control of the situation. Tony was the same and I respected him enormously as both a safe and fast rider.

Even so, I once had a big moment riding over to Shelley's. Coming out of a roundabout with the bike leaned over, I opened the throttle and started to accelerate hard. Suddenly the bike went sideways and I shut off instinctively. When the sliding rear gripped again I was spat into the air and then landed heavily – and without much grace – back on the seat, heart racing and adrenalin flowing like never before. I wondered what had happened and it wasn't until I started road racing years later that I realised this had been my first highside.

I'd got away with it more by luck than anything else, and I knew I'd just escaped a big incident. When you consider that my riding kit was jeans, jacket, baseball boots and a helmet, I was very grateful indeed. At that age and with limited experience, I'd thought I was invincible, that nothing would happen and I wouldn't get hurt. Nowadays with bikes a lot faster, the roads much busier and – to be blunt – with far more ignorant car drivers on them, I wouldn't venture out in anything less than full leathers. But, back then, there was nothing Shelley and I liked more than to take off on the bike on a summer evening or at the weekend. She enjoyed riding pillion, and together we visited pubs and devoured winding roads with a voracious appetite.

I'm sure our enjoyment of road riding helped in my later racing career. Whenever fans at race meetings came up to me in their leathers, carrying helmets, their faces red with excitement, I'd know exactly what they were feeling because I'd been there myself. I could empathise with their enjoyment and would genuinely be interested in their ride to the circuit or what bike they owned. They were living the life Shelley and I enjoyed for several years and, while they may have longed to be out on the track racing, on more than one occasion at a circuit I wished I was back riding with Shelley, with no pressure and enjoying a motorcycle on the open road.

I've led many ride-outs since I started racing and at the beginning I was worried that other bikers would view me as a target to overtake. Some did and still do. They'll tear past me at 100mph and as I watch them disappear I tell myself that it's not worth it. If they're lucky enough to make it to their destination, I'd advise them to try a track day to see just how fast they really are.

My strong feelings about rider safety on the roads have recently led me to represent national rider safety groups like Think! and Bike Safe as well as the Shiny Side Up campaign in Nottingham. I've received a royal award for this work but what really motivates me is the hope that the message may have helped save lives. I love motorcycles as much as anyone else and hate to hear of fatalities on the road.

If you think you're fast, then go to a track day and ask an instructor to follow you round. He'll give you guidance and if you have any ability you'll be able to nurture it on the track without fear of cow-pats, oncoming traffic and Volvo drivers.

If you want to ride a modern superbike to anywhere near its potential, you need to go on a circuit anyway. It's the only place you'll learn about its limits and characteristics, and what you learn there will make you a better and safer road rider.

If you just enjoy road riding, though, then stick at it. Few experiences can rival a ride through the Dales on a hot summer day, wind cooling you down while the road twists and turns like a snake into the distance, and a pub with a garden waits to welcome you for lunch. That's motorcycling at its pure best. I'd put it right up there with winning a Superbike race.

Although my first car, the scrapper Ford Escort that I worked on with dad, always played second fiddle to my Honda CB900, I took a great deal of pride in it as well. Dad sorted the bog-standard 1300cc engine while I painted the bodywork – a skill that came naturally to a signwriter. We stripped the car to a shell and rebuilt it from the ground up, adding new wings. In true boy-racer fashion, I fitted alloy wheels, bucket seats and a roll-cage, and finished it off in RS2000 rally car colours. It was pretty slow but it looked the business and that's all that mattered to me.

I moved up to a Ford Granada after that. I had to fit a rear spoiler to it – the racer inside me must have been shouting for attention. Then for my 21st birthday dad bought me a BMW 528i. It was a well-used second-hand car, but it was absolutely fantastic and a proper performance car – I didn't need to modify it.

My 21st birthday was a work day. Tony was still working at Phillips Signs, landscaping the sites where our signs were erected. That evening Phill asked him to stay on and finish a job, but Tony replied that it was my birthday and he couldn't. Phill asked again, making it very clear the job needed to be finished. Tony shook his head, packed his tools away and told Phill what he could do with his job. He always was a strong character…

That night at the pub Tony hatched the idea of 'Buggymania'. His dad had recently sold his estate agency business and loaned him the money to buy half-a-dozen 70cc kiddies' three-wheelers – so Tony already had his new career lined up. He'd work on the business all week, and then at the weekend I'd join him and we'd pack the trikes into the van and go to local fairs. We had a regular pitch at Watnall Market and we'd charge £1 a go.

It proved popular. In truth, though, we were the biggest kids around. We set up a little off-road course and we'd race round. Having given up competitive motocross, I was able to get my fix of racing on those little trikes. Often a family would come up to us and, although they were the paying customers, we almost wished they'd go away so we could keep on playing.

Then Tony had the idea of running the business at Skegness – I guess as an alternative to the donkey rides. We drove out there once and it was a successful day, so on the way home we pulled into a Ford dealership in Lincoln and, heady on the thoughts of huge profits and wealth, we asked if we could buy two new Escort XR3s on the business. The salesman raised an eyebrow and asked if we were VAT-registered. I said 'yes' and simultaneously Tony said 'no'. The salesman nodded, took another sip of coffee and we left.

Those were great days, but I still had an itch to make something more of my life. My work ethic was non-stop and that's why I didn't mind sacrificing my weekends. More than anything, my parents had taught me how to graft and the importance of earning my own way in life. But Buggymania wasn't the replacement for racing for me, nor was it a money-spinner. Tony bought a Jaguar XJ6 with our profits but the venture died shortly after that.

A gifted signwriter is a pleasure to behold working. The deft flicks of the wrist, the artistic eye and the individual flair are incredible skills. By the time I was 21 these skills were mine, but they were made redundant almost overnight thanks to the introduction of computers.

I was one of two signwriters at Phill's. When the computer arrived it reduced the need for us both and we knew it, so we started putting a lot of effort into being busy and indispensable. Phill taught me how to use the computer to design and write signs, and that was my new job. But anyone could have done this – it didn't need a trained signwriter. All of a sudden it was no longer an art form. I was punching keys and then the end drawings would be produced in a different room.

Phill was great and stood by his staff, myself included. He didn't let any of us go, although I'm sure he could have justified it on business grounds. But a lot of my pleasure in the job had vanished. I felt removed from the production process and my eagerness to get up in the mornings took a dent.

It was during an evening out with Shelley, talking about the possibility of going road racing, that I had a brainwave.

'Dad has an old Velocette in the garage that he used to race,' I told her. 'What if I raced that in the vintage class? It could give me a foot up into racing. All I need to do is get noticed and I could make it.'

Shelley thought this a good idea and, looking back, I consider that evening as one of those life-changing moments. I made the decision there and then. I wanted to road race and I realised I needed to get my dad involved. It was the only way I could ever achieve my goal, so I started scheming. If I could prove myself in the vintage class, maybe dad would buy me a Yamaha RD350 and I could go mainstream racing...

A week or two later dad went off to watch a vintage race meeting, and that night at the dinner table I mentioned my idea. He liked it but was a bit cool, because of what mum had said previously about leaving home if I road raced. Mum had also spent 13 years travelling around watching my motocross racing and really enjoyed it, but towards the end she preferred to stay at home. Then, when I stopped racing, she had dad at home most of the time – which is what she wanted. It took quite a bit of effort from me to convince dad that vintage racing would only take up about six weekends a year and we would have a great time. It wasn't fair of me, hitting him below the belt like that concerning something he enjoyed anyway, but that was just part of my scheme to get on a road race bike.

When dad eventually relented, he and mum had serious disagreements about it. He told her I was my own person and made my own decisions. Later in life, I found out that she actually did leave home, but came back the next day.

I remember asking her what she thought of the idea of vintage racing. She turned away and told me she wanted nothing to do with it. It sent a shiver down my spine but I pressed on regardless, and it's only now that I really understand her fear and feelings. She was frightened and scared for me, and did everything she could to dissuade me. As the years went by and I won races and championships, that fear remained with her but it began to mingle more with pride. Early on she came to one meeting and, sod's law, I crashed right in front of her – she never came again. Right up to my final race weekend in 2005, she'd always say before a race meeting, in all seriousness and completely at odds with my instinct as a racer, 'Don't go too fast.'

I couldn't have gone racing if mum hadn't come home that day. If she'd stayed away and made a bigger issue of it, then I'm sure road racing would never have got off the starting blocks for me, because dad wouldn't have allowed the family to split up. I really appreciate all the support and caring that my family gave me. I couldn't have achieved my success without both of my parents behind me. Now's a good time to say, 'Thank you for everything, and I love you both more than you can ever know.'

Dad took me to see the vintage race organisers and we presented photographs of the Velocette to them. When dad raced it in the

1940s and 1950s, he'd removed the solid rear frame and fitted his own design of cantilever suspension. It was years ahead of its time but was a modification that wasn't allowed in vintage racing. The only way we could race the bike now was to prove that it had been raced previously with the suspended rear end. We searched high and low for anyone who might have photographic proof, but found nothing. So we had to revert to the rigid rear frame – a real shame for my dad.

By now my enthusiasm for road racing was running at full steam ahead. Tony and I had chatted about trying out the Chas Mortimer race school at Donington Park and now we signed up. Dad came along to watch. It was my first time on a proper race bike, a Yamaha RD400 complete with race fairing and exhaust. Compared with my Honda CB900 road bike, it felt light, nimble and incredibly fast. Although we were there to have a good day out and enjoy ourselves, I also wanted to find out if I could actually cut it as a road racer.

Chas followed us around the track for 20 minutes, and I spent the rest of the time learning the circuit and perfecting what I thought were the best lines. The day, which was cool and dry, went by in a blur of excitement, concentration and sheer pleasure. Tony and I were evenly matched but he lapped two-tenths quicker than me. At the end of the day Chas spoke to all the riders and commented on what it takes to be a racer. Right at the end he pointed at Tony and me and said: 'You two have a lot of talent and might want to try racing. You're not fast yet but you're smooth and tidy and that shows a lot of potential.'

It was October, but for me it felt like Christmas Day. I had confirmation from a real racer that I might have potential and should try racing. I looked over to dad and he frowned. But with hindsight, I'm convinced this was what actually persuaded him to commit to the vintage racing. He knew there was a glimmer of talent and was as excited about unearthing it as I was.

Chas said I'd lapped the short circuit at 1 minute 38.2 seconds. He said that was quick for a novice and I was delighted. Instead of keeping my mouth shut, I asked him what fast riders would lap at. He said a top RD350 rider should go round in about 1 minute 21 seconds. Where I'd been going through Craner Curves in fourth on mid-throttle, he told me the racers would be in fifth, and accelerating hard. After the initial pat on the back, this news felt like a real kick in the groin. How you could ever go 17 seconds a lap faster on similar machinery was just beyond me. But, by rationalising that it was my first time on the circuit and on that bike, I remained quite happy with the day. However, even as I enthused with Shelley that evening, I had lingering doubts that I kept to myself. Was I up to the job? Did I really have it in me to find 17 seconds or more? I decided there was only one way to find out and that was to try vintage racing.

Not long after that I bumped into an old motocross friend called Johnny Johnston. I told him I was looking at road racing now, and he said he'd grown up with the Haslams and would introduce me to Ron if I liked. My mouth went dry just at the mention of one of my heroes. Soon I was at the Haslam farm sitting at a table with my idol, eating chips and chatting about my hopes and dreams!

Ron was brilliant and I was blown away by the visit. He suggested that I try production racing, and then gave me a vital piece of advice that's still as true today as it was then: if you want to race then you must be prepared, and be able to afford, to crash.

I give similar advice to young hopefuls today and I only hope I come across as accommodating and encouraging as Ron was to me. As we were leaving I thanked him and he said I could come back again any time to chat. He also said he'd be at Donington Park the following week for a test with one of his relations, John Gainey, and asked if I'd like to come along. As I got into the car he told me to be sure to bring my helmet and leathers.

I went home that night filled with hope. I'd been given personal advice from one of the best riders in the world and was going to join him on a test. I was ready to ride my luck and opportunity with Ron as far as I could go. If I had talent and he noticed, maybe I could make a career out of it.

The following week, with dad and Johnny, I turned up at Donington to meet Ron. I had a set of leathers with me that I'd bought off Tony for £20, and my own black Arai helmet. I'd stripped the helmet down to primer ready to paint it in Freddie Spencer colours and it was still in pieces – I reckoned that if I did get the chance to ride I could put it together in a couple of minutes. We watched the test all morning as Ron and John went out on the track, and I loved every moment. As they talked in the garage, I listened. They were the experts and I was a sponge soaking everything up.

Then, at lunchtime, Ron said that if I got changed he'd take me round for a couple of laps. I put on my leathers and went to rebuild my helmet, but Ron stopped me and told me I didn't have time. For a moment I was gutted, but thankfully John offered me his brand new white Arai and I was ready to go.

Ron gave me a little 80cc Yamaha race bike and he got on a Honda VFR750. The plan was that he would lead me for a few laps so that he could gauge my ability. I had to pinch myself that I wasn't dreaming and off I went, on track with my hero receiving one-to-one tuition. The track was dry and the surface cool, but I hardly noticed as I followed Ron. We swapped positions a couple of times and I used all the experience of the Chas Mortimer school to go as quickly as I dared. After a while I knew the session would soon come to an end, so I decided to dig in and really impress Ron. I was going as hard as I could when I came over Coppice too fast and lost the front end. It all happened so quickly that there was nothing I could do apart from bite the gravel and wait for the world to stop spinning.

I sat up in time to see Ron come to a halt, flick out the side stand and walk over. I was mortified, and all I could think of was what a prat I'd been for crashing. He asked if I was OK and checked the bike. The silencer had come off, but otherwise it was fine. He told me to remount and then he pushed me back to the pits. Rolling into pitlane was a very embarrassing and painful experience. My dad stared as I was pushed past him, the look on his face telling me I was in big trouble. I parked and took off John's helmet. There was a long gouge down the outside of the shell. I gave it back to John and mumbled an apology. I was ready to cry. Luckily John smiled and said it was OK, and then Ron patted me on the back and reiterated his advice – don't race if you can't afford to crash. This time I was lucky, and Ron told me he could fix the Yamaha without any cost.

I called Johnny that evening to see if he'd spoken with Ron after we left the circuit.

'Yeah,' said Johnny. 'He says you could be good if you don't crash your brains out.'

I hung up and punched the air with joy. I had another very significant endorsement under my belt and the crash was soon forgotten. During the following weeks I made many impromptu visits to the Haslam home. I didn't want to make a nuisance of myself but I wanted all the advice I could get. I told him about my plans to go vintage racing and that's where my friendship with Ron began.

After dad had returned the Velocette frame to rigid, as required by the organisers, he told me we had one chance to try the bike on track before the winter. It was an autumnal Thursday afternoon at Cadwell Park, dry and crisp, and we were the only people there. As I was unloading the bike from the van, dad asked me not to use the seat to jump-start the bike as it was made of thin wood and he hadn't had time to reinforce it. In my excitement, though, I immediately jump-started it, landing on the seat and snapping the wood.

Dad and I had a big argument there and then. He was furious that I'd broken the seat after warning me minutes earlier. The fact is that when I get my racing head on I become much more aggressive – it has always been that way. Mix that with feeling stupid and angry at myself, and I shouted back at dad. My racing career nearly came to a premature end right there, but after a few minutes we both calmed down. I apologised and dad fixed the seat.

I had access to the short circuit at Cadwell Park – the old version where Mansfield doubled back on itself and took you back up the hill. After my previous two track experiences, I had the notion that I'd like to get my knee down. If I could do that I'd be one step closer to being a real racer, because that's what real racers like Ron Haslam could do. Much to my disappointment it would be some time before I lost my knee-down virginity.

Cadwell Park was where I'd shortly make my race debut in a vintage meeting that autumn, so there was good reason for our test. For the first time since quitting motocross, I really enjoyed myself. I was in my element, learning the lines and imagining I was leading a race. By modern standards the Velocette was slow, but it could still top 100mph on its fully treaded tyres. Originally its gear and brake levers were on the opposite sides to what I was used to, but dad had adapted the bike so that the gear lever was now on the left. It worked a treat. At the end of the day dad and I were happy not to have broken anything.

As the date for my first venture at Cadwell Park drew nearer, I'd lie in bed wide awake, forehead damp with perspiration and mind racing with fear. I'd think to myself that racing would be fantastic if it was safe. I still harboured a hidden terror and couldn't imagine myself riding as fast or fearlessly as the top men of the day. It wasn't until I started racing that I realised the perceived danger is actually part of the excitement. I quickly discovered that when racing you're the one in control of the bike and there aren't many things to fear. The riders around you are, by default, similar to you and can, for the most part, be trusted. The only thing you have to fear is making a mistake, and that comes back to your own control.

My philosophy on control has been a long time in the making, with nearly 30 years of racing to back it up, but when I lined up for my first ever road race I was more excited than ever before – and, quite frankly, scared silly.

Chapter 5

FIRST STEPS

The sky was clear blue, stained by wispy white clouds. My breath was fogging the inside of my visor slightly. I could hear my heart pounding and dad was staring at me, his eyes alive with excitement as he clung to the pit wall. There I was, having drawn lots for grid position, in the middle of 30 other vintage racers, sticking out like a sore thumb in my orange novice's bib and concentrating intently on a nondescript man in country casuals who was walking to the side of the track, a Union Jack in his grasp.

I'd just completed the warm-up lap for my first ever road race, in the late autumn of 1986, and I was the most excited man on earth. I'd arrived at the holding pen, where you gather before being allowed on track, long before anyone else. I'd sat there on the Velocette for 15 minutes, feet tapping the ground, butterflies somersaulting in my stomach – and I'd fought the urge to go to the toilet one last time. For the warm-up lap the Velocette started on the first bump and I followed the other racers round the track before we gathered again on the grid and cut our engines.

The man lifted the Union Jack again and then dropped it quickly. I took half-a-dozen running steps and bump-started the bike on the first try. Despite my cracking start, all of my rivals had matched it and I went into the first corner firmly welded to the centre of the pack. On the first straight, though, it became crystal clear that the Velocette was very slow compared with the competition. Even with the throttle wound right open, I was a rolling chicane and bikes simply drove past me. But going into corners, particularly the hairpin, I was able to pass a lot of them again, holding off the brakes and carrying more corner speed. They'd drive past me once again on the next straight, but I felt I was racing and thoroughly enjoyed myself.

There were three races that day and I never got a sniff of the podium. I didn't get my knee down either, which was really disappointing. However, I'd just experienced my first real road racing and was thrilled. Nothing else mattered. Shelley had joined us for the day out and she too was excited by the racing and right behind my hopes – but she'd noticed the bikes streaming past on the straights and thought it was unfair.

In the van on the way home dad admitted that the bike was well down on power, and the next day he went into the garage and started working on the engine. Our objective for the coming winter was clear – more horsepower. All my hopes and dreams were tied up in that vintage racer and I watched its development with fervour. When I wasn't in the garage with dad, I could most likely be found at Ron Haslam's, asking questions and learning about racing.

At what seemed a snail's pace, 1987 arrived and our next meeting was at Mallory Park. During practice the bike felt livelier and faster, and, coupled with the slightly smaller and tighter nature of that circuit, the power deficit compared with the competition was not quite as apparent as at Cadwell Park. I was a slightly faster rolling chicane this time, particularly for the 500cc machines that were allowed to compete against us.

The schedule for the day meant you had to qualify to get through to the final, so it started off with heats. I had learned a bit from Cadwell Park, and when it came to picking lots out of the hat for our starting positions, I looked down, saw a front-row slot and picked it out. Was that cheating? No more than every other person who drew from that hat. I was just lucky to get to pick early.

In my first race, and from the front row, I made another great start and was in the leading group straight away. Down the main straight the 350cc bikes would creep by and the 500cc bikes would blast past contemptuously, but I made up the deficit at

Gerard's, the first corner and one of the most exhilarating in the world. Through that long 180-degree right-hander, which can be taken at extremely high speed, I rode underneath or round the other riders, while the bus stop and hairpin corners worked further to my advantage. The fast-in-a-straight-line riders were soon behind me and I found myself in second place fighting for the race win.

I was up against a 65-year-old character, complete with comedy handlebar moustache, on a much quicker 500cc race bike. He'd overtake me on the straight and then I'd get him back at the hairpin or bus stop. I remember thinking to myself that I had to break him if I was going to win. The finish line was halfway down the straight and he would out-drag me to it every time, so I decided I needed to overtake him through Gerard's and then hold that advantage to the hairpin and bus stop. If I got clean runs through those corners I reckoned I might have enough of an advantage to stop him retaking me on the straight.

Such tactics meant going into Gerard's faster than ever before. I bit the bullet and went for it. My heart was in my mouth, the tyres stuck and I rode round the outside of him. I held him off through the esses and once I was through the hairpin I knew I had him. He didn't pass me on the straight on that lap, and I was able to extend my lead further through the corners.

I crossed the finish line in a euphoric haze. Can I compare the feeling to anything? Try bungee jumping, losing your virginity and winning the lottery all rolled into one. It may only have been a heat but I'd won! I'd qualified for the final and my hopes were high even after the rain started to fall. As I'd never raced or even practised in the wet, this was going to be a new experience.

The next race started and after a couple of laps I found myself in second place again, catching the leader quickly through the turns. I didn't have time to think I might win. On the next lap I flew into Gerard's and my front wheel ran over the slippery black over-banding, which is the same as the shiny black stuff you see on roads today. In the dry it's bad enough, but in the wet it's lethal. Before I knew it, I'd lost the front wheel and was sliding through the gravel trap. I came to a stop unhurt and with no major damage to the bike, the only casualty being the rev counter gearbox coming off the side of the engine. It was such a mild crash, without any repercussions, that I actually found the incident exciting, a bit like a fairground ride.

I'd experienced my first race win and suffered my first race crash on the same day, and thanks to my good luck and lack of injury I felt invincible and ready to race again. Dad had other ideas. As soon as I got back to the pits he told me that it was all over for the day – no more racing for me. He'd seen the crash and was worried sick for me. I think he was also worried about what mum would say when we got home.

'Dad, I'm fine, nothing's hurt or badly damaged,' I said. I picked up the rev counter drive. 'I don't need this anyway, so there's not even anything to fix on the bike.'

He scowled at me, but relented almost instantly. Perhaps my enthusiasm and excitement from the day rubbed off on him. Maybe he realised I was going to continue racing regardless of what he said. I wasn't being disrespectful – just totally determined and focused. I'd tasted my dream and wasn't about to give it up without a fight. Either way, he nodded and said he needed to strip down the bike before racing at Cadwell Park a fortnight later.

That evening we told mum I'd crashed. She frowned but accepted it with grace. She was interested in my racing but just didn't want to see me getting hurt.

Cadwell Park was my third road race meeting and it represented a major milestone. Steve Tombes was the rider who everyone in the class wanted to beat. He was cleaning up virtually every race he entered and he was my target.

For this meeting Ann Haslam gave me a set of Ron's old leathers. They sported the Shell Pharaoh colours and were a huge source of inspiration for me – real leathers that had been used by one of the best riders in the world. I imagined a bit of his genius might have rubbed off on them and bring me good luck.

Ann was a real rock of support as I clawed my way into road racing. Both Ann and Ron could see my hunger and had decided together that they'd help nurture me. While Ron was still in the thick of his career and travelling a lot, Ann found in me a receptacle for all the lessons they'd learned in the early years. She talked me through everything – what to expect, what to look out for, how to present myself – and today I can reflect on how many of her observations came true and how much her advice shaped my career.

Ann told me there were always people watching and listening. Benefactors could be anywhere at any time, but they'd never provide support to anyone who behaved badly or might represent them negatively. This was something I understood early on and it has stuck with me as one of the vital lessons for a modern road racer. In every paddock I've ever been in I've found at least one rider who disgraces himself in public, and I've seen talented riders disappear into oblivion because of their tempers.

Road racing needs to be entertaining to attract the crowds, and with the crowds come commercial opportunities. Whether the commercial element is one individual wanting to be involved or a huge conglomerate seeking to promote its brand to millions of people, both want a racer they can present to customers, media, friends and family, and not have to worry about covering the kids' ears. Given that you ultimately cannot race motorcycles without money or commercial interest, this remains one of the key lessons for any road racer.

At Cadwell Park I donned Ron's leathers with pride and honour. Many of the other racers would deliberately want to pass me because of the leathers but I didn't care. Besides, I was focused on Steve Tombes and had the optimism that only inexperience can bring.

I didn't win that day but I did have another major achievement. During the main race I fought my way through to second place and was trailing Steve by 100 metres. I was determined to try to reel him in. As we came down the hill at the bottom of the Gooseneck I went into the corner faster than before. My left knee scraped on the ground for an instant until I picked the bike up again. The next lap I went in faster and again my knee touched the Tarmac, only this time for longer.

I'd got my knee down. I felt like I was a real road racer at last. The leathers didn't have any sliders on them and every time my knee touched down I was wearing a hole in them, but even as I did it I knew it was a badge of honour and just rode harder. I buried my knee into the ground and was riding faster than ever before. By the chequered flag I was only a couple of bike lengths behind Steve and had made a huge leap forward.

Just as in motocross many years before, I suddenly knew I could run with the best. That confidence helped fuel my ambition even further – that was when I thought I really could be a road racer after all. With Shelley in the pub that evening, all we could talk about was the racing. She'd watched and was just as excited as I was.

'I love road racing,' I confided in her. 'Now all I need to do is get into club racing. That's what Ron advised as the best way to get noticed.'

Snetterton came next, and it was to be a weekend of contrasting fortunes. The long straights of the airfield circuit meant the Velocette's engine was going to be under a lot of pressure and needed to be at its best for me to stand a chance. Riding on a wave of optimism, I set off in practice. After a couple of laps the engine exploded – the barrel blew straight off the top of the crank. It was terminal. We scoured the paddock for anyone who might have a spare engine, but in vain.

We watched the racing and set off for home disheartened. To be at a race meeting and not take to the track has always been difficult for me, but never more so than on that day. Back home, dad gave me a cup of tea and told me he thought I had a lot of promise. But when he said the damage to the bike would be very expensive and time-consuming to fix, my heart sank faster than the tea I was gulping down.

Then he said that rather than spending time and money on the Velocette, he was instead going to buy me a Yamaha RD350 to race. I leaped for joy. My scheming was coming to fruition – I was going to be able to club race just as Ron had advised. There was just one catch. While dad would buy me the bike, a huge investment on his part, I was the one who'd have to pay the running costs, including race entry fees, tyres, fuel and anything else that was needed.

I agreed to dad's terms straight away and early the following week we went to our local bike dealership and bought a brand-new RD350. Dad made a big sacrifice as he had to sell his Honda road bike to buy my new racer, and in due course I'd also have to sell my BMW to help fund my racing. We put a race fairing on the RD350 but didn't touch the engine, as dad thought it was quick enough in standard trim.

For my first outing on the RD350 we went to Mallory Park to test, two weeks after the disastrous Snetterton weekend. On the Velocette I'd been able to lap Mallory in about 1 minute 7 seconds. I knew the top 350cc racers were hitting 56 or 57 seconds and I wanted to see how close I could get. At the end of my first session I came into the pits bewildered. The RD350 felt like a rocket ship compared with the Velocette but my best lap was still three seconds away from the quickest times. I needed more horsepower already!

I joined Derby Phoenix Racing Club and remain a member to this day. I had my race licence and was ready to try proper club racing. I started racing every weekend and entered the 350cc, 500cc and Open classes just to build up experience.

After my session at Mallory, dad worked on the engine and gained a few extra horsepower, and then I went to my first race at Donington Park. Trevor Clow was the man to beat and a certain Matt Lewellyn was racing at the time as well, so I was in a new league of ability.

During my day at the Chas Mortimer race school I'd recorded 1 minute 38 seconds on the short circuit. I started the weekend on the RD350 with 1 minute 27 seconds and ended with a best of 1 minute 25 seconds. In my opening race I finished third, and then in the second race I ran off at McLean's, a fast right-hander that demands full commitment. I rode onto the grass and instinctively held the bike upright. The scare didn't help for the final race of the day, and I ended up just bringing the bike home for a mid-pack finish.

Back in 'The Royal Oak' with Shelley, I was starting to scheme again. Even though I hadn't ridden the RD350 much, the financial burden was immense. The sport was getting serious now. It was costing everything I had just to turn up and race, and I dreaded the thought of the extra expense if I was to end up crashing. As Ron told me, you need to be able to afford to crash, and I knew I would struggle. In fact I only crashed once while racing the RD350 and was lucky that the damage was only superficial. It was at Mallory Park the weekend after Donington and I highsided coming out of the hairpin, putting a dent in the tank. I got back on the bike and kept on racing.

As we sat scheming I realised that I couldn't afford to race for very long. I was working six days a week and barely keeping out of the red. I needed to start winning races and get noticed fast, or it would be curtains to our dreams.

Vintage racing had been a stepping stone to club racing, and the dream was now very much alive and kicking. But just as a newborn baby needs oxygen, my racing needed financing, and I was going from weekend to weekend on a wing and a prayer, glad to still have the chance to be competing. Looking back on those heady, stress-filled days, I was sustained by all the support I had from dad, Shelley, friends and others. When Ron wasn't at a Grand Prix, he'd come along with Ann to watch John Gainey and me.

Ann gave me a second set of Ron's leathers – jet black Elf leathers from a previous season. They must have been a target for other riders, but I didn't care – all I wanted to do now was to get rid of my novice's bib. They were my first leathers with proper knee sliders. As the originals wore out, I'd turn them round and swap knees to try to make them last a little longer as I couldn't afford to replace them. It sounds grim, but that's what we used to do with the tyres as well. After a meeting we'd turn the tyres round so that I could get the benefit of the other side of the tyre for the next event – you could squeeze enough life to make tyres last two or three race meetings that way.

My third club race meeting was at Mallory Park, and I was riding down the straight at 110mph when the wind tore off one of my knee sliders, which by then were wafer thin. When I came into the pits I was summoned on the PA to visit the organisers. I thought maybe they'd recovered my slider for me, but when I entered the room several angry people were waiting. My slider had just missed hitting a marshal. One man waved the offending slider at me before coming over and unceremoniously ripping the remaining slider from my leathers. 'These aren't safe. Get new ones or don't wear them at all,' I was told.

By now I'd established myself as a winner on the RD350. I was quick but, more than that, I was brave. I missed apexes, rode off the racing line, went into corners too quickly and made a lot of mistakes. I lacked technique and experience, but my bravery was pulling me through and I was starting to turn heads – just as I'd hoped.

A couple of weeks later, in June, racing guru Vic Lamb called dad and told him about a chap called Barry Coxhead who sponsored Dean Robinson with a Yamaha TZ350. Dean had been forced to stop racing and the bike was up for grabs. Barry enjoyed taking his wife Chris and family to the races and having an interest in a rider taking part. There was nothing commercial to it but if I was interested in borrowing the bike then I should give Barry a call – which I did right away.

Barry had been expecting the call and after a brief conversation he said he'd come and see me at Cadwell Park the following weekend. He wanted to meet dad and Shelley as well, to see what sort of people we were. I guessed he wanted to know if he could make friends with us and be able to relax in our company as he watched the races. When we got to Cadwell I was more nervous about meeting Barry than the racing itself. He shared a cup of tea with us and we chatted until I had to get ready for the races, then he excused himself and we didn't see him again that day. Back at home that evening, he rang and congratulated me on my results – a couple of wins and third places – and offered to lend me the TZ350. That capped a pretty good day.

I'd dreamed of having a proper race bike. Now, parked in our garage, I had a TZ350 complete with fairing and clip-on bars. Apart from the funding I'd received from dad, this was my first sponsorship of any serious kind. With the TZ, however, there also came much more responsibility. It wasn't my bike and I had to take care of it. I had to run it and cover all expenses on top of my RD350. It was only a matter of three months since I'd started racing and my finances were already stretched thin. Now they went into the red. I was earning £120 a week but spending £150-£170 a week on racing.

There's nothing like going into debt to focus your mind and priorities. It would have been so easy to walk away and say I couldn't afford to race, but I thought differently. Things were getting interesting and putting myself into some debt for the rest of the year was worth it if I could get noticed by a big team.

Time was limited, though, as I couldn't race for long like this and needed sponsorship fast. What the TZ allowed me to do was to enter the British Championship and gain access to a bigger audience that was more valuable to sponsors. Before that, however, I needed to get 10 signatures on my licence so that I could ditch my novice's bib.

By now my entire life revolved around racing. Shelley and I couldn't afford to go out on a Friday or Saturday night, and if dad hadn't helped me I don't think I'd have made it through that period. He put in a lot of time to help with the bike and lent me money when I was really desperate.

I went to another practice day at Mallory Park and was riding the TZ when Andy McGladdery came past me at a ferocious rate on a Honda Superbike. I tried to hang on to him but didn't stand a chance – he was gone. That evening I wondered how anyone could go that much faster than me on the same circuit. I was going quickly on my TZ but it was many seconds slower per lap than the Superbike. I wondered how fast I'd have to go before I could be termed a 'good' rider. Was I as good as I needed to be? I was plagued by self-doubt but I refused to tell anyone about it, simply locking it away inside.

Another thing that the Superbike showed me was a new direction for my racing career. Superbikes were not only fast and exciting, they were attracting sponsorship and money. If I could get onto a Superbike then I could make the step up from club racing.

I had a friend called Tony 'Stick' Evans whose father started to take an interest in my racing. Denton Evans offered to help me look for sponsorship. He knew Tony Delahunty, a DJ at Radio Trent, and he got me mentioned on the radio. On one occasion my race boots were destroyed in a crash and I couldn't afford to replace them, so Denton bought me a new pair. He was my first financial sponsor.

My first race meeting on the TZ was entirely forgettable. I had problems with the fuel line and couldn't get off the grid. I was 12th going into the first corner, and you can never win a race from there in just five or six laps, no matter how fast you are. Back at home dad found a blockage in the fuel line, so he fixed that problem, but that didn't cure the bad starts.

We took the TZ to the Watnall Brick Yard every evening for the next week, spending two hours each night practising my starts until we'd both had enough of it. I needed to be able to sit on the bike and paddle off just like my rivals, but my legs were a little on the short side. It took a lot of practice but eventually I got it right and at the next meeting I started to win races.

Towards the end of the 1987 season I took part in a race at Donington Park and Suzuki's Grand Prix hero Niall Mackenzie was the star guest. He was the big name who'd come to watch a club meeting, and he smiled and nodded at me from a distance. At the end of the day he awarded the 'Man of the Meeting' prize to the race winner on an RG500 Suzuki. That irritated me a little, as I felt I'd deserved the award for putting up a fight and finishing second to him on my smaller-capacity bike.

By the end of the season I finally got rid of my novice's bib and achieved my national licence. I was planning a proper attack on the British Championships in 1988 and spent the winter working and saving.

Watching television one weekend I saw Rob Orme and Steve Hislop racing at Cadwell Park and wanted more than anything to be with them. They were racing heroes at the top of their game and doing what I wanted to do. I aspired to be able to give up signwriting one day and join them in the ranks of professional racers. Although I still had some of that self-doubt, I relished the thought I may race against them one day.

For 1988 dad bought me a Honda CBR600 to race in the cleverly named 'Honda CBR600 Challenge' and also in Seniorstock racing. Dad and I both knew the future for racing was in four-strokes, so we thought the CBR600 was a good move. Again, I had to fund the running of the bike, and all the money I'd saved through the winter was already spent by the time the first meeting came around. I was facing what I knew was going to be my make-or-break season. If I didn't get noticed now, I wasn't going to be able to afford to race any more.

To enter the CBR600 Challenge, the rules stated that you needed a dealership's support. Someone had told me to speak to Peter Padgett, of Padgett's Motorcycles, so I rang him and he agreed to lend his name to the bike to get me on the starting grid. I'd also race the TZ because as far as I was concerned the more laps I completed the more I was learning.

My first ride on the CBR600 was at Donington Park and the class of field in the British Championship was leagues ahead of anything I'd encountered before. Eric Macfarlane won the race and, although my lap times were just 1.5 seconds slower than his, I finished way down in 19th place despite riding as hard as I could. I was devastated, and on the way home from the meeting I voiced my self-doubt for the first time to Shelley and dad. They convinced me that I'd done well for my first attempt on the bike and in the class, and that my expectations had been too high. I decided they were right and kept at it.

I won the 350cc British ACU Star Championship on the TZ that season to confirm my credentials as a road racer. It was by remaining competitive in this class that I kept myself sane and moving forward. It was my second British Championship title after winning in schoolboy motocross and I was delighted. But my aim remained firmly on four-stroke racing by now, and with the financial pressure so high I needed to get into that class if I was going to make it.

Halfway through the year on the CBR600 I was finishing anywhere between 12th and 15th on a bog-standard bike. I was fighting a losing battle against the professionally tuned and better-funded teams, including the factory-backed racers.

At Cadwell Park I was facing another frustrating weekend of mid-table results when Vic Lamb, who was working with Team Green Kawasaki, said there might be a chance for me to race a factory bike. Vic was an important figure in my career. We'd met when his son Wayne and I raced together in schoolboy motocross. The two significant moves I made in the early years – Barry Coxhead and Kawasaki – were both introduced by Vic, and I'll never forget his help.

Roger Hurst and Ray Swan were the two official Team Green factory riders, and Roger had crashed in morning practice for the races. His ZX10 and GPX600 bikes were available. Vic spoke with Kawasaki team manager Colin Wright. Colin was new to team management and called his dad Alec, who was in Europe managing Kawasaki's motocross team. When he hung up he told me I was being given the chance to ride the GPX600, just hours before the race was due to start.

Despite having no practice on the bike or with the team, I wasn't going to turn down an opportunity like that. The Team Green Kawasakis were much faster than my Honda, so here was my chance to see what I could do with similar machinery to the front runners. I finished fifth in the race. Although no fairytale start, it was a huge step forward and showed I had the potential to run at the front.

Despite everyone's best efforts, however, it was getting close to the end for me. Through 1988 I had two bikes that I personally had to pay to run, and all of my money, and a lot of dad's and Shelley's, was going into keeping my hopes alive. If I wasn't noticed and sponsored soon, then I was going to end up flat broke. I was now working every hour I could to earn a few extra pounds to put towards my racing. I was still enjoying my signwriting job and had no intention of packing it in despite my rapid progress within racing. For a start I couldn't afford to do that, and, secondly, my nature is always to look for security. Shelley and I hardly had time to scheme in the pub any more, and when we did have the time we agreed that we couldn't afford it.

I needed some big breaks. Luckily, they came quickly.

Chapter 6

THE BIG BREAKS

A week after my stand-in ride at Cadwell Park with Team Green Kawasaki, I was asked to visit Kawasaki in Slough. There I was given some fantastic news. Colin Wright offered to lend me a GPX600 for the rest of the season, and would also cover the cost of running it. This was my first big break.

The GPX was the best 600cc bike of its time and dad and I knew it would be more competitive than my Honda CBR600 in Seniorstock racing. My plan was to go into the races as hard and fast as I could and target wins every weekend.

From Kawasaki's point of view, I think I was a pretty shrewd investment. It allowed them to stake a claim on me should I ever be a success. Colin and Alec Wright could keep a close eye on my progress and see if I had what was needed to win. If I didn't, they could walk away at the end of the season after minimal expenditure. The way I see it is that Kawasaki had cast its fishing line and was waiting to see if I'd bite. I was biting all right – champing at the bit would be closer to the truth. I was very aware that this was my opportunity to prove myself and the pressure was enormous. I dreamed of being taken on as a regular rider for Kawasaki and being paid to race motorcycles – if I could do well I might even be able to secure a job for the following season.

Dad was tasked with tuning and preparing the GPX, which was as close to standard as you could get, and set to work in the garage at home as soon as we got hold of the bike, after its outing in the production event at the Isle of Man TT races. Team Green Kawasaki shared information with him, and provided a Pro-Flex shock absorber as well as some new fork internals to help with suspension tuning. Dad has a great engineering brain and worked tirelessly on that bike, coaxing as much horsepower from it as he possibly could.

Dad has always been a fantastic mechanic and has made some cracking innovations in his time. Once, at a schoolboy motocross meeting, I remember mum saw another child crash and hit his jaw on the handlebars, smashing out his front teeth. The next weekend I had sponge on my bars – I don't know if dad was the first person to come up with the idea but now all the 'crossers have sponge on their bars. Despite mum's best efforts, I ended up smashing my front teeth out a year later while ice skating, and no amount of sponge would have helped when that happened...

The two Team Green Kawasaki riders, Roger Hurst and Ray Swan, gave me a hard time. I was a hungry young racer looking for a break and they were the two established stars trying to hold down their jobs. I guess if I proved myself then one of them would be looking at the axe, and that's not a comfortable situation. We weren't friends and there was little chat between us. In fact they were quite openly hostile. I was disappointed in them as they wouldn't even give me the time of day, but I didn't give a damn how they treated me. I wasn't at the races to make friends – I was there to do a job. If their attitude had any effect, it got my back up a bit and made me even more determined to run with and hopefully even beat them.

My first outing was at Thruxton. I'd raced there before and it was a bumpy track. It's still a bumpy track but back in 1988 it was a lot worse than now – you could call it a Tarmac motocross circuit! Fortunately, thanks to my motocross upbringing, I was quite happy with the bike moving around a lot underneath me, and the bumps didn't phase me one bit. Something clicked there for me and I went from an also-ran to a race contender. After qualifying well, I got a good start and went away with Roger and Ray, who were going for the championship and were the men to beat.

The three of us built up a lead and I was thoroughly enjoying myself dicing with them. I was riding within myself and the capabilities of the bike, yet I was able to stay with them and even to set the pace when I hit the front. I was in a comfort zone, and that's a wonderful place for a racer to be. I knew if I had to dig a bit deeper and find some extra speed I could – I didn't have to ride at 100 per cent to maintain the pace.

On the final lap I drafted the other two down the straight and took the lead with just Club Chicane to go to the chequered flag. I left my braking as late as I dared and, as I turned in, Ray Swan came underneath me, his bike sideways and out of control. He banged into the kerb – how he stayed upright is a mystery to me – but he made the pass stick. I followed him in and, on the exit, Roger Hurst went for an equally desperate overtake and got on the throttle too early. He highsided in a spectacular crash and rolled across the finish line behind me, on his backside in third place.

I returned to the pits barely able to contain my joy. Second was my best result yet, and in my heart I knew I'd taken a step up in performance and could run with these riders and challenge for victory. Roger and Ray had nearly killed themselves trying to pass me and my relationship with them suffered a turn for the worse, but I honestly couldn't have cared less. I'd made a breakthrough and was too busy celebrating.

Not long after the podium celebrations Alec Wright came to see me. He took me to the rear of the awesome Team Green Kawasaki truck and told me that what had happened in the race had not been to plan. Roger and Ray were going for a championship and that's what was important for Kawasaki. I received a right rollicking for my efforts. But then, just before he walked away, he smiled, looked me straight in the eye, and said, 'Bloody good ride though.'

Dad and Shelley were worried I might have blown my chances with Kawasaki. I was as well, but I can look back now and see that the rollicking was a formality, given with tongue in cheek, and there was as much praise as damnation in Alec's words. The meeting had been televised by the BBC and provided enormous media exposure for the team. I learned another vital lesson that day. I wasn't club racing any more – I was part of a bigger team and a bigger picture. On this stage, bike racing wasn't just about going as fast as I could. There were other factors: television, team-mates, manufacturer and sponsors were all political forces that needed to be weighed up. My transition from privateer to factory racer had started.

While the factory stars were staying in fancy motorhomes or hotels, we were still sleeping in our Iveco van, dad and me in the back and Shelley in a hammock in the cab. While they had workshops to tune their bikes, we had the garage at home. While they trained all week and focused solely on racing, dad returned to the Coal Board, Shelley to her job at a chartered surveyor's office and me to Phillips Signs. But that was all I knew at the time and I didn't knock it. I still dreamed of being paid to race and giving up my day job, and was just thankful that I was now on a level playing field. I had the same bike and equipment as the leading riders and could show off my talent against the best in the country.

There were only two more meetings that year and I finished fifth in both of them. At Mallory Park my lack of experience showed through on what is without a doubt one of the hardest circuits in the country. You must be prepared to hit fairings and elbows and force your way through if you want to win there, and I was up against some of the toughest riders around. I did my best, and later in the day dad told me a story that proved it to me. He'd been viewing the race from Gerard's and was standing beside Roger Hurst's mother, although she didn't know who he was. A couple of laps into the race I made a hard pass on Roger going into Gerard's, overtaking him at one of the fastest and scariest parts of the circuit. His mother turned to dad and said: 'For goodness sake, he's hungry isn't he?' I felt proud when I heard that.

My final race of the year on the GPX was at Brands Hatch, and it was a similar story. I could run with the leaders and was right on the pace, but I was still learning racecraft. Sheer determination saw me through to fifth.

In between those British Championship Seniorstock races, I went to Scarborough for the Gold Cup meeting. It's more of a road circuit, and it was one of the first times I'd come up against Jim Moodie, one of the best riders of that decade. 'Mad Dog Moodie', as he was called, put us both into a hedge at the hairpin, and that began a long series of clashes between us. For me, I was simply riding my heart out and giving it my best. Whenever Jim and I came together on a track, it invariably ended up in a crash. Even to this day, I'd hate to be racing against him. I just think there's no give in either of us on a track, and that has led to more crashes than I can remember.

One week after Scarborough, Padgett's, the motorcycle dealership that had lent its name to my racing in the CBR600 Challenge, asked if I'd like to ride a Suzuki RG500 two-stroke at the following weekend's round of the European Championship at Donington Park. I jumped at the chance. This was another of my dreams coming true. There was no payment – just the opportunity to ride. I'd watched Barry Sheene race a 500cc Suzuki and now, ten years after him, I was getting a chance to ride a descendant of his machine. Grand Prix was, and remains, the highest class in the world and I was desperate to see what I could achieve on a real two-stroke racer.

The fact that the European Championship was at my home track was a bonus and when the event came I was fired up. The circuit was wet but drying through the race, and I fought my way up to third place – and then started the last lap. I flew past the pit wall where Martin Cutler – a local lad, friend and mechanic who helped me out – was standing. He was going mad, waving his hands and jumping up and down with excitement, and I took that to mean there was a rider right behind me. I thought I'd have to ride the lap of my life if I wanted to keep my podium place, so I got my head down and went into Redgate corner faster than before.

In the dry I'd have got away with it, but in the damp conditions I was a fraction too fast. I hit my apex and drifted out to the edge of the track, my wheels just touching the painted kerbing. I was going fast and utterly committed to the corner, so when the bike let go violently on the slick paint I never had a chance of catching the crash. I slammed into the Tarmac while the bike bounced into the gravel.

I was knocked senseless and woke up in the middle of the track with bikes coming at me at high speed and barely missing me. I wobbled, crawled and ran to the side of the circuit, thankful that no other racer had hit me. Once I got to the wall I sat down and a bloke I didn't know started talking to me, but I could hardly make out a word. Eventually he asked me what day it was. I looked round and, because I was at a race track, guessed it must be Sunday. He nodded and started talking again, and it dawned on me that he was either a medic or a marshal.

Then another man came up and started talking. I was feeling pretty bemused by now. He was asking how I was and I replied with whatever I thought they might want to hear. Yes, I was fine, I felt great, of course I could race again that day. But I knew deep down that something was very wrong. The second man kept talking to me and was treating me as though I was familiar to him. I asked him who he was. It turned out he was Doug Hogg, a friend of the past 15 years and a near neighbour. I didn't recognise him at all after the crash and that confirmed my fear that I was badly concussed.

By the time I got back to the pits Peter Padgett was at our garage and pushing for me to race in the F1 World Championship on a Honda RC30 later in the day. I desperately wanted to start the race, but by now my vision was blurred and I was feeling pretty sick. Another doctor came to see me and said there was no chance I could race again that day.

It was a double missed opportunity. Not only was I dazed, confused, concussed and bruised, but I was hurting inside from missing a podium and a chance to race in a World Championship event. The F1 World Championship was basically a precursor to World Superbikes and featured great riders such as Carl Fogarty, Joey Dunlop, Mick Grant and Rob McElnea. I'd missed my chance.

Clive Padgett, Peter's son, was cool about the crash and told me I could have the Suzuki RG500 for the next race at Cadwell Park. I felt as though I'd just had a 'get out of jail' card.

At Cadwell Park the Suzuki wouldn't start for the opening practice session, and Clive had to push me all the way through Hall Bends before it fired into life. Annoyed that I'd missed the first minute of the session, I took off as fast as I could. I got to the Gooseneck, which is a sharp left-hand downhill corner. There aren't many left-handers at Cadwell, and I went in far too fast for the still-cold tyres and lost the front, crashing heavily without even completing a lap. I learned a lesson that day about warming up tyres.

I also broke my right wrist and that led to serious repercussions with Kawasaki. Alec Wright told me I shouldn't have crashed and if I wanted to race for Kawasaki then all my other racing activities would have to stop – whether F1 or anything else. I understood completely. Kawasaki was expecting me to deliver week in and week out. I couldn't do that if I was injured.

I was beside myself with disappointment and for getting into such a compromised situation. Call it youthful exuberance or over-zealousness, it didn't matter, either way I needed to calm down or I'd be out on my ear. After two crashes on the Suzuki RG500 I was also aware I was breakable and not invincible after all.

I'd also destroyed my Arai helmet in the crash and things were so tight I couldn't afford to buy a new one. The Blanchard family, very close friends, came to the rescue and bought me a replacement. That meant a lot to me, and I could race again once I was fit.

I was out of racing for five weeks while my wrist healed. I tried riding but the pain was incredible and I couldn't operate the throttle and front brake. When I came back it was near the end of the season and I needed to show my talent and ability quickly if I wanted a job for the following year. There's never a good time to break your wrist, but the end of the season when contract negotiations are rife is probably the worst.

In Seniorstock racing I was running with established riders and felt as though I was a front-runner on merit. Luckily for me Kawasaki agreed – and was willing to invest in me.

I visited Kawasaki's team HQ at the end of the season and Alec Wright told me that Kawasaki wanted me to run and race my own GPX600 in 1989 – and they'd pay me. The wage they offered was the same as my job as a signwriter, and on top of that they'd pay dad to maintain and work on the bike. Dad immediately told me I could have his money, and by the end of the day I was set to be earning more from my racing than my full-time employment.

As we were leaving Alec told me I should get my van painted in team colours and he'd cover the cost. I was delighted, but a lot more than a paint job was needed to keep the van on the road and looking good. We ended up replacing panels and wheel arches, and I guess it wasn't far off a complete rebuild. When I eventually showed him the invoice for all the work, he just shook his head and told me he'd expected to pay for paint, not a complete refurbishment. I didn't complain – after all I was now earning a very good living from racing.

But the money wasn't life-changing. It was the equivalent to a decent salary, but certainly not enough to convince me to give up my day job. I wasn't about to take anything for granted, and there was no way I was giving up signwriting. Racing was fickle and the wages from Kawasaki were heavily performance-related. That was too much of a risk for me, especially after my experience with the broken wrist.

My life for the next year was fairly well set out before me. I'd work from Monday at Phillips Signs, and then we'd travel to a race meeting on Thursday evening. On Sunday night we'd get home late and it would be up early the next day to start the next working week. That sounds like hard work, but in fairness

I've never felt that racing a motorcycle is work – it has always been pleasure.

During the working week I'd spend the first two days thinking about my last race meeting – what I could have done better and what I needed to work on. For the next two days I'd focus on the next race meeting and visualise myself at the circuit and racing. On Thursdays, the end of the day couldn't come quickly enough for me to get home, load the van and get to the next circuit.

What the money from racing did give me was light at the end of the tunnel. Shelley and I had dreamed of me being paid to race bikes. Now it was happening and it was another tick in the box on my list of ambitions.

When the contract was drafted and signed I couldn't wipe the smile off my face. I was being paid to do what I loved. I'd roughed it but now I was making it.

As well as having the van painted in team colours, I could now afford a new awning to keep us dry. I was given team clothing to wear instead of jeans and a T-shirt, and, most important of all for me, I was given my own made-to-measure leathers in team colours and with 'Reynolds' written on the back. That was a major step forward. I was like a child at Christmas who has just got all the presents he could have wished for. Until then I'd still been using Ron Haslam's old leathers, covered in black duck tape to conceal sponsors that clashed with Team Green Kawasaki. Now I had my own leathers and felt I was really going places. Not only was I racing with the leaders, I was looking like a winner as well.

At the beginning of 1989 I was a sponsored 600cc and 250cc rider. I'd achieved a lot but my sights were still set on racing a Superbike and I told Colin Wright, the team manager, that this was my aim. He smiled and told me it was my job to win the Shellsport 400 British Championship on the new Kawasaki KR1 and to race in the Seniorstock on the GPX600.

If, at the start of 1989, I'd had to write a list of all my hopes and dreams in racing, I'd have been about halfway down it, and more determined than ever to prove my worth and get a Superbike ride.

Going into 1989, my social life was non-existent, but I was as happy with Shelley as she was with me. We shared the dreams, hardships, ups and downs. There was no more talking in the pub about racing: my budget, my time and the need to be physically fit meant that socialising over a pint of beer was a thing of the past.

Between racing and working I didn't have a spare minute. Even my holidays from work were booked to coincide with test sessions or race meetings. If I did get a moment of spare time, I often used to go and see Ron and Ann Haslam, who'd become more than mentors and were now good friends. Ron and I would fly remote-controlled helicopters at his farm and shoot the breeze about life in general. We no longer talked as much about racing – there was no need.

I had my head down living the dream, and those were happy days of hard work and great personal reward and achievement. I was mixing with riders who were my heroes.

Dad never told me what he really thought of the Kawasaki deal for 1989. He said it looked great on paper, but it's in his nature to be very cautious. It's from him that I get my attitude of taking nothing for granted and not getting too excited. During that winter of 1988-89 he simply put his head down and worked on the race bikes for me, still using his garage as the team workshop.

Mum was proud of my achievements. She was still scared of the racing, but it was established within our home now and was no longer an issue.

It was around this time when I was racing at a minor meeting at Carnaby in East Yorkshire when a spectator came up to me holding a book and a pen. I said 'hello' and he offered me the book.

'What's that for?' I asked.

'Can I have your autograph?'

I was stunned. I didn't have an autograph or even a half-legible signature, but I was honoured to have been asked. He noticed my pause and said, 'I think it may be worth something some day.'

During 1989, being asked for my autograph became a regular occurrence, and I also found that the media wanted to talk to me. My first interview was with Julian Ryder for the now defunct *Motorcycle Weekly*. He wanted to know where I'd come from and how I'd made it so far so quickly.

Right from the outset I promised myself that I'd always make time for the spectators, fans, sponsors and media. As far as I was concerned it was thanks to all of them that I was able to do what I loved and I respected them all for that, and still do.

I was an up-and-coming racer and everyone was supporting me. Julian's article was very positive and after it was published I was asked for autographs more frequently.

Just before the start of the new racing season, Colin Aldridge, who sponsored Ray Swan and Mark Farmer, made me a very lucrative offer. He had a 750cc F1 Kawasaki in a Harris chassis on full slicks and wanted to know if I'd ride it for him. An F1 bike is basically a Superbike and here I was, a lot sooner than I'd imagined, being offered the opportunity to race one, not in the Superbike class but in F1, which back then was equally prestigious. I asked Colin Wright for permission and he agreed, as it was a Kawasaki that I'd be competing on.

This was a lucky break. You can call me lucky or naïve, and I may be guilty of both, but one thing I never did throughout my career was push myself in the paddock or to teams. All the opportunities I had actually came to me, rather than resulting from me looking for them. Anyway, I wouldn't have known how to push myself forward, as self-publicity isn't a strong point and never has been. I was fortunate to be picked up early on by Colin Wright, so I didn't really need to push myself to team bosses. Whenever an opportunity presented itself I took it and made enough of an impression to step up the ladder one more rung.

I could have made a lot more friends in the paddock over the years. Some riders are brilliant at this: they know all the team managers and send them Christmas cards, and are always high on everyone's list of desirable candidates for their teams. But that has never been me. I was in the paddock to do a job and win races – anything else was a distraction. I'm sure I've lost out on opportunities and potential earnings because of this, but I'll never complain because it has worked for me.

People got to know me through my riding, not because of my socialising or politics. I never had a manager and in some ways that may have been a bad thing, but I never felt I needed one. I conducted my own negotiations and made my own decisions.

Vic Lamb was the first person to give me an opportunity by introducing me first to Barry Coxhead and then to Colin Wright. We weren't the best of friends or anything, but he recognised that I had talent and he gave me the introductions. In a way this proves that it's who you know and not what you know that matters in racing. But I maintain that the people who could seriously help you need to recognise your talent otherwise they'd never push you forward. No matter how well you know someone, if you aren't performing then you won't make it. Vic Lamb, Colin Wright and Ron Haslam all saw the talent in me, and their belief, along with the right contacts, helped me to advance.

I firmly believe a rider can still follow this sort of career progress today. Although the paddock is now a much more commercial place, a determined rider can still catch the eye of a decision-maker and prove that he has talent. Two names spring to mind as riders who've enjoyed fast rises to stardom – Casey Stoner and Shane 'Shakey' Byrne. In just a few years they both won British Championships and were catapulted into the big time.

I know for a fact that Paul Denning at Crescent, the organisation behind the Rizla Suzuki Superbike and MotoGP teams, is always looking at promising new talent. He put Tom Sykes and James Buckingham on his Rizla Suzuki Superbikes when they were on the rise and put them into the limelight. If he sees someone going well he'll give them a chance to prove himself, and at that point it's up to the rider to take his chance.

My advice to would-be racers is to take the job seriously, don't annoy people and seize your chances. It worked for me and I still think it can work for young riders wanting to break through.

It also helps to have a mentor. Ron and Ann Haslam helped me no end and gave me fantastic advice. I'd like to think I'd be the same towards a young enthusiastic rider if he came to me and asked for help. Obviously a rider must have the talent to back up his request for advice, and the onus is always on the rider to take the initiative. Top riders and ex-champions don't go looking for the next big stars – the hopefuls must approach them for help and work on the relationship.

That's how I went about my career, and it led to my big breaks. The 1989 season was going to be a very busy one, especially when the opportunity to ride the TT came along as well.

Chapter 7

THE ISLE OF MAN TT

At the start of 1989 Kawasaki asked if I'd be interested in racing at the Isle of Man TT, and I said that I would. There'd be no pressure on me to win – I'd just go to the island and see if I gelled with it. I was excited to think I'd be racing against living legends like Steve Hislop, Carl Fogarty, Robert Dunlop, Trevor Nation, Brian Morrison, Jamie Whitham, Phillip McCallen and Nick Jefferies.

There has long been debate about whether or not the Isle of Man TT should be maintained as a road racing event. I believe that as long as riders want to race at the TT, then it should have a place on the calendar. We live in a free society and we shouldn't be legislating against riders who want to go to the Island and take it on.

My parents took me to the TT four or five times as a child. It was our annual holiday and, along with the bike racing, there was a brilliant carnival atmosphere that we all enjoyed – there's a lot more to the TT than just road racing. I admire the riders. They are fantastically skilled and have courage by the spadefuls to do what they do.

Ever since those early visits as a child, the romantic notion of the TT circuit being the most difficult and challenging in the world has flirted with me. It teased me and invited me to take part. So, before the short-circuit season started, I took Shelley across to the Isle of Man and we spent a few days driving a car round the TT circuit and enjoying a rare break, as holidays were few and far between at this time. My appetite for the racing was whetted. Driving the circuit at 40mph can do that for you – it's when you're doing it for real at 140mph that it becomes a lot more serious.

Back on the mainland, I started to concentrate on the circuit racing. Brands Hatch was the opening F1 race on Colin Aldridge's 750cc Harris-chassis bike, and right from the start it didn't go as planned. On the Saturday there was a problem with the engine that forced us to drive all the way back to Colin's garage in the evening. He was up all night working on the motor before driving back down to Brands for the race on Sunday. I struggled with a poor starting position and a still unfamiliar and under-performing bike, and ended up 22nd. On my first outing on the KR1 I finished second and was much happier.

At Mallory Park, my first proper race on the F1 bike, I was mixing it with the main stars of the day – Steve Spray and Trevor Nation. I took second place, and my plan to prove I was good enough to race Superbikes was back on course.

The next outing, at Brands Hatch, was my first ride that year on the GPX600 and I won the race. Third was all I could manage on the KR1 and, knowing this was my main priority, I told Colin Wright I thought it needed more horsepower. His response was to tell me to ride it faster through the corners and not to believe what the pundits were saying about its lack of power. I wasn't sure how to respond to that, so I said nothing. The bike was slow and I think we both knew it.

Barring a few glitches on the circuits, it was a good start to the season, so it was with light hearts and open minds that we went to the Isle of Man in May. If nothing else, the break from the daily grind of work was enticing. Shelley and I stayed in a hotel, but dad decided he'd sleep in the truck with the bikes. It had been ten years since we'd last come to see the TT as a family, but there was still the same friendly atmosphere. This time, though, there was the looming spectre of the racing itself. I wasn't watching any more. Instead I'd be taking part on the most difficult and dangerous track in the world. Still, there were no nerves as there was no pressure to win. It was all a new experience and I was proud to be there.

After we'd unloaded the bikes, I put a number plate on the production bike and told Shelley to jump on the back – we were going to do a lap of the circuit. She looked slightly puzzled, but I urged her to get on. It was a full-on production race bike with the speedo taped over and race numbers on the fairing, and the inclusion of a number plate made no difference to its legality on the road – it was completely illegal. I didn't care, though, as I wanted to ride the track for the first time, open roads or not.

We took off down Bray Hill full of excitement. On the approach to Union Mills the road widened a bit and I came into the town flat-out in fourth, in complete control and on my side of the road. A copper was standing in the middle of the road with a speed gun pointed directly at us, and, despite sitting up and braking as hard as the bike would allow, I was collared. There's no question I was speeding – call it the enthusiasm of the young and inexperienced. I took off my helmet and gave him my best 'sorry officer' face, but it was to no avail.

'Do you know how fast you were going?' he asked.

I glanced guiltily at the taped-up speedo and said, 'Not really, maybe 40 or 50mph?'

'Try closer to 90mph,' he advised, getting his book and pen out of his pocket.

I finished the lap at a much more sedate pace and rolled into parc fermé, where dad was waiting. When I told him what had happened and that I was going to appear in court in two days' time, he was less than impressed. It turned out I wasn't the only rider to get caught speeding before the event began, and we all ended up in court. The judge – not a bike fan – gave me a hefty fine. Ouch!

Once the practice sessions started, I was able to ride the circuit with complete confidence on closed roads. This was another of my dreams coming true. I'd always wanted to race at the TT and now

I was doing it. As a child, all the racers who took part in the TT had been heroes to me, gods on two wheels, and now I was riding with them. I was utterly caught up in thoughts of conquering the track and overcoming the dangers. On my first lap, I used the entire width of the road and all of my knowledge of the circuit, gleaned from many laps in a car, to best effect, registering a 90mph average speed – which I was pleased with for a first attempt.

On that first lap I found that there's a huge difference between riding a race bike on closed roads and driving a car when the roads are open. Although I knew my way through Bray Hill, Union Mills, Kirkmichael and the Mountain in a car, Bray Hill looks completely different when you arrive at 160mph on a bike. The speed paints an entirely new picture and it takes some getting used to. On a bike I was getting to Union Mills four minutes ahead of my fastest attempt in a car – the world had been put on fast-forward and I couldn't keep up.

I can clearly remember coming out of Union Mills on my first lap, concentrating 100 per cent, and being struck by the realisation that I didn't have a clue where the next corner went or where I was on the circuit. I had no choice but to roll off the throttle and feel my way through the corners until I came upon a more familiar section. I ended up following the white line in the middle of the road all the way to the Mountain before I could attack the circuit again.

I was used to laps of between one and three miles. The TT is 37.75 miles and around every corner is the potential for danger and the unknown. As a newcomer I was lost for most of my time riding the circuit. Even at the end of the fortnight I couldn't say I knew the circuit well. The faster you go the more it changes, and that means relearning parts of it all over again.

In one of the early-morning sessions I started out at five o'clock and was riding the F1 bike hard, but well within my limits. It was a cold, clear morning with moisture in the air. At well over 100mph I was approaching Barregarrow, a section where you come out of a corner and down a hill. There's a steep dip that quickly levels out, and too much speed here can really upset the bike when you leap out of the dip and land hard. Coming up to the dip, I eased off the throttle and started to brake. Half a second later a bike came past me at a ferocious speed, far faster than I would have thought possible.

It was Steve Hislop on a quick lap. He didn't roll off the throttle for even an instant. He flew off the dip and landed in a puff of tyre smoke, the suspension bottoming out and the bike slewing from side to side. As soon as his rear tyre touched Tarmac he was accelerating again.

I rode through the dip as fast as I dared, feeling the bike go light and then compress, before starting down the road after Steve, but he was already out of sight.

I'd just witnessed what it takes to win a TT, and I was left short. Not just slightly off the pace, but strides away from the commitment needed to compete. I knew instantly that I was incapable of riding at that pace. My sense of self-preservation is too strong. On a proper race circuit I can ride to the very limit, and sometimes beyond, but on the road, where any mistake could be your last, there was no chance, particularly with no pressure on me to perform.

My first session on the 250cc KR1, again starting at five o'clock in the morning, was a bit easier. It wasn't as fast as the F1 bike, of course, so I felt I had a bit more time to think things through. I was enjoying it, but when I went through a wooded section close to Kirkmichael a bird flew straight into the top of my helmet. I was lucky to stay on the bike.

The KR1 had a small fuel tank so I needed to come in at the end of every lap for more petrol. As I pulled in, Shelley pointed at me saying, 'Oh my God!' There was blood all down the back of my helmet and leathers, and it was extremely unpleasant to look at. Once they knew it was a bird's and not mine, they cleaned me up and set me on my way again.

Later on, again in practice with the KR1, I was concentrating so hard that I rode straight past the pits, forgetting that I had to stop for fuel. I only realised what I'd done when the bike started to misfire, passing the Bungalow about 30 miles later. As I struggled on from the Bungalow, trying to coax the bike closer to the pits, Rob Orme came past and disappeared round the corner. I later found out that he'd crashed at high speed and was in a bad way. I pulled to the side of the road, ignorant of what had happened and with the bike completely out of fuel.

Back at the pits, dad and Shelley were beside themselves with worry. They knew that I'd be around the Bungalow area by now and that there'd been a bad accident there. When the air ambulance was sent up, they were frantic.

By now I'd also pieced the situation together and thought they might be worried, so I caught the attention of a marshal and asked him to relay a message back to dad in the pits to say that I was OK, and that he should stay put as I could hitch a lift back with my bike in another van. It was 20 nervous minutes of waiting for us all before the message got through. As soon as dad knew I was OK, the rest of the message fell on deaf ears. What followed was like something out of a Benny Hill show.

Dad set off in the van to collect me, with Shelley in the passenger seat, while I got back to the pits in a borrowed van only to find there was nobody there. By this time I'd been up two hours, in the freezing cold, without any breakfast – and I was starving. Now I was furious as well because they'd gone to get me when I'd told them not to. I drove back to the Bungalow to fetch them, but they weren't there. Realising I was back at the pits, they'd returned as I went back to find them…

We can laugh about it now, but that morning we all ended up very grumpy, hungry and angry with each other. It took about three hours before we stopped running from one location to the next looking for each other.

Every lap I completed was faster than the one before. After starting at 90mph, I recorded my quickest, 110mph, during the F1 race. I was pleased with my progress, particularly considering how much I was having to alter my riding style and how hard the track was to learn. I was quick and smooth, but I was also mindful of taking as few risks as possible. Having seen Hizzy roar past me, I knew I was never going to be able to win a race, so I was riding well within my abilities and enjoying the experience.

I was paired with Jim Moodie in the F1 race and by the time I got to the bottom of Bray Hill he'd already disappeared from my view. I had a problem with the bike during the race. Halfway along one of the straights on the second lap the engine felt as though it was running on two cylinders, and I was forced to roll off the throttle. It seemed to fix itself, but then it happened again on the last two laps. Later we worked out that, as the fuel level decreased, there wasn't enough pressure to push fuel through the carbs when flat-out on the straights, so the engine was starved. I finished 24th, with a healthy dose of respect for the riders ahead of me. This turned out to be my only race on the F1 bike, as Kawasaki pulled out of the Senior as a mark of respect for a top-level factory employee who'd died suddenly.

To race an F1 bike round the Isle of Man is something special. It's a blindingly quick motorcycle and to hit the 120mph average needed to win takes a lot of commitment. Now the TT riders are knocking on 130mph average, which I find absolutely incredible. I can't imagine the feeling of lapping at that sort of speed – it's scary.

My best result of the week was ninth, using the KR1 in the 250cc race. It didn't feel as fast or intimidating as the F1 bike and I wasn't as scared of the speeds, which were still over 100mph. Kawasaki won the team award in the Production race, but it was a hollow victory. A team needed three riders to finish and we were the only team to achieve that. My bike wasn't handling well and I finished a long way down.

There were six deaths at the TT that year and the news hit us all hard. Shelley had been sitting with one of the rider's wives when a marshal came and told her that her husband had been killed in a crash. She was distraught and Shelley was extremely upset. As we packed the van to go home she came up to me, the memories of the deaths on her mind.

'If you ever think of racing here again I'll leave you.'

I nodded in total agreement. The TT wasn't for me and I knew it. I didn't have the commitment necessary to win and wasn't prepared to put my neck on the line. Put simply, I didn't have the balls to be a TT legend. Dad agreed, and wasn't keen on coming back to race either. So that was it – decided.

I won the 'best newcomer' award at the TT that year – something I'm very proud of. It's the only trophy that visitors to my home will see, as I keep it on display downstairs. All my other trophies are in a dedicated room that serves as a record of my racing career. Despite that pride, I was happy to walk away from the TT, the experience under my belt and another box ticked in my career and ambitions.

I've been back to the Island several times, on promotional duties for sponsors, and I love to watch the racing. It's still exciting and you feel part of something special. I've even completed a few demonstration laps and really enjoyed them.

By their very nature, bike racers need to be selfish in order to do their jobs. We need to put all other considerations, including the dangers, to the back of our minds and get on with it. TT racers, I think, need to be even more selfish, especially if they have families, because the dangers are even more apparent and understood by all. At a circuit, if you make a mistake or something on the bike breaks, there's usually a run-off area with a gravel pit. At the TT, it's more often than not a brick wall – and the threat of horrendous injury or even death. The level of danger is increased still further when accidents happen because of oil spills or people walking on the circuit while bikes are racing.

I understand the romance and appeal of the TT and other classic road races, but I've always preferred circuit racing. I have the utmost respect for the riders who race there and Hizzy, the man to beat when I was at the TT, was a hero of mine, but most of my heroes were from Grands Prix or Superbikes.

After two weeks of riding and racing at the TT, my next event was at Donington Park and I finished well down in the Supersport

400 race. I couldn't get my head round the change in riding style. I was dead slow and riding defensively as though I was still on open roads, and giving the apexes a wide berth as if they were walls or hedges. I'd forgotten how to race to the limits. This was another factor that cemented my decision never to race at the TT again – it messed up my circuit ambitions.

I started the F1 race at Donington frustrated and pushed myself to go faster. As it was I pushed too far and crashed at Coppice, breaking my collarbone. Afterwards Colin Wright told me I wouldn't be able to race the F1 bike any more, as it wasn't a priority for Kawasaki. That was a big blow for me as F1 and Superbikes were the classes I really wanted to race in, and I'd just ruined my chance for the rest of the year.

At the end of the season I was offered the opportunity to race at the Macau Grand Prix and, despite it being a road circuit, I accepted. I fancied the experience of going to Macau, and I spoke with a couple of the riders who told me there was a gentleman's agreement that we'd ride fast but not actually race. That appealed to me. We'd go quickly but not actually risk anything, and it would end up being a bit of a foreign holiday.

Most riders who go to Macau don't take their girlfriends, for a variety of reasons, but I took Shelley with me. It wasn't much of a break for her. That week was one of the worst of my life. I contracted salmonella poisoning on the flight and thought I was going to die. The connections, including ferry journeys, to our hotel took for ever, and I was extremely ill. I spent six days in bed suffering and got to see very little of Macau. Shelley spent the time at my bedside putting damp cloths on my forehead and making sure I was still alive.

I came round just in time for practice and managed to get on the starting grid. I felt truly awful and could have happily forgotten the race, but I felt a duty towards my sponsors and Kawasaki, who'd paid for me to be there. I started the race thinking we were putting on a fast but controlled exhibition. As soon as the green light flashed up it was apparent the gentleman's agreement was out of the window and the riders took off like bats out of hell, racing full bore. I finished well down, in sixth, and the best part of the trip was when I got on the plane to go home.

I finished the season with second place in the Supersport 400 class – a good result for the KR1 and Kawasaki. At the end of the year the team ran me as a wild card in a Superbike race at Brands Hatch on a GPZ750. I was very excited and wanted to show I could cut the mustard with the big names. I finished sixth, a result that didn't get me a full-time Superbike ride for the next season but helped to cement my position as a paid rider with Kawasaki.

Chapter 8

BRITISH SUPERSPORT CHAMPION

Going into 1990, I was pretty excited about the season ahead. That year Kawasaki introduced the new KR1S, which was expected to be better in almost every department than the bike I'd ridden in 1989. Then there was the new ZZ-R600, which Colin Wright invited me to test on the road prior to providing a written report. I went down to Kawasaki's HQ in Slough and took it out, and after half an hour of steady riding I returned and stupidly told Colin it was good enough to win the British Championship. That statement would haunt me and was a rod for my own back. And I was also going to be given an F1 GPZ750 to race.

At the first race of the season, at Castle Combe, I went out on the KR1S and it wasn't as good as I'd hoped. It felt slow, but when I said this to Colin he replied that there was nothing wrong with the bike. This was the second time that he'd given me this response, and I was riled by it. I was going through the corners as fast as I could, but the bike lacked grip from the Pirelli tyres and just felt plain slow. I went out and proved to him it wasn't a rider problem by winning the 600cc race on the ZZ-R600's debut.

The F1 race at Castle Combe was an important milestone in my career. It was my first permanent Kawasaki-supported F1 ride and I was able to race at the front, dicing for the lead with the JPS Nortons of Steve Spray and Trevor Nation, who were top-level riders. I enjoyed every minute of that race and wasn't even too bothered that I ended up third, as I'd proved beyond any doubt that I had the ability to run with them and felt I'd publicly made the step up to being a real contender in the big-bike class. It was good news for Kawasaki as well because, up to that moment, the GPZ750 had never looked like it could win a race.

Priorities changed instantly after Castle Combe, and Colin Wright told me I wasn't going to be racing the KR1S and instead would concentrate on the British Supersport 600 Championship and F1. Colin knew my target of becoming a Superbike rider and he made it clear that if I were to win the 600cc series, then I'd have a Superbike ride in 1991.

I relished that challenge and when I told Shelley it all clicked into place. We were taking another step forward and all our efforts were simply increased. I was being given a serious opportunity and was more determined than ever not to let it slip by. On top of having the Superbike carrot dangled in front of me, I also knew that the new ZX-R750 due out for 1991 was being touted as a massive improvement on the GPZ750. I believed it would be a contender from the outset and wanted to secure the ride so much I could taste it. Only two years previously I'd sat with Shelley in 'The Royal Oak' and we'd talked about my dreams of being offered a Superbike ride, and now it was within my grasp.

I was battling for the British Supersport 600 Championship with quality riders like Jamie Whitham, Mike Edwards and Jim Moodie. By mid-year I was leading the championship and then we went to Thruxton, where I was expecting another titanic race. It was here that the season took a turn for the worse and I was left with a very sour taste in my mouth.

Phil Borley, my main rival for the championship, put in a protest that the handlebars on my bike were not within the regulations. The team had dropped the bars down the forks to make the bike handle better and in the process had fitted new non-standard clip-ons. He was right, the bars weren't legal. Knowing that we were about to be disqualified, I discussed options with Colin Wright but there was nothing we could do. It ended up with the team pulling out of the race, so I left Thruxton without any points and also a reduced lead in the championship.

I was livid as there'd been no intention to cheat or do anything against the rules, but our arguments fell on deaf ears. The whole incident fired me up more than Phil could ever have guessed. We went back to stock handlebars for the next meeting and I wiped the floor in the race, winning easily. I made sure Phil knew his protest had exactly the opposite result to what he wanted. The standard bars gave a performance edge over the ones I'd been running and it had backfired on him completely. He had antagonised me in the worst possible way and I was prepared to pull out all the stops to beat him after that.

It's a base thing to say, but when I won that race with the standard bars I felt a sort of satisfaction I hadn't experienced before.

In 1990 there was an F1 and a Superbike Championship. In August I won an F1 race at Pembrey, but it was against a weak field of riders, and despite it officially being my first F1 victory, I felt it was a slightly hollow one. I wouldn't count myself a winner until I'd beaten the best in the business, and that didn't happen until Oulton Park late in the season.

It was a televised MCN Superbike race and the Cheshire circuit was wet, but drying. We all started out on wet tyres, and Trevor Nation took off on the JPS Norton while I settled into a comfortable second place. By the end of the race, Trevor's tyres were shot and I caught and passed him, my wet Pirellis standing up well to the conditions. It was my first win in the F1 class against strong opposition, and I backed it up later in the day with a fourth place in the second race.

One week later, at Donington Park, I beat the established stars again and it looked like I had a legitimate claim to be a Superbike race contender. Donington was also the round where I could win the British Supersport 600 Championship and secure my Superbike ride for the following season. The race came directly after my F1 victory and I was nervous. I needed to finish in front of Steve Ives and the pressure was enormous.

The conditions were damp and tricky. I always like to feel my way into this sort of race as it's all too easy to crash out with very little warning – and that would have been disastrous. I decided to take a cautious and calculated approach, and finished with an uncharacteristic fifth. But I was ahead of Steve. I'd won the British Supersport 600 Championship.

To say I was happy would be an understatement. At that moment in my life I thought things couldn't get any better. Not only had I won a major British Championship at my home track, but I'd booked my ticket into Superbikes. I was chasing my dreams and catching up with them.

That evening the whole team enjoyed a massive night out in Nottingham. I don't think anyone was sober and I certainly drank far more than I should have, but I couldn't help myself. I was the happiest man alive and was being bought drinks by all and sundry. When I got back to the hotel in the small hours I managed to suffer my only crash of the weekend. There was a Lego statue of a robot on display in the reception area, and despite it being huge, clearly marked and well out of the way of guests, I was so out of control I walked straight into it and collapsed in a heap of Lego blocks, hitting my head hard. Shelley helped me back on my feet and, as there was no-one around, we staggered off to our room where I fell into unconsciousness as soon as I got into bed.

I woke the next morning with a stinking hangover and the pillow stuck to my head with dried blood. I'd gashed myself badly and still have the scar to show for it. I was ill for most of the day but it didn't stop me enthusing with dad and Shelley. My list of achievements was growing and I was now about to be named a bona fide Superbike rider. There'd be no more 250cc or 600cc races for me – I was going to be concentrating on two Superbike races per weekend and nothing else.

My new contract tripled my wages overnight and after two hard years of debt, grafting and roughing it, there was a lot of light at the end of the tunnel. When I'd sold my BMW to stay in racing, I honestly thought it would be the last decent car I'd ever own. Now I could afford to buy a good car again and that felt brilliant.

At the start of 1990, Shelley and I were still living at our parents' homes. We were very happy together, but hadn't spoken at all about moving in with each other. Then one evening in January we met up after work and she told me she'd seen an appealing house just round the corner, only five minutes from her parents' home, and wondered if I fancied having a look at it. She worked in a chartered surveyors' office, Goddards, and her father had been an estate agent, so she knew what was what.

It was a little three-bed semi-detached with a garage, and as soon as we saw it we both fell in love with it. I thought it was absolutely perfect – if we were going to move in together it couldn't get any better. All we ever discussed was racing and how we could keep trying to achieve our dreams, so seeing a house and falling in love with it was a surprise to us – but the time was right to get our own place. While we got on brilliantly with our respective sets of parents, our relationship had naturally progressed and we were ready for the move. I was certainly very conscious of staying at Shelley's parents' home all the time during the week, and I didn't want to be seen to be taking advantage of their generous nature.

On top of that, our new position of actually having money to spend on things other than racing made buying a house together possible. For the past four years every spare penny had gone into racing. We'd gone into the red and clawed ourselves back into the black, and now for the first time it looked like we'd be ahead of the game, and a house was the first thing we needed.

We were already engaged to be married as, four years earlier, I'd decided to ask Shelley to be my wife. That was in 1986, when I'd just started out on the dream of being a road racer and she was an integral part of my ambitions and security. I'd like to say it was a romantic proposition, that I took her to a waterfall on a hazy sunny day and got down on bended knee with a rose in my mouth and asked her to be my wife, but, when you're a motorcycle racer putting every penny aside for tyres and fuel, you just can't afford that sort of thing.

Instead, I took her to a local pub, the 'Burnt Stump Inn', for a meal. As the name suggests, it wasn't even that posh, but it was quite pleasant and served good food. I'd been thinking about asking her for ages – I couldn't imagine my future without her. Shelley, on the other hand, had never mentioned marriage or even hinted that was what she wanted, but I wasn't about to let that stop me trying.

Over steak and chips, I didn't get down on one knee, but instead smiled at her and said a little bit too quickly: 'Do you fancy marrying me?'

I was actually quite shy and quiet, so it took a big effort to ask Shelley, and she knew it. We'd been together since 1982 and I wanted to make a commitment to her. In a way it was also a method of making a commitment to racing because I knew she was right behind all my ambitions.

I'm aware that in motorcycle racing some guys have an exceptionally good time with plenty of girls. Motorcycle racing is a dangerous, exciting world and that attracts some women. Success is also a turn-on. But I'm not that sort of guy. I'm the bloke who took Shelley to Macau and didn't think twice about it. To put it mildly, very few men would ever take their wives or girlfriends to Macau as the local entertainment is more than enough to suffice – but I did. I've never been a womaniser, and with Shelley I knew I was on to something good and didn't want to let this slip away. I had two loves in my life. One was racing, the other was Shelley. I was happy with that. It ticked all my boxes.

I've seen a lot of energy being spent by talented riders as they chase women, energy that could have helped them in their careers. To function well, I craved stability and security with someone who understood and shared my dreams. Shelley was that person and her support let me get on with racing without any distractions. I'm quite serious when I say that without Shelley the racing would probably never have happened – or not in the way it did. With her my personal life was sorted out. That allowed me to concentrate 110 per cent on the racing and my professional life.

We'd argue sometimes, of course, but I can't remember any major occasions when we fell out. There were a few incidents when one of us would get a little jealous or over-protective, but they never got in the way of our relationship – we were simply young and daft.

There's one area where Shelley has an understanding of me that's unique and has helped to keep us together for all these years. Normally I'm placid and easy-going. Not much fazes me. It takes a lot to get me angry and even then I prefer to walk away from confrontations. Except, that is, when I'm racing. In a pit garage I'm utterly determined and do whatever it takes to win. I can be very selfish, angry, volatile or aggressive. All I think of is winning – nothing else registers on my radar.

I've lost count of the number of times I've been nasty to Shelley in the pits. It's often easier to lash out at those closest to you when you're under stress. To her eternal credit she recognised this shift in my character early on and dealt with it in the most efficient manner possible. If I started to rev up at her, she'd simply smile, turn round and walk out of the garage. Not only did that help us avoid a lot of hurt and anguish, but it allowed me to return to the job in hand immediately and focus my energy on going faster, working with my mechanics or figuring out what changes needed to be made to my bikes.

There aren't many women who could take that sort of grief and simply walk away. There are fewer still who, later in the day, would behave as if nothing had happened. She knew I was a different person while racing and I didn't have to apologise for that, although many times I did.

Shelley and I set out our ground rules very early on. We were in Belgium for a motocross meeting and it was Shelley's job to prepare my goggles. She'd apply the Fairy Liquid and make sure they were clean and ready for the race. One meeting I suffered bad fogging in my goggles and when I came in after the race I threw them at her in disgust. Shelley picked them up, walked over to the nearest dyke and threw them in the filthy water. 'Sort them out yourself in future,' she told me, and walked away. That was the day I knew I'd met my match and, by default, my perfect support as a racer. She can be fiery when she wants to be, and I learned to respect her just as she learned to avoid me when I was in the garage.

Shelley always shared my dreams for racing and being the best, but she told me that it was only part of the package. She said she'd enjoy living any dreams with me, motorcycle-related or not. That means a lot. We are best friends as well as husband and wife.

At the 'Burnt Stump Inn', Shelley did say she'd marry me, but then hit me with the bombshell that I'd have to ask her dad. As I was shy, I hated the prospect of having to do that. We went back to Shelley's house and sat down.

'Dave, I've got something to ask you,' I said.

'What's that then, John?'

'I'd like your daughter's hand in marriage.'

'Fantastic.'

His reaction wasn't really a surprise as we all got on so well and had been on holiday together as a family. I was just uncomfortable asking and glad to have it over and done with.

During the next couple of days we went out looking for a ring. One thing I'd learned early in my relationship with Shelley was that no matter what I picked for her it was always wrong, so I hadn't got a ring before proposing. We ended up spending £110 on a diamond solitaire and we both looked at each other and knew we couldn't afford it. Every penny was going on racing. But we made this exception and it was easily the best investment I've ever made.

So in 1990, four years after our engagement, we finally bought our first house together. After viewing in January, we moved in during April. It cost more than most first-time buyers would spend and we needed a mortgage for it. Although I was earning decent money from Kawasaki by this time, it was Shelley who paid the first few instalments while I got back on an even keel after years of dipping into the red to fund my sport.

Moving into the house was very strange for us. I was 27 by now, but that didn't stop me from running a bath that first night, locking the door and crying into my hands as I came to terms with the fact I'd just left home. Suddenly the emotions were just too much for me. We both got on so well with both sets of parents that moving out was a big deal. We were cutting the apron strings and it hurt. Shelley felt exactly the same, even though the house was only five minutes from her parents' home. It probably hit her mum, Maureen, the worst – Shelley would 'phone every day and her dad would say that her mum had been crying again. A week later, however, we were revelling in having our own space and freedom.

Chapter 9

JOHN REYNOLDS –
SUPERBIKE RACER

At the end of 1990 Colin Wright of Team Green Kawasaki told me I'd be concentrating solely on the Superbike class for 1991, and I was determined to make it work and become a successful Superbike rider. I was going to be part of a two-man factory team in the biggest, best-publicised motorcycle racing championship in the UK.

There were, in fact, two Superbike Championships running side by side in 1991 and I was in both of them. There was the televised MCN Superbike series and the Supercup, which was the established British Superbike Championship. Both had more or less the same field of entrants.

Until I was offered the Superbike ride, I'd been chasing after a dream with help from Shelley and dad, but it was always tantalisingly out of reach, beyond our hopes or financial means. Then it was upon us and suddenly I had a new dream – to win in the pinnacle class of British motorcycle racing. In many respects this dream was exactly the same as the one I'd had when I first rode my three-wheeler round the block all those years ago – I'd found something I was good at and wanted to be the best.

Failure did cross my mind, but I tried to lock it away quickly and use my own experiences to bolster my confidence. I was a triple British Champion, in schoolboy motocross as well as the road racing 350cc and 600cc classes, and told myself I deserved to be in Superbikes. I'd earned my chance, and from my wild-card rides in the F1 series in 1990 I thought I could run with the best riders in the country. But I was being taken back to square one in a class where I had no history and where I'd be competing against a lot of riders with pedigree. I've stated before that I never take anything for granted, and that's how I approached 1991. I felt I was going into a make-or-break year for my racing career: if I did well then the sky was the limit but if I screwed up I'd end up as just another rider in the pack.

The early winter couldn't go quickly enough. I was really excited about the new bike that was due to arrive. The GPZ750 was being replaced by the much harder-edged, performance-orientated ZX-R750, and we had high hopes. Even the name of the bike sounded faster to me and I couldn't wait to try it out. All the reports we'd heard from the factory were of big steps forward and that was just what I wanted – a bike with the potential to run with the Yamahas, Hondas, Suzukis and Nortons that were dominating racing.

Until then dad had worked on my bikes, and I trusted him implicitly, but now I had a team of technicians – another affirmation that I really was a professional rider in a top team. I had to learn to work with my new mechanics, professionals whose jobs were to make my bike fast. Luckily that proved easy as I got to know them – they wanted to win just as much as I did.

When the 1991 season started I was incredibly focused. I just wanted to be the best and I was ready to pour absolutely everything into achieving my goal. The trophies themselves meant little to me: Shelley and I had no cabinet for them in our new house, and, if I won any, then mum would take them back to her house. What mattered was going to a race meeting with 300 other racers and coming away having set the fastest lap of the day and winning the races I took part in – that way I'd have beaten every single one of those other racers. This goal drove me on constantly.

When my Team Green Kawasaki team-mate, Tim Bourne, ended a practice session, I'd still be out there, trying to go faster. If there was anyone quicker than me on the timesheets, I'd stay out until the chequered flag, pushing my limits, probing to see where I could steal a few tenths or hundredths of a second and go faster.

As the years went by I learned to control this need to be the best every day and in every session. I began to see that there was a bigger picture, and accept the situation if I wasn't fastest in practice or qualifying. Even at the end of my racing career I still didn't like being topped on any sheet of practice times or race results, but age and experience taught me to cope with it and to channel my energies more positively. That's just as well, because I'd have ended up a nervous wreck if I'd carried on trying to win every session I ever entered.

Back in 1991, though, I was raw and had to be the best every single time I took to the track, otherwise I was bitterly disappointed and angry. A big reason for this was my need for security. I figured that if I won every session and was the number one rider in the country, then I'd have a better chance of keeping my job for 1992 – even before the season started that was a key aim for the year.

Tim Bourne, my first ever team-mate of any sort in racing, was a really nice guy. He was flamboyant and witty, a rider who enjoyed the lifestyle in a way I never could. Winning was too important to me to waste time socialising in the paddock, but Tim loved that side of the racing and was superb at it. Right from the start I got on well with him.

I feel bad stating this, but I knew Tim was never going to be a Superbike winner, not while I was there anyway. I'd do anything it took to beat him, and that meant early nights, more laps, meticulous preparation and applying all of my determination to the job. There were very few times Tim out-qualified me, so I won my first battle in the Superbike class – beating my team-mate. In racing you always want to win, so along with that comes the requirement to beat your team-mate – that's how I see it.

In fairness to Tim, he tested a lot of parts that I ultimately benefited from. Together we were developing a new bike and I certainly couldn't have been as competitive as I was without his help trying new settings and parts. In that way, having a team-mate was a real bonus. If he found a technical advantage, it was only a matter of minutes before the information would be shared with my crew and we'd be able to use it as well. That was the way Colin Wright ran Team Green Kawasaki – as a team, not two individual riders. I liked being part of the team and felt as though I belonged.

We all had corporate team clothing to wear at the races, something that not too many teams did at that time. It was terrific when the boxes of kit arrived. Shelley and I opened them and couldn't believe the amount of gear we were getting, how good it looked and how much it must have cost. I had shirts and jackets with my name on. Although I'm not into bullshit in racing, that meant a lot. Someone had taken the time to produce these garments and make it very apparent I was part of a team. I was immensely proud when I first wore the team clothing and couldn't stop grinning. I was also instructed to wear team clothing instead of casuals when I was making an appearance for Kawasaki at dealerships or shows. I loved it – I was just so happy to be part of something bigger.

That year Shelley and dad would come to the races just as fans, for the first time without jobs to do. They both decided early on to stay out of the team environment as much as possible, as they knew the team and I had a job to do and they didn't want to get in the way. They remained like that right through to the end of my career. If I needed them they were nearby, but mostly their support was from the fringes. They'd come into the team garage when I was on the grid and leave when I was on the cooling-down lap. We all knew of riders who'd been sacked because their family or friends encroached too much, and dad and Shelley obviously didn't want that to happen to me.

Right from the outset dad's distance from the team caused us to have an argument. The team had provided Shelley and dad with jackets with their names on, which was a really nice touch and made them feel they belonged. But dad didn't want to wear his. The clothing was very bright green and by nature he's a shy and understated man. He wanted to blend into the background, but that wasn't an option for him when his son was a factory rider for a top team and lots of people knew him to be my father. By wearing the branded clothing, you're endorsing and promoting the team and its sponsors, and this is an important aspect.

He chose to wear a Ron Haslam jacket or something else related to my earlier career, and that didn't impress Kawasaki. I remember mentioning that he needed to wear the Team Green clothing but he wasn't keen as he didn't want to stand out from the crowd. When I told mum, she was really upset with him and told him to play ball. Next time out he was wearing the corporate clothing.

At the start of the season we had the new ZX-R750 to develop and we were told we'd be running Pirelli tyres. The first test was a private team stint for three days at Knockhill in Scotland during January. Normally you'd expect the weather to be wet in Scotland at that time of year, but when we turned up it was like the sun had come along to join us – although it was by no means warm. During the first morning we all had to help chip ice away from under the bridge, where the track was in shadow, but there was just enough temperature that day to keep the tyres warm.

It was a brilliant test that allowed us to get to know the ZX-R750 very well indeed. Almost immediately its lap times were faster than those of the old GPZ, and we all knew there was a lot more still to come. I was consistently faster than Tim, my team-mate, and happy with that as well. The only downside came on the final day when we decided to run the new bike against the previous season's GPZ in a straight drag race from the hairpin to the finish line. We wanted to see just how fast the new bike was in a straight line.

I rode the new bike and Tim the old one. We came out of the hairpin side by side and accelerated as hard as we could up the hill. The new ZX-R and old GPZ couldn't be separated. That hit the whole team because we all wanted to believe the new bike's top speed would be higher. Obviously, because our lap times with it were quicker, the ZX-R was a better bike for cornering, braking and acceleration, but when it came to top speed it wasn't the quantum leap forward we'd all hoped for.

There was a serious amount of testing early in the year to get us, as riders, up to speed and to learn about the bike. I had my work cut out putting in the laps, but I enjoyed every one of them. I was a Superbike rider and I was happy. At the start I spent time learning the bike, how fast it was, the way it turned, the limits of the suspension and the brakes. Once I was comfortable, we started to alter settings. Footrests, handlebars, exhaust pipes and seat position were all altered and tested.

The day after Knockhill we went straight to Cadwell Park for a one-day national race. It wasn't as strong a field as you'd expect at championship level, but it was still a good starting grid. This was my first race as an official Superbike rider – and I won it. That was another special day for me, one when I particularly enjoyed the feeling of winning.

As a team we also knew the ZX-R750 was a bit special. We knew we had a bike and package that would allow us to compete in the two major Superbike Championships, but, despite winning that first race of the season, I was really still a 'nobody'. Colin Wright, the team boss, knew very well that I was just another rider who he was giving a chance on a Superbike. He pushed me and worked me hard for the whole year, never cutting me any slack.

Shortly after that we went to Donington Park for the first round of the televised MCN Superbike series. I was up against my heroes, riders like Rob McElnea, Steve Spray, Jamie Whitham, Trevor Nation, Carl Fogarty – and even my friend and mentor Ron Haslam. It was amazing to be racing against all these guys, but I was dumbfounded to be lining up on the same grid as Ron. Only five years previously I'd been watching him on television in awe at what he could do on a bike. He'd given me my first try on a race bike and watched me crash. Now he was a good friend and I was competing against him. And I wanted to beat him.

But at Donington I didn't get the result I wanted, finishing seventh. After that it was off to Pembrey for another one-day national and I took second place, although it was not a full-strength field. The season progressed and my seventh place was joined by an eighth, but those were my lowest results of the year. I started recording seconds, thirds, fourths and fifths in both the MCN Superbike and the official Superbike Supercup Championships.

On top of that I had the great honour of being included in the Transatlantic team for Great Britain alongside Carl Fogarty, Ron Haslam, Niall Mackenzie, Brian Morrison, Trevor Nation, Terry Rymer, Ray Stringer and Jamie Whitham. It would be run over two legs at Mallory Park and Brands Hatch, and it was a big deal to all of us riders. We badly wanted to beat the Americans.

At Mallory Park, Ray Stringer was on fire and he won everything. I finished second overall on the day, a brilliant result. The fact that there was a big cash prize was even better because I was eager to earn as much as possible. My great hero Freddie Spencer was racing and finished way down, but I didn't really count this as a proper race for him – can you imagine what might go through a World Champion Grand Prix racer's mind when turning up at Mallory Park and seeing the very basic facilities?

That day at Mallory Park will always remain etched in my memory as one of the scariest moments in my riding career. Coming out of the Devil's Elbow, I was two bikes back from Superbike legend Miguel DuHamel when he crashed. It happened well into the corner at maybe 120mph. He went into the barrier and his bike followed before bouncing back out on the circuit. I was still accelerating hard at 130mph. I'd registered the crash and then, when the bike bounced back out, reacted by rolling off the throttle – all of this took maybe half a second. Miguel's bike slid in front of my Kawasaki and I missed it by just an inch or two.

I was petrified. If I'd hit Miguel's bike it would have been very messy. Being a racer, though, I shut out such thoughts, got back on the throttle straight away and continued to race. It was only later, when I recalled the moment, that I started to shake.

I'm sometimes asked if crashes or moments like that hold you back as a racer and the answer is 'absolutely not'. Having a short memory helps, but it's important to be able to deal with the fear and lock it away.

At Brands I finished third overall behind Rob McElnea and Ron Haslam, securing second overall in the series for me. Team GB stuffed the Yanks out of sight. We had 625 points compared to their 161. I've always been proud to be an Englishman. Whether it's football, cricket or rugby, I will always cheer on England. Motorcycle racing, however, is one sport where opportunities to race for your country are few and far between, and I was privileged to be part of the Transatlantic squad.

Back in domestic racing, I was getting fantastic starts, taking off from the front and running with the best riders in the field. Then, as races wore on, my tyres would start to lose grip and slide. I still rode as hard as I could, but there simply wasn't the grip to keep me at the front towards the end of races. It was very frustrating and I complained to Colin about it, but he blamed me for fading towards the end of a race.

It got to the stage at Oulton Park in August that either something was going to have to happen or we were going to have a big falling out. It was the Saturday and Colin was giving me a rollicking. I cut him short and said, 'Colin, put Dunlop tyres on the bike and I'll win.' I was red-faced, angry, defensive, righteous and ready to prove I was right. He stared at me, then walked away. As soon as he'd gone from the garage I remember thinking, 'What on earth have you just said? What have you committed yourself to?'

We had Pirelli as a sponsor, and it wouldn't have been happy about us switching to Dunlops. But, an hour later, Colin came back and told me I'd be out on Dunlop tyres in the morning warm-up next day. He was calling my bluff and I knew I'd have to deliver. I went out with Pirelli stickers on my bike but Dunlop rubber on the wheels. I was quickest in the warm-up and that got me Dunlop tyres for the first race.

I took off from the front as usual and this time, when it came to six laps to go, I didn't fade. The tyres were still gripping and giving me feedback. I knew what was going on and could control it. I won the first race, and finished the other race in second place.

Until then the ZX-R had been a good package. Now, it seemed, I'd found the missing ingredient. The grip on the front through the corners allowed me to carry more speed, and it felt like the bike was on rails. Crucially, the Dunlops also let me carry that speed for an entire race distance.

After that we went public about the change from Pirelli to Dunlop because we didn't want to do anything underhand. It had seemed OK to test the Dunlops without anyone knowing, but if we were going to start competing for wins regularly then it needed to be official before anyone found out.

After Oulton Park I won four of the remaining six races, and the two I lost were down to my own mistakes. I was beating the cream of the crop regularly and I was building up my credibility.

Before the end of the season it was very clear I was the team leader, and I knew by September 1991 that Team Green Kawasaki wanted to keep me for 1992. That was a huge step for me, and satisfied my need for security. I was no longer the wet-behind-the-ears rookie surviving on talent and determination. I was a real contender and I knew it. If I was on top of my game I could compete with the very best riders in the UK.

If I had to put my finger on a moment when I made the transition from fast rider to real contender, then it would have to be that weekend at Oulton Park when I tried Dunlop tyres for the first time. I was using all of my talent and ability in combination with the experience I'd gained to solve the problem of grip. I could identify the problem and work it out. Instead of missing apexes and riding off line, I was by then more precise and calculating. I'd developed consistency and control during the previous five years, and had become a much better rider. I was actually altering my riding style to suit the bike and conditions, and I was being precise with everything I did on the bike. Instead of making ten mistakes per race, I'd reduced the number to eight, then six, then four. And the mistakes were different. When I started racing I'd miss an apex by three feet and be overtaken as a result, but now I might miss an apex by six inches and not be overtaken.

Talent is absolutely required to be a racer, but it's paper-thin. It's raw and has no depth. What I'd been doing was turning that sheet of paper into a book with depth and many different levels. If something goes wrong and you rely solely on your talent, it's easier to fall off. If you add the layers and depth that come with experience, you can dig into the volume of the book and find a solution on page five that'll allow you to stay on and avoid a crash.

Through 1991 I really enjoyed racing with riders like Rob McElnea, Jamie Whitham and Ron Haslam, and the fact that I started beating these consummate professionals towards the end of the season was brilliant. But I was already looking towards 1992 with the same team and, just five years after first dreaming about it, I knew I could seriously compete for the British Superbike Championship titles.

During 1991, believe it or not, I was still working full-time as a signwriter, even though I earned a lot more money racing a Superbike for Kawasaki. But I knew bike racing was a volatile career that could turn upside-down with a single crash or a poor season, and that made me keep my day job for the time being. I decided to put aside as much money as possible, just in case.

Money was never part of my dream, although in truth it was an excellent spin-off as a good Superbike racer can make a very decent living indeed. Despite the new financial freedom, however, I didn't squander a penny. Living on a shoestring teaches you the value of money, and I wasn't about to waste any of it. Dad had also taught me that no matter what I spent, I should never come home penniless.

Continuing with my job at Phillips Signs was difficult during 1991. There was a lot of testing on weekdays and my holiday allowance, and more, was used for this purpose. To make up time I ended up having to work on Saturdays when I wasn't racing.

My accountant told me it wasn't tax-efficient to have two jobs, and through 1991 my wages from Phill were basically going straight to the tax man. Despite that, I remained determined to keep the signwriting going, and it wasn't until the spring of 1992 that I actually gave in and resigned.

Phill taught me a lot. Before meeting him I'd led quite a sheltered life, and mum and dad had paid for a lot of what I wanted. Then Phill taught me about hard work and earning your own living. He pushed me hard and made many demands on my time and commitment. He encouraged me – sometimes forced me – to become a better person with hard-working values, and I respect him for that because they've been vital ingredients in my success within racing. He also stuck by me despite the demands my racing put on him and his business. He'd even given me that second chance when I'd asked to become a signwriter, having previously turned down the opportunity.

Chapter 10

BRITISH SUPERBIKE CHAMPION

Early in 1992 I went to Florida to race in the Daytona 200, and Freddie Spencer was taking part. Freddie had been my biggest hero for a long time. I'd often watched him winning races on TV and dreamed that one day I might be as good as he was. When I was starting in racing I'd painted my own helmet in his colours because I couldn't think of a better racer in the world. I can remember clearly how much in awe of him I was as I took to the track for first practice.

During one of the early sessions I was drafting Freddie and got close enough to read his name on the back of his leathers. As we came off the banking towards the infield section at nearly 180mph, something made me decide that I was going to outbrake him into the next corner. I really wanted to pass the man who'd been my idol for so long and was prepared to risk everything to do so. When he sat up at the end of the straight and braked, I held on for a fraction longer and went underneath him. I held it all together and passed him cleanly, my heart racing because of the late move.

It wasn't fair on Freddie. He didn't need an upstart risking a crash just because he wanted to say he'd overtaken his hero. I realised later that it had been a stupid thing to do, but somehow I'd needed to do it. How many people could say they'd overtaken Freddie Spencer when he was trying hard? Not many. All of a sudden it made Freddie, who I worshipped, seem like a mere mortal, and that was the moment when I began to see that my big heroes weren't so untouchable any more. In a way it was a sad moment for me, and Shelley felt the same.

The race at Daytona ended prematurely thanks to overheating. On the banking the bike would be running at 90 degrees, and then when I entered the infield it would jump up to 100 degrees. The temperature fluctuated all the time and when I came in for the first fuel and tyre stop the bike actually boiled over. I only managed one more lap before it broke down. I was bitterly disappointed as this was an early-season race and I was hungrier than ever to make my mark, and I'd also been the fastest British rider all weekend.

It was at Daytona in 1992 that I first met Ben Atkins, and little did I know then what an impact he'd have on my later career. He was over from England with his wife, June, to watch the races and, as a fan, he came up and asked for my autograph on a brilliant photograph of me in action. After I'd signed it for him, he thanked me and presented me with a framed version. I was touched by this generous gesture, and we got talking. It turned out that he originally came from Nottinghamshire, not far from where I lived.

We agreed to meet up later on, with Shelley and June, at the MCN party. As Brits abroad we were glad of each others' company, and the night flew by in a haze of good food and conversation. We became friends, all four of us, and gradually the friendship blossomed into easily the most valuable prize I've taken from racing.

At first I thought I'd met a decent fan. Ben didn't have the look of a stalker about him and we shared the same views, values and beliefs on many things. Initially we just talked about bikes, but that passed and soon we were chatting like any other couples out for a meal together. From the sound of Harley-Davidsons to the weather in the Midlands – it all came easily and naturally. One thing we didn't discuss much was motorcycle racing, and that suited me down to the ground as it was my job and I was glad to have a break from it – Ben had figured that out early on.

We found that we had a mutual friend, Clive Corah, who lived close to us in Kimberley. Clive had joined them to watch the

Daytona races and it was good to see him again as well. Clive had actually been the one to introduce Ben to motorcycle racing and had told him all about me, the local lad from Nottingham who was doing a lot of winning and was a favourite for the 1992 season. Clive knew me from his business as he owned Nottingham Insulations, and Phillips Signs used to do all of the sign work for them. He'd obviously taken more interest in me than I'd thought.

I went about my racing and didn't see Ben or hear much from him through the early part of 1992, and thought that was the end of that. I later found out that Ben was in awe of me as a motorcycle racer and thought I was the best rider in Britain. He ranked me right up alongside the likes of Mike Hailwood. When he approached me he was actually meeting one of his heroes.

Ben went out of his way not to be pushy. Back in Britain, he'd come to race meetings in 1992 and deliberately avoid my caravan. If he saw it in the paddock he'd take a half-mile detour just to avoid walking past and perhaps be seen. He didn't want to be perceived as a hanger-on or become a nuisance, as he knew what some fans could be like. But every now and then Ben and I would bump into each other in the paddock, and each time we built a little more on the friendship we'd started at Daytona.

Eventually his inclination to avoid me faded. When Ben invited us to a barbecue at his house in Polebrook, on the day after June's birthday, I presented her with a huge bottle of champagne that I'd won the previous weekend, and once that popped the party really got going.

Ben and June introduced us to their friends, and how well we were welcomed. They barely knew motorcycle racing existed and treated us like normal people, and we adored it. Although I loved bike racing with a true passion, I'd suddenly found friends who weren't really interested or bothered. They spoke to me as a companion, not as a hero. I could lose myself in an evening of conversation without my prospects in the British Championship being brought up for the hundredth time. These times were a precious escape from my day-to-day preoccupations.

Every time Shelley and I got together with Ben and June, as well as their daughter Karen, the weather would be brilliant and there'd be a magical atmosphere. That barbecue was no different. It was like a scene from *Darling Buds of May* and I can remember talking with Shelley on the way home about possibly living in the same area as our new friends. For a while we seriously considered a move, but our family ties in Nottingham were too strong for both of us and we ended up contenting ourselves with frequent visits.

Picking up little clues, we gradually realised that Ben and June were extremely successful in business with a mechanical and electrical installations company called Vogal. It never really occurred to Shelley and I, though, that they were any different from us, and we were as happy for them about their growing business as they were for me about my racing success.

Thanks to my 1991 results I was earning decent money from racing and, having finally made the decision to leave my day job, I was free to focus on winning the 1992 Superbike Championships. My social life took second place to my racing as I was training hard for race fitness and didn't want anything to get in the way.

My new team-mate for 1992 was Brian Morrison. He was altogether a different rider from Tim Bourne but, as with Tim, my first priority was to beat him. Brian was quick, though, as proved by the numerous World Endurance Championships he has won. I still had it in my head I wanted to top every time sheet or test session, and it was a lot harder with Brian as my team-mate. Literally I'd need to stay out for the last seconds of a session to beat him. He pushed me harder than Tim had ever done.

Brian always carried a £50 note in his back pocket. That sounds flash, but it was more about saving money than spending it. Any time he wanted to buy a sandwich or a drink, he'd pull out his £50 note, shake his head and ask if someone could lend him a tenner as he didn't want to break into the £50. It worked a treat. I don't think he ever had to use that note, and it's probably still in his back pocket. He was a nightmare to hang about with – it cost a fortune.

The MCN-sponsored TT/Superbike Championship started early in the year at Thruxton, and the event was both a disaster and a lesson learned for me. The weather was atrocious – as close to flood conditions as you could get – and Brian was taken to hospital for an operation after he crashed in practice and hurt his elbow. Along with most of the other riders, I agreed it was too dangerous to race on the day. True to our word, Colin Wright packed up the garage and put the bikes in the back of the truck.

As we were getting ready to leave, the first race was about to start and we decided to watch. I think I was the only rider who failed to take to the grid. I don't know the reasons, but the riders who'd been so vocal earlier in the day were lined up ready to race.

That showed me I couldn't trust anyone in racing. By sticking to the agreement, we'd lost the chance to win points in that race, but the team vowed it would never again make the mistake of packing my bikes away.

After that we entered the World Superbike round at Albacete in Spain. That's when we had an inkling that our luck was changing. I was up against some cracking riders, including Fabrizio Pirovano, Carl Fogarty, Aaron Slight, Doug Polen, Terry Rymer, Scott Russell and Raymond Roche. Right from the start I was dicing with these guys at the front and found myself in the lead of a World Championship race.

It was a wet track, but drying, and I was on wet tyres. I think I may have panicked a bit and wondered what I was doing at the front. After four hectic laps in the lead, I lost the rear end on a closed throttle and crashed out, bitterly disappointed but elated at the same time. I was amazed and delighted that I'd led a World Championship race for four laps.

The second race was a bit more ordinary and I went out determined to finish. I came eighth, which isn't bad when you consider the quality of opposition and the fact that it was my first visit to the circuit. It was a tantalising appetiser to World Superbikes and I couldn't wait to try it again.

We returned to the UK for the next round of the MCN-sponsored championship at Oulton Park. After what had happened at Thruxton, where we'd packed the bikes away because of the weather conditions, I had a point to prove. I won both races and closed the gap on Jamie Whitham, who was leading the series after the first round. It was a great day. I beat Carl Fogarty into second place in both races.

After that, World Superbikes came to Donington Park and I took 13th and ninth places. I approached the event just like the previous one at Albacete and with a bit more confidence under my belt after winning at Oulton Park, but I couldn't make a dent on the results despite being at my home track. I tried my hardest, as I always do, but it just didn't work for me. I remember telling a journalist afterwards that I hadn't gone any slower – it was just that everyone else had gone a lot faster. I added the comment that I didn't think I was ready to compete at WSB level, and went home dejected.

Our next race outing was at Snetterton and, after a few nights sleeping on my WSB performance, I decided the best way to respond was to come out fighting. I hate being beaten on a bike – it's close to physical torture for me. Some riders might struggle to find their confidence and form after taking a pasting like the one I received at WSB, but for me it's different. My poor results ate away at me and I had to do something about it. Rather than worrying any more about what I'd done wrong, I concentrated on Snetterton and what I had to do there to be the best again.

I won both races and took the championship lead, and as far as I was concerned I was back where I belonged. I was the hungriest and most determined rider on the grid on the day, and nothing was going to deny me victory. That's not conceit, it's simply a reflection of how hard I worked and the determination I applied to the job. In my own mind nothing but winning would suffice.

By now I was beating some fairly senior names. Yesterday's heroes were now my competitors and, more often than not, I was leaving them behind and winning.

With hindsight, I look at my results at the Donington WSB round and think my explanation, that I wasn't quick enough, wasn't an excuse after the event but instead the reason why I performed so poorly. I went into the race thinking I couldn't cut it with those guys – and that came true. My feet-on-the-ground mentality worked for me most of the time, but perhaps that was the occasion when it backfired and I needed to be more aggressive.

The next event the team entered was called the International Shoot-Out Races and there was a decent prize fund of £5,000. It was at Brands Hatch on one day and at Donington the next, and all the big names were there from short-circuit and road racing. Steve Hislop wasn't in the Superbike Championship on a regular ride, but he was in this event. I had a great battle with him on the first day, and I just took the win. The next day, at Donington, my bike's engine seized, but I'd taken home a decent pay cheque and was happy.

Then it was back to World Superbike racing at Hockenheim. I retired from the first race when the clutch cover gasket failed, and finished eighth in the second race. It was an adequate result, but didn't really reflect my form at home, where I was now winning almost every race I entered.

I think our participation in the WSB races was actually intended to be a series of tests for me and the team, rather than events we seriously went out to win. We had a plan to ride, test and race as much as possible, and the WSB races fitted into that. Our focus was still squarely on the British Superbike Championship and that was when we got very serious indeed. It goes back to a version of the old saying, 'The more practice we do, the luckier we get.' We practised a lot in 1992 and were very lucky indeed.

Hockenheim sticks in my mind today for reasons other than racing. Our hotel was lovely, and Brian and I decided to go down to the swimming pool and sauna to relax. I left Shelley in the room, took my towel and met Brian. We had a quick dip then wrapped our towels round our waists and went into the sauna to sweat a bit. We sweated a fair bit more than we anticipated. We opened the door and walked in to find a room full of naked German women. We almost walked straight back out, but they were smiling at us and we felt obliged to sit down for a few minutes. It's true what they say about German women – I saw hair where I didn't think it could ever be grown!

When I'd returned to Britain it was back to the serious job of winning championships. I was doing everything I could to win races and was regularly topping the podium. If I didn't win, which was rare, then it was normally because of something out of my control. I enjoyed a very impressive winning streak that season. In the televised Supercup series I won every race I finished.

Held at Donington Park, the first round of the Supercup series was, however, nearly my undoing. I crashed in the first race, but was determined to make amends in the second. After a couple of laps I felt there was something wrong with the front brakes, and after four laps I decided to pull in to the pits. To me this was a simple survival instinct. There seemed to be something wrong with the bike and I didn't want to risk a crash. The fact that I was uncompetitive simply added weight to my choice to pull in.

Colin Wright was furious with me. He sent me a severe letter the next day telling me the team never expected me to retire from a race like that, and saying I should have stayed on the track and scored points. I thought it was very harsh, but I could see I'd made a rookie mistake and learned a lesson. Colin was looking at the big picture, where a couple of points could mean the difference between success and failure in the championship. I was lucky that I never again had a similar problem while racing, but, given the same circumstances again, I'd have ridden for as long as possible, safety permitting, just to get to the finish.

It was in 1992 that my obsession with helicopters began. Ron Haslam and I would spend hours on the fields with our remote-controlled helicopters, and one of the biggest accidents I had that year involved a model helicopter.

Ron taught me how to fly the models, and we'd share the controls of the same helicopter while I was learning. He'd take off, then I'd quickly take the controls, and we'd carry on taking turns. In one of the changeovers, we were both holding the remote, but there was a mix-up – I thought Ron had the controls and he thought I had them. We watched as the helicopter fell out of the sky and smashed into the ground. After crashing the first race bike Ron allowed me to ride, I'd now destroyed his model helicopter as well. I dread to think what was going through his mind, but we moved on and eventually I started to crash my own model helicopters.

I also got the chance for a real helicopter flight that year with an RAF Air/Sea Rescue crew. That was when I made the decision that I needed to learn to fly myself. I was smitten and, after that, if I could find any PR activity that involved helicopters or flying of any sort, I was the first in line to do it. My love for flying seems to be reciprocated by a lot of the pilots I meet. Whether helicopter, plane, jet or RAF, it seems professional pilots enjoy the thrill of riding motorcycles just as much as I enjoy flying. It means I've made some good friends over the years, and these experiences have enriched my life enormously.

From basic 'up and down' flying to simulated battle manoeuvres, I've done the lot, and even now I go to bed at night dreaming of aerobatics. In 2004 I was taken up for a battle simulation and Tony Carter, at the time a journalist for *Motorcycle Racer*, was in another plane. Within five seconds my heart was soaring as high as the plane as we pulled huge G-forces, and I was willing the pilot on to more daring feats. Within five seconds Tony had already thrown up in the cockpit.

I like to think there's a link between motorcycle racers and pilots. We have love of speed and the ability to control machines built into our brains. I respect pilots just as much as my fellow racers.

My 1992 season, meanwhile, was going from strength to strength, and at the age of 29 I was about to win my first Superbike Championship. When I say that I was 29 in 1992, that may come as a surprise to some of my fans. Back then my age wasn't a concern to me – I was still relatively new to the sport and was able to make a successful career out of it.

In today's world it seems that you risk being written off as too old if you're out of nappies. I think this could be the Valentino Rossi factor. A World Champion in his teens, Rossi is already one of the most successful racers of all time, yet potentially he still has another ten years or more of racing ahead of him. In age terms, he became a World Champion years before I'd even sat on a road race bike.

As the years rolled on in my career, it became increasingly apparent that the sport was becoming younger, that people wanted to cheer on young exciting talent. It has now almost got to the point where you're seen as too old if you're over 25 – certainly that's starting to happen in MotoGP. Eventually I had to take a look at myself in the mirror. In 2002, ten years after winning my first British Superbike Championship and immediately after securing my second, I knew I could still race and win, but I decided I needed a revamp. I subtracted a couple of years from my age, becoming 37 instead of 39. I figured that being nearly 40 was likely to work against me in trying to get a seat on a competitive race bike. It worked, as I was given a berth at Rizla Suzuki, one of the most competitive and professional teams in racing.

It was incredibly easy to pull off my change of age without anyone noticing. Even the press and media pundits couldn't have told you my real age. They may have suspected a ruse, but never got close to the truth. I can even remember watching a re-run on TV of the 2003 WSB round at Brands Hatch and listening to the commentators arguing about my age. It was all good-humoured and in the end they settled on what my press release said – 38. I was actually 40 and racing against riders half my age, and beating them. I'm not sure whether the sport would have taken that on the chin, but I wasn't going to try to find out. What I didn't want was people telling me it was about time I retired. I didn't want to be written off because of my age when all I wanted to do was continue to race motorcycles.

I'm not the only rider who has pruned his age to play to the crowd and keep himself in the shop window. I'll bet that there are riders disguising their age in every paddock in the world.

I can tell the truth now I've finished racing and it no longer matters. So, to put the record straight, I was 42 when I retired – not, as most people thought, just turned 40.

I clinched the 1992 MCN TT/Superbike title at Cadwell Park in August. This was an important championship but wasn't seen as the real deal. Although it was every bit as competitive, it didn't have the heritage of the Supercup.

I won the first race and finished second in the next to take the title. It was a non-event really. I didn't class it as the championship the team was really aiming to win. The second race was an epic, though, and one I'll never forget. I got a horrendous start and was pushed onto the grass. I rejoined in last place and spent the rest of the race overtaking people as fast as I could. I got up to second, but couldn't quite catch Robert Dunlop, who won. Two more laps and I'd have had him – it was one of my best rides.

I won the Supercup Championship at Brands Hatch in September. By then names like David Jefferies, Sean Emmett and Michael Rutter – riders I'd spend the next decade battling with – were starting to break onto the scene. It was an important day, and Duran Duran's Simon Le Bon was in the garage with Yasmin Le Bon. I won the first race and then had to beat Brian Morrison, my team-mate, in the second. I went out intent on finishing in front of him, but he crashed out and I ended up riding round knowing I was the new champion. Even so, I went for the win, partly because Yasmin Le Bon was going to be presenting the trophies. I got a kiss on the cheek for my efforts.

The Race of the Year at Mallory Park came next, and this was another successful outing. I won both races and added my name to the trophy alongside Giacomo Agostini, John Surtees, Mike Hailwood, Derek Minter, Kenny Roberts, Randy Mamola and Jamie Whitham. I did the first 100mph lap of Mallory Park and won a decent cash prize of £1,000 for that. Brian Morrison set a new lap record on the next lap but missed out on the prize because it was for the first lap at 100mph, not the record-holder. He was very disgruntled and thought he should have had the money.

Then it was off to Ireland to race at Kirkistown. I got a fracture in my left leg in the first race after suffering a huge highside going onto the main straight. It was a big blow to me and to the Irish fans attending the event. The doctor said I'd broken the smaller of the two bones in my lower leg. We strapped it up for the sake of the fans, who were absolutely brilliant and had given us such a warm welcome, and I started the second race.

It was painful and I didn't really enjoy the race, but I still managed to take third place in the main Sunflower meeting, beaten by Brian Morrison and Rob McElnea. It took a lot of effort to finish the race and I won't pretend it was great fun, but it was appreciated by the crowd and I think I made some good friends that day. Even now, when I return to Ireland to shows or events, the fans are very knowledgeable and easy to get on with. They remember the races and effort, and are some of the best fans in the world.

The next race was scheduled to be Brands Hatch for a Powerbike meeting, but I wasn't able to ride because of my healing leg. Kawasaki wanted me to attend in a promotional capacity so I made the trip – and it was one of the worst weekends of my life.

If there was one person in the paddock I didn't get on with, it was Sean Emmett. He was cocky, arrogant and, to cap it all, very fast. He was writing for *Fast Bikes* magazine at the time and was trash-talking about how great he was. He'd say the only reason I was beating him was because his bike wasn't good enough.

I didn't know Sean then, but there was something in his character that brought out the worst in me. Everything he did just irritated me. And the worst thing I could imagine happened that day – Colin Wright gave him my Superbike for the meeting.

I had to sit in the garage watching him compete on my bike and, to add insult to injury, by the end of the weekend he'd recorded a faster lap time than I'd achieved earlier in the season. He gloated about that, making the most of it as I looked on in agony with my broken leg. He didn't win the races, but he did a good job – and for me that made it even worse!

The season was coming to an end, and Kawasaki still hadn't offered me a job for 1993. Despite winning just about everything I entered, and taking both Superbike titles, discussions for the following year were always being put off.

In fact that didn't bother me at all because Clive Padgett had approached me during the British Grand Prix, around the mid-season point. Through Padgett's dealership, I'd had my first entry into the Honda CBR Challenge a few years earlier, and his team had also given me a couple of outings on a two-stroke Suzuki RG500. This time he asked if I'd like to race full-time in Grands Prix in 1993, and without even pausing for thought I said 'yes'.

After accepting Clive Padgett's offer I felt a little awkward at the thought of Colin Wright raising the issue of 1993, and I tried to avoid it as much as I could. I was so grateful to Kawasaki for giving me my break into road racing, and deep inside I felt I was betraying them in some way. My nature is to be loyal and, just as in my relationship with Shelley, when I'm happy and content I don't want to rock any boats.

But the chance to go Grand Prix racing was something I just couldn't turn down. It was a huge opportunity, and the competitive part of my character jumped at it. I liken it to when Kawasaki offered me the chance to race the 600 at Cadwell Park four years earlier. I'd decided it would be better to try and fail rather than never to try at all. Just the thought of being a real Grand Prix racer set my pulse racing.

Then, at the end of the season, just as I was working myself up to call Colin and tell him I was moving on, he called me. I was wondering how on earth I was going to break the news to him after everything he'd done for me. I was in turmoil. But, before I could utter a word, he spoke.

'John, I've got some news for you.'

'Yes?' I replied.

'I started the job with Kawasaki and now I'm finishing it.'

'Oh, that's a shame,' I said, unconvincingly.

I was off the hook. Kawasaki was pulling out of British racing and he didn't have a job for me. I was so relieved. I'm sure he must have wondered why I wasn't disappointed. Then he spoke again.

'We've been thinking about it, Alec and me. Why don't you buy the bikes and race transporters off us and we'll continue to support you?'

I politely declined. As far as I was concerned I'd earned money from the team and wasn't about to give it all back. I was a racer, not a team owner or team manager.

Two days later I made the announcement I was going into Grand Prix racing with Padgett's Motorcycles. I didn't speak to any other teams or consider any offers – I was determined to become a Grand Prix rider. In contrast to the glitz and glamour most people may expect, the meeting to finalise the deal with Clive Padgett took place at a fish and chip shop.

To my mind I was progressing. My Superbike dream had been realised and I'd won both the Supercup and the TT/Superbike series. Now I had a new challenge – to go to the very highest level of racing in the world and see what I could achieve.

The offer from Padgett's was very basic, and different from what I'd enjoyed with Kawasaki. I'd have a bike to race, but I wouldn't be earning a wage and I'd need to cover my own expenses. I weighed up the options and thought the risk was worth it. I'd been paid well by Kawasaki in 1992 and had topped that up with prize money as well. Shelley and I were now comfortable financially, and I reckoned it was worth giving up a salary for the opportunity. If I could make waves in my first year, then my earning potential would be so much more than in Superbikes. If I failed, then at least we had a bit of money in the bank to fall back on and we needn't worry.

It was a decision that put racing ahead of earnings, and that has always been the way I've approached the job. I thought, at least, I'd be able to get some income from a helmet and leathers deal.

So, I was sorted. I'd have a Harris-chassis Yamaha-powered 500cc racer for Grands Prix in 1993. I couldn't wait to get going. A world of opportunity, excitement and adventure lay ahead of me. Little did I know that, after tasting the highs of Superbike Championship victories and making a decent living, my career was about to take a serious turn for the worse, and that the next two years were to be a less of an adventure and more of a nightmare.

Chapter 11

GRAND PRIX RACING

My first Grand Prix was at Eastern Creek in Australia in 1993. I was amazed by the stars I was rubbing shoulders with in the paddock, but the one I really held in reverence was Barry Sheene. Ever since I was a little boy I'd idolised Barry. Shelley and I often joked that it would be great to meet him properly. It was a pipedream we hoped would happen one day, but Barry had retired years earlier and we didn't take it too seriously.

After walking Eastern Creek with Shelley, we'd returned to the garages to find some sort of presentation going on. It was like a 'who's who' of racing at the time, including Kevin Schwantz and Wayne Rainey. Barry, who by this time had emigrated to Australia, was also there as a commentator for Channel Nine, the Australian TV channel that covered motorcycle racing.

'Shelley,' I nudged her. 'That's Barry Sheene over there.'

We walked past looking at him, but quickly looked away when he clocked us. Even as I looked away he spoke. He said: 'John Reynolds?' I nearly fell to the floor. I was astounded he knew me. He came over to talk. That moment, and the conversation we then had with him, made the whole experience of competing in Grands Prix worthwhile. I'd met my greatest hero – and he knew me.

The 1993 Australian GP doubled up as our honeymoon. After a fantastic 1992, we decided to get married in February, and, as it was only a week and a half later that I was due to race at Eastern Creek, we elected to have our honeymoon in Australia. The wedding, at Kimberley Church, was big and a lot of local media attended. It was nothing like the Posh and Becks wedding, and I certainly didn't earn millions from *Hello* magazine, but it was a great occasion for us and we loved it.

Shelley did everything for the wedding. While I was busy sorting out my Grand Prix career and training for the season, she organised the whole thing, from arranging the church and flowers through to food, cake, suits – the lot. Luckily I turned up on time and smiled at the right moments – and it was a brilliant day.

After that wonderful start to the year, I was going into Grand Prix racing with a glimmer of hope. I'd been lucky in everything I'd done so far in my racing career. I'd kept myself clean, tidy and out of trouble, and now I had an opportunity on the biggest stage of all. I was hoping and praying I could do a good job, get picked up by a factory team and move on from there. That was the plan.

Grand Prix racing was, and is, the elite of the elite in motorcycle racing. The bikes are the fastest in the world and the hardest to control. Just getting a Grand Prix bike set up to go fast is a skill, and then the rider has to be good enough to exploit it. I knew it wasn't going to be easy, but this was exactly what I wanted. Even if I couldn't beat the best riders in the world, I still counted myself incredibly fortunate to have the opportunity to race them at all.

Mum and dad were cautiously happy for me, but dad thought I was on a hiding to nothing. I told him he was probably right, but felt it would all be worthwhile if the plan worked out. When I thought of factory race bikes and support, I couldn't help but dream of winning races and championship titles. If those ever came my way, then so would the financial rewards.

Looking back, I can see a lot of naïvety in my approach, but I had to go through the experience to learn that. In 1993 I still believed talent and determination would see me through. Ben Atkins had advised me to seize the moment and see what happened. And it's in my character to take chances when they're offered. If the worst came to worst, at least I'd have tried. No matter what I chose, Shelley supported me through thick and thin and I was grateful to her.

By now I rarely met up with my mates, but when I did it was just like old times. They never held me up above my station as 'Superbike Champion' or a 'Grand Prix rider' – to them I was simply John Reynolds. As I've said before, they're a great bunch of guys and have helped me keep my feet planted on the ground. Whether I was to end up a multiple champion or on the dole, I always knew they were there for me. With success comes the opportunity for arrogance. It's easy to delude yourself that you may be better than others but, thanks to my family and friends, I sincerely hope I've never shown any of those traits. I take nothing for granted and, to my mates, I never really changed from the schoolboy they knew.

In 1993 I was a columnist for *Motor Cycle News*, the national weekly bike paper. The experience was new to me and I hope I don't get anyone in trouble when I let you know I didn't actually write the words myself. I'd meet up with one of the journalists each week and tell him my thoughts, and he'd make sense of them for me on paper. They wanted to follow my progress in Grands Prix. I wanted to share the story with everybody. It never occurred to me to ask for payment, despite finances being incredibly tight as I was no longer being paid to race.

When, late in 1992, I mentioned to Ben Atkins, as a friend and in confidence, that the deal would provide a ride but no salary, he immediately offered to support me financially in return for a badge on my leathers. That was a strange moment. Someone I valued as a friend had, all of a sudden, mixed business with pleasure. Ben said this would be a great way for me to put myself in the international shop window and prove what I could achieve. That idea excited us both.

I accepted Ben's generous offer, and, with hindsight, it's just as well I did. Ben became my major source of income for 1993, and beyond. I lived on sponsorship money from his company, Vogal, plus a few other endorsements that came my way, such as FM helmets and Fieldsheer leathers. Together they paid me a wage and without them I wouldn't have been able to race – I was, and remain, massively grateful for their support. I was never going to be rich, but it allowed me to pursue my dream a bit longer, to see if I could measure up against the best in the world.

Apart from keeping me solvent, the sponsorship from Vogal also gave Ben and June Atkins the perfect excuse to join us at all the race meetings. They travelled the world with us and we had some great laughs on the way. He remained my personal sponsor the following year as well, and we did it all again, except this time we were even firmer friends and his whole family were part of the globetrotting entourage.

Before a race, Ben and I'd ride round the circuit together on scooters, and it was at Mugello, in Italy, that he asked where I'd start braking. He told me to shout to him and he'd see if he could brake in time for the corner. The little scooters could only hit 15mph flat-out, so off we went. Before we came to my braking marker on the straight, where I'd normally be going at closer to 160mph, he asked if we should be starting to brake. I said 'no'. He continued and eventually, when I told him to brake, he pulled up, looked at the corner and asked me how on earth I could make it braking so late. I told him the apex of the corner was actually out of sight, and he simply shook his head and smiled. I did the racing and he did the thinking – that made us a good team.

The first season in Grand Prix racing was always going to be a learning year. The second season would be the time to go for results. If I got results, this might in time lead to a big payday. The rewards where there for all to see in the Grand Prix paddock – Ferraris and Lamborghinis, and some of the most spectacular motorhomes you could imagine. My lifestyle, of course, didn't compare with those of the big stars. I had a secondhand VW Golf GTI parked at the airport and lived out of a small caravan at races. This was all I could afford, but that never bothered me. Just because I was a Grand Prix rider didn't mean I had a God-given right to be rich.

I often looked at the trappings of the top riders and thought that if I could take two seconds off my lap times then I could be living like them. But finding a second a lap is tough. Two seconds is harder still. Even finding the last tenth of a second, the bit that makes you a champion rather than an also-ran, is difficult. Given the machinery and tyres I had access to, the millionaire lifestyle was always going to be just out of reach.

Despite my dreams, I never was, or will be, a flash person. I've never gone out and spent everything I've got – that's something my dad bred into me from an early age. If I went out with ten pence, I always made sure I came home with a penny in my pocket. I didn't need flash cars or mansions and never was jealous of anyone else. I can remember thinking, why on earth would I want an expensive sports car? It would be parked at airports for most of the year.

I knew of the Padgetts before I ever raced for them, as the family owned large bike dealerships. The first time I came across them was when I was motocrossing. Peter Padgett seemed to be a hard man – he shouted at one of his lads because he wasn't winning – and the family appeared to be ruthless. I was a bit intimidated when I first signed up for the team, but as I got to know Clive Padgett I found that he was solid gold, through and through. He was a character, and the whole family was great to be with and full of laughs.

The Padgett's team was good – there was no way I'd have signed up otherwise. Although it was a privateer team, I could see resources and effort being put into the racing. They were up for the job and so was I. The crew they put around me was good as well. Padgett's imported the YZR500 engines and Harris supplied the chassis, so, on paper, everything was sweet.

I knew Jamie Whitham had ridden a similar bike in Grands Prix and set myself the target of matching, or maybe even beating, his results. That would prove I was a decent rider. If I could get in the top ten on a privateer bike, I reckoned I'd be doing well.

Looking back, I think the whole Grand Prix world took a major step forward between 1992 and 1993. A significant advance in technology – the introduction of 'big-bang' engines – meant that the bar was raised by more than the standard increment. The factory teams moved a generation ahead of the machinery that Padgett's had. Right from the gun it meant that my job was hard. As hard as I'd expected – and then some.

The first time I rode the Padgett's 500 was at Mallory Park. The difference between a four-stroke Superbike and a two-stroke Grand Prix bike is huge. Not only do they sound distinctly different, but they're dynamically very different as well. At the time, both bikes made the same sort of power, somewhere around 160bhp, but the delivery of the power was very different. The four-stroke Superbike would rev to 13,500rpm, while the two-stroke managed 11,500rpm. The four-stroke was tractable from low down, while the two-stroke didn't start to go forward with any urgency until 8,000rpm and then tailed off towards 11,000rpm. But when it pulled you knew all about it – the power would tear your arms out of their sockets. That fierce power delivery was also married to a much lighter bike: compared with the 160kg Superbike, the 130kg Grand Prix bike would accelerate faster and harder. At Mallory Park, coming out of Gerard's and onto the back straight, I cracked open the throttle and the front wheel lifted while the bike shot forward – that had never happened to me on a Superbike. I giggled inside my helmet, partly through excitement, and partly fear.

A two-stroke engine is very different from a four-stroke. On the Superbike, if you shut the throttle then the engine would start to brake the bike. On the Grand Prix two-stroke there was no engine braking. Roll off the throttle and the bike would coast, much like pulling in the clutch on a four-stroke – all the deceleration had to be done on the brakes. And the brakes were seriously different from a Superbike's. Instead of steel rotors, these were carbon and needed plenty of temperature in them to work. When they did work they were astoundingly powerful – like hitting a brick wall.

The contrast between the bikes was night and day. They just couldn't compare. But I was quick to adapt. I'd come through the ranks of racing two-strokes in motocross, and competed on RD350 and TZ350 Yamaha road race two-strokes early in my career. I knew how to ride two-strokes.

That first day at Mallory Park, when the Yamaha-powered Harris-frame Grand Prix bike was wheeled out for me to ride, I was shaking like a leaf. It was November, and freezing cold, but dry, which was the main thing. But there was a problem before I even sat on the bike. Throughout my career I've always used a road bike gearshift pattern – one gear down and five up. It makes sense to me that when you brake you should go down the gears and follow the direction of the bike rather than using the traditional racer gearbox, which is the exact opposite. Of course, this bike had the racer gearbox and I had to concentrate doubly hard not to make a wrong shift because we didn't have time to change it on the day.

I took it pretty steady on the bike and soon I was loving it. This was unquestionably the fastest motorcycle I'd ever ridden and it lit a fire in me. Ultimately, if you want to go round any race track quickly, regardless of the type of bike, the same principles apply. I'd instinctively known those principles as a young child racing around Gloucester Avenue on my bicycles. To go through a corner as fast as possible, you need to go from kerb to apex to kerb. You need to be on the brakes for as little time as possible and on the throttle for as long as possible. On the Grand Prix bike those same rules stood, and, although braking markers may have moved a few yards further back and corner speeds risen, I felt at home.

Our first proper test in anger was organised by IRTA (International Race Teams Association) at the Jerez circuit in Spain. In two days I crashed three times, and that was completely new to me. I rarely crashed. Each crash was a front-end crash, when the front wheel slides away from you and there's nothing you can do about it. I couldn't work out what was going on.

If there's a problem with the rear, generally you'll feel it slide and be able to compensate with the throttle to control it. Rear-end grip problems can still end in crashes, but if you have good feel on a bike then you can predict, control and save the situation. A front-end problem is much more severe. When the front wheel loses grip it slides and tucks, and there's not much you can do about it. Yes, it's possible to save it by digging your knee into the ground and fighting to stay upright, but in my entire career I only managed to do that a handful of times. The fact is, front-end slides happen instantly and normally at high speed. At that stage you're a passenger and usually you'll crash.

It's extremely important as a rider to have good feel and feedback from the front end of the motorcycle in order to avoid crashes and to have confidence to go through corners. On the Grand Prix bike I had no idea what was going on with the front end. It would simply let go without any warning and, no matter what we changed, it stayed that way all through the season. We changed offsets, yokes and swing arms, but nothing cured it. On a bike with a front end giving good feedback, you can go into corners hard, slam the bike on its side and know you'll get away with it. You think there's no way it can make the turn, but you do, and you exit with lots of confidence, knowing you can do it again. I never had that feeling on the Yamaha 500.

I had to ride it with a degree of caution and within my limits. Instead of pushing it to 100 per cent, I'd need to go through the turns at 95 per cent, and that was never going to be competitive. Luca Cadalora, Wayne Rainey, Kevin Schwantz and Mick Doohan are some of the greatest riders of all time, and there was no hope of hanging on to their coat tails unless I had the utmost confidence and feel in my bike.

'Feel' is a word that motorcycle racers use a lot. It basically means a rider's ability to understand and decipher the feedback a bike is giving him and, using that information, to go as fast as possible without crashing. When you're racing at the highest level, you're always on the edge of the laws of physics, daring the tyres to slide and challenging gravity to stay upright. A rider with good feel can tell when the rubber is about to let go and take remedial action in the hundredth of a second before it does, and stay upright.

I've always been blessed with good feel, but I just couldn't gel with the front end of this particular bike. It surprised me every time it crashed, so I ended up approaching it defensively. I had to, just to survive. Even then it would still catch me unawares. I'd go through a corner at the same pace 20 times without as much as a hint of a problem and then on the 21st time, for no obvious reason, it would crash. Riding a bike at less than 100 per cent was hard for me – the numerous crashes I suffered in 1993 bears testimony to the number of times I thought the problem was sorted and could push a little harder. Out of 15 starts, I ended up in the gravel five times.

In 1993 I didn't have a team-mate in the Padgett's squad, but I counted Sean Emmett as the next best thing. He was a fellow Brit racing in Grands Prix, on similar privateer machinery from Harris, the firm that supplied the frame of my bike, and he had been a serious rival to me in the UK. He was also someone I instinctively didn't get on with. It was my mission in life to beat him.

In the races we both finished, I think Sean only beat me once that season. I was on Dunlop tyres and he was on Yokohamas, and I should have beaten him thanks to my rubber advantage. In fairness he rode well, but beating him was, for me, some sort of a goal achieved. In the grand scheme of things, though, it made barely a dent in what turned out to be a hard season.

In Australia I started the season with a lot of fire in my belly and a determination to prove myself. During practice and qualification I'd managed to push to the limits of the bike and stay upright. I'd had my scares but went into the race hoping my luck was changing. It wasn't. Turn one at Eastern Creek is probably one of the fastest corners in the world. Coming off a straight, it's a committed left-hander at around 120-130mph. During qualifying I'd gone in as normal and lost the front end but managed to hold it. I hauled the bike upright, streaked across the grass and rejoined the circuit at the hairpin, my heart beating at about the same 11,500rpm as the bike. I'd worn a massive hole in my boot and, although I'd held the bike together, this reinforced my fear of the front end.

I qualified around 12th or 13th, which I was pleased with. Niall Mackenzie was just in front of me on the grid and I had my carrot. He was the established Grand Prix star who I desperately wanted to beat on my privateer machinery.

The factory teams in any race series tend to be the best of the best. With the manufacturer supporting the team, they have a technological advantage. The factory bikes have the best suspension and more horsepower than the privateer machines. They also have the very best tyres. I had good Dunlop tyres, but in Grand Prix racing there was an established hierarchy and it was something you had to live with. I knew my tyres were good, but factory riders on Dunlops had access to newer technology, construction and rubber. At best I might hope to be only a second off the pace, and that was all down to the tyres.

The race started and I kept my carrot in sight and, as the laps ticked by, I started to reel Niall in. I was comfortable keeping station with him, but catching him was very difficult. About eight laps from the end I was doing everything I could, and had visions of passing him in my first race. It wasn't to be. Instead of the front end washing out on me, I came out of a corner and opened the throttle a little bit too hard, highsided and crashed.

It was a big crash out of 12th place and the first highside I'd experienced on the bike. I walked to the side of the track and can remember not having a clue where I was. Bikes were racing, so I guessed I was at a race. I even recognised some of the riders but I couldn't have told you their names. A little later, when it dawned on me I'd just crashed out of a race, I headed off in the general direction of where I thought the pits were. As I walked back, holding my battered helmet and nursing a sore head, the Australian crowd went mad. They started chucking beer bottles and calling me a Pommy wanker.

I was a bit taken aback. This was a whole new world to me. All I'd done was give my best in a race, crash my brains out and now

I was being pelted and abused for my efforts. I thought, 'Heck, what have I done? It's not like I've taken out Mick Doohan or anything!' I guess I ended up entertaining the crowd...

In the first four races I crashed three times, but after that I settled into results in the mid-teens and was pretty much the best privateer. Assen, in the middle of the season, saw me creep up to tenth place, and I followed that with a career-best ninth at the British Grand Prix at Donington Park. I loved Assen as a fast, flowing circuit, and Donington, of course, was my home track and I knew it well. Two more ninths followed, at Laguna Seca and Jarama.

To get into the top ten in Grand Prix racing on a privateer bike is a big achievement. But for me to get into the top ten, I needed some of the factory riders to fail to finish, otherwise there was no chance – my best would be a standard 11th or 12th place. I only ever beat established factory riders when they crashed.

More than anything, by the end of 1993 I wanted to get better tyres. I needed the same tyres as the factory riders so that I could see how I really compared. Eventually I did get a set of good tyres from Dunlop. It was the final race of the 1994 season at Albacete, and I was presented with two secondhand race tyres that one of the factory stars had discarded. I fitted these for qualifying, went out on track, and the increase in grip simply blew me away. Even though the tyre was well-used and past its best, it was better than anything else I'd ridden. Albacete was an invitation end-of-season event, but a lot of the big names were there and it meant something that I put the YZR500 on the front row. There were two races that day and, although I had to go back to my normal privateer tyres, I recorded my best-ever finishes of fourth and fifth, purely because of my good position on the grid.

I reckon those used tyres were worth a second a lap, every lap of the race. Compared with the tyres I was used to, the gulf was huge. I only wished I'd been given the opportunity to use them at a full Grand Prix or, even better, had the chance to try new versions of the same tyres.

When you look at my results and the problems I was having with tyres and the bike's front end, you'll understand why I didn't enjoy 1993. For me, racing isn't about finishing halfway down the field. I was in it to win, and deep down I knew I didn't stand a chance with the machinery and equipment at my disposal. I tried to fool myself with goals of beating Sean Emmett and finishing as top privateer, but on a subconscious level that wasn't what I wanted. The fun had been taken out of it and, for the first time in my life, racing had become bloody hard work. I had a plan, though, and I was sticking to it. I wanted to prove myself and maybe, just maybe, I'd attract the attention of a factory team. If I did, then it would all be worthwhile. Thinking about the future was the only way I could cope mentally with my position. I kept giving it my all and looking for light at the end of the tunnel. Every time I felt disheartened, I picked myself up more determined than ever to succeed.

At the end of 1993 I was offered the chance to stay on with the Padgett's team. It may sound bizarre after the season I'd just experienced, but that was exactly what I wanted. I'd now ridden all the circuits, familiarised myself with the bike and achieved a few top ten finishes. With that experience behind me I wanted 1994 to be the year I proved myself and made a mark.

The terms were the same. I'd need to live off my personal sponsorships, so I knew I'd be facing another year of standing still financially, but that was OK. In any case, there was no real alternative. British Superbikes was going through the doldrums and World Superbikes was packed with riders, so I had nowhere else to go. The deal was done and my three main sponsors stayed with me and paid the mortgage for another year.

During 1993 the factory teams had developed 'big-bang' engines, where the firing order of the cylinders is changed to improve traction and grip, and the big advance for me in 1994 was that I'd have one of these engines as well. Along with the experience I'd gained in my first year at Grand Prix level, this gave me hope for achieving better results.

Approaching the second year of Grand Prix racing had other plus points. Both Shelley and I loved travelling the world, seeing new places and meeting new people. In many ways it compensated for the hard work. Driving through Europe with a caravan was great fun. It was fascinating to experience new foreign cultures. Even the long-haul flights could be enjoyable. Not many people get the chance to see the world the way we did and we felt privileged. But it changed the way we viewed holidays.

Before the Grand Prix years we'd look forward to breaks abroad. Now, when we did go home, all we wanted to do was batten down the hatches and relax. People would ask if we were going anywhere on holiday and we'd look at them as if they weren't sane. We're pretty normal people at heart and sometimes it's wonderful just to sleep in your own bed, watch trashy daytime television and make your own sandwiches for lunch.

I love flying, which is just as well, given the job. Shelley is OK with it as well, but there was one time that neither of us will ever forget. During the winter Ben Atkins had introduced me to an old school friend called Colin Barnes. I was on the breadline and he was a prospective new sponsor. Ben took me to a local pub and, as we were walking in, a red Ferrari came around the corner sideways, tyre smoke everywhere, and hurtled into a parking space. I smiled and Ben knew instantly that I was going to like Colin Barnes.

After some discussion Colin decided he'd support me through his building contractor firm, Barnes & West, and, there and then, wrote out 12 cheques to cover the coming year. He remained a personal sponsor right up until my retirement. Although his backing in 1994 didn't make me rich, it did make the mortgage payments a little easier and allowed us to order a coffee on the plane rather than going without.

We became mates and I soon found out that Colin owned a microlite aircraft. On one occasion he took me up in it from its base at Caunton chicken farm, and he started mucking around, asking if I knew where the runway was, that sort of thing. It was my first time in a microlite and I was already suffering from vertigo and felt a bit worried, but soon realised this was just his sense of humour.

Colin offered me the chance to learn to fly and loaned me the microlite. In 1995, after I'd passed my exams and obtained my microlite pilot's licence, I called Colin to say it was my turn to take him up in his microlite, and we met at Caunton later that day. I'd got to the farm early and went through all the pre-flight checks. My wrists were sore from an accident on the bike so, instead of turning over the prop to fill the float bowl with fuel, I removed the float bowl and filled it from the petrol tank I'd brought with me, and then bolted it back on. It seemed like an easy way of saving my wrists from grief.

When Colin arrived, I strapped him to the passenger seat and took off down the runway at full power. All went fantastically well until we were at around 150ft and then the microlite lost power. It was mushing along, neither gaining nor losing altitude. You're never supposed to turn an aircraft round when that happens, but we were heading straight for power lines and I needed to do something. I performed a flat turn and, as soon as the crosswind got a hold of the microlite, we accelerated up to 85mph flying downwind.

'Colin, we have a problem,' I shouted into the headset.

'Yeah, right, whatever,' he replied.

'We have a problem, I mean it.'

'Stop joking and just fly the thing,' he laughed.

I thought my time was up and brought the microlite down towards a ploughed field. When I shut off the engine he stopped laughing and knew it was serious. Just 15ft from the ground I shouted into the headset that he should take over and land. I can't remember what he said, but I don't think he thanked me for handing him the responsibility. We hit the ground hard and eventually came to a halt in clouds of dust. We knew we'd come very close to killing ourselves. Typically, Colin laughed.

A couple of minutes later we dusted ourselves down and checked the microlite. One of the propeller blades had been shortened by an inch in the crash. Colin got out a hacksaw and reduced the other blades to match and then told me to give it a test flight. I refused. Colin took it up and landed without incident and urged me to go up again. By now I'd recovered from the scare and went to get the bucket of sand I used as ballast in the passenger seat. He said I didn't need it and I believed him. The trouble is, when racing I weighed only ten stone soaking wet, and Colin was a fair bit heavier than me.

When I took off, without the bucket, the microlite went nearly vertical. I throttled back to try to stop that and when I came off the throttle it tried to stall. For the second time that afternoon I was terrified. I got to 500ft and tried to bring it in to land, but it just refused to lose height. I had to put it into a steep dive and when I eventually got back on terra firma I was relieved just to be alive. Colin laughed. I never flew the microlite again.

Colin had been a keen biker from an early age. When he came to races I always made sure I spent time with him and that wasn't just out of duty – we really did become good friends. During the summer, when testing at Darley Moor before the 1994 British Grand Prix, I suffered a massive crash. I badly smashed up the bike, my new helmet and myself, and was properly out of sorts for the race five days later. In that whole muddle I forgot completely about Colin during the weekend.

After the race, on Sunday night as I was driving home, I realised I hadn't seen him at Donington Park and phoned him. His partner, Anna, answered and gave me both barrels. Colin would never say anything, she said, but he was really hurt that I'd ignored him all weekend and she couldn't believe how I'd treated him. He had to buy his own passes and watched from the crowd, cheering me on.

I was completely disgusted with myself. I'd let a friend down. So, as an apology and to make up for my forgetfulness, I immediately hatched a plan. I bought Colin tickets for an all-expenses-paid trip to join us for the next round at Laguna Seca. We had a great time together in the States. On the plane for the flight home from San Francisco, Colin's sense of humour struck again. He couldn't resist winding up Shelley just before we took off.

Going down the runway we were messing around and in good spirits. But about 15 minutes later, at 20,000ft, we felt a cold wind blowing through the cabin. Colin and I looked at each other and I said, 'That isn't right, is it?'

'No,' he replied, without any humour at all.

A couple of minutes later, the air stewardesses came to our seats, right at the back of the plane, and started unloading emergency equipment. Colin had a serious look on his face and was watching intently. They left a minute later and then the air brakes went on. Almost immediately the engines started to roar and vibrate and we could see fuel being dumped.

'Colin,' I said. 'Do we have a problem?'

'This is it,' he replied. 'We're dumping fuel. That means we're going to crash land.'

'What did he say?' asked Shelley.

'That's it, we're going to crash, we're probably going to die,' I said.

The noise from the engines was deafening, the passengers were now shouting and the whole plane was shaking and vibrating violently. We sat there, waiting for the worst to happen. Shelley simply buried her head in her hands. I think we all said our prayers.

Thankfully, the pilot came on the speaker system a couple of minutes later to tell us a door had been left open on the front of the aircraft and we would be returning to San Francisco as a precaution. He told us the engines were on full power to burn fuel quickly.

By the time we landed Shelley was very ill. She'd vomited, was suffering from a migraine and generally felt in pretty bad shape. We were shepherded off the plane and then put onto another. Flying was the last thing any of us wanted to do now, but we had to get back to England. Shelley still being sick and a stewardess offered to upgrade us to first class as that might help.

It certainly helped me and, while Shelley tried to recover, Colin and I were wined, dined and entertained on what turned out to be one of the better flights I've taken.

My only other memory of flying during the Grand Prix years was when a bike-enthusiast airline captain invited me to see the cockpit as we came in to land. I jumped at the chance and was fascinated right up until we touched down. The first officer was flying and he made an extremely heavy touchdown that nearly knocked my teeth out.

Wherever we went in the world we'd take our own English tea bags. As I've said before, we're pretty normal people at heart and when we visited a faraway place like Malaysia we'd often find the local McDonald's for dinner. I love Indian food and over the years I've tried just about every sort of cuisine, but nothing beats familiar tucker.

People may talk trash about our lifestyle, TV shows and weather, but I wouldn't change England for anything. I love the place. Being born and bred in the Midlands, I've had salt-of-the-earth people round me all my life and there isn't a place in the world I'd rather live. If I were ever to be evicted from England, however, I'd pick Australia as my next favourite place, despite my first Grand Prix experience there with the crowd. Those guys were pissed and thought it was a good idea to hit a rider, but once you get beyond them you find a fascinating and friendly country. I've got a lot of friends in Australia and some great memories from the times I've visited.

When you go to different countries, the race organisation puts together publicity stunts, and the best for me were always in Australia. On one occasion the riders in the 500cc class were all invited down to Sydney harbour for a boat race. I can remember sailing out in the harbour on a fast boat, with Mick Doohan and Kevin Schwantz and the rest of the stars alongside in their own yachts. It was a beautiful sight. In many ways, as a privateer I was in the wake of the factory riders at these sorts of publicity stunts, but that didn't stop me from enjoying them. Although I wasn't being paid at times like that, looking at the Sydney Opera House while on a yacht, and being treated like a king, was well worth it.

If Australia is the second best place in the world, then one of my favourite nationalities, and certainly the most genuine, is the Japanese. It's so refreshing to go to Japan and know you can leave your car open overnight, with the keys in the ignition, and it'll still be there in the morning. Theft seems to be non-existent.

As well as the strict Japanese discipline and work ethic that you regularly hear about, I think there's a good deal of western humour in their culture as well. Just look at Yukio Kagayama, my factory Suzuki team-mate in 2003 and 2004. He'd laugh at all the same things we would. He's one of the funniest riders I've ever had the pleasure of knowing. He knew exactly what he was doing when he mixed up his words and pretended he didn't know the meanings.

Looking back on these memories, I wouldn't trade them, but I'm aware that I wasn't an ordinary tourist. I love Australia but I only ever got to see the very best parts. As a Grand Prix rider I was insulated from normal life. If you spend a lot of time in a country then you'll start to hear the gripes and groans and find it's pretty much like normal life in the UK. Taxes, the cost of petrol, crime and politics are issues wherever you are in the world. The only difference with Australia is you get to moan in the sunshine.

I guess the acid test for Shelley and me was that, no matter where we were in the world, however pleasant it was and friendly the people were, we could never wait to get back home to Kimberley. It sounds difficult to believe but it's the honest truth. You don't realise how much your roots mean to you until you're half a world away.

At the end of my first year in Grand Prix racing I rode a Honda NR250 at Brands Hatch at a national event. After the first session I came into the pits and told my crew that the 250 was much more comfortable than my 500 race bike, and they took the measuring tape to it. It was set up almost exactly the same but, crucially, the footrests were a couple of inches further forward. It sounds very simple, but that small change to the footrest position cured the front-end problems when I next tried the 500. It altered the centre of gravity on the bike and settled the front forks. It gave me feedback on what was going on at the front end and allowed me to control my pace through the corner to the grip level of the tyres and circuit rather than having to guess. It was a major breakthrough for the team.

My second year as a Grand Prix rider had to be the season I proved myself and earned a factory ride, and I was more determined than ever – I'd never previously failed when I put my mind to road racing. But, despite all my efforts, the year was a hard slog right from the start. It began with a 10th place in the opening race in Australia, and I didn't get a better finish that season. When your commitment, sacrifice and dedication result in just 10th or 12th place, you can't help but let your head drop. You forget what it was like to win. You go out and ride fast, but if you aren't in contention then the shine becomes tarnished – and that happened to me. There's no substitute for competing at the front to keep you on form and fighting fit. If you go into a race thinking you can win, then you may indeed do that, or at least come close. But if you can't think positively, you're not going to perform as well. It's simple psychology.

After a year and a half of battling for 10th place, I was sick of racing. My state of mind was perilously negative. No matter how self-motivated I tried to be, it eventually came home to me that I was on a hiding to nothing. The Italian Grand Prix, the eighth race of the year, was the turning point. I'd finished the first six races and had confidence in my bike, with four 10ths and two 12ths. I went to Mugello cocooned from reality, still thinking I could make it in Grand Prix racing.

I wrote off a bike in a heavy crash in the Sunday morning warm-up. It was a real mess and the whole team was down, but they pulled through and worked their fingers to the bone to get me on the start line. Butch Cartwright, my mechanic, had the bike ready about a minute before pitlane was due to close. After about four laps in the race I crashed again and the bike caught fire. It was completely destroyed. The crash had been caused by one of the hoses coming loose from the water jacket and spreading fluid over the rear tyre. The fire and destruction was testament to the speed and manner of the crash. I'd highsided and the bike slammed into a tyre wall at a horrific speed.

I didn't know the reason for the crash and – lying in the gravel, bruised, battered and beaten – I was in the grips of despair. Eventually I got back to the pits and dad was there waiting for me. He said, 'Son, you might as well give this game up.' I was furious with him and told him so. I was blinkered to the reality of my position. I'd let my determination blind me to what was really going on. Even *Motor Cycle News* had seen the writing on the wall and stopped publishing my column. I was a club rider in the professional world of Grand Prix racing.

Dad told me the truth. He'd watched me hitting my head against a brick wall for the previous 18 months and it finally got too much: he had to let me know. Given how quiet and reserved my dad normally is, this was a huge statement and it provided me with a reality check. A couple of days later I accepted that he was right – and that was when I decided I wouldn't race in Grands Prix with Padgett's in 1995.

Ben Atkins had been so positive and was always telling me I'd be at the sharp end next time around but, after Mugello, I told him I didn't believe that any more. Although Ben was a sponsor, he was also my friend and, more than anything else, I wanted advice from someone I could trust. What should I do? Where should I go? He admitted it was time to stop being optimistic and start being realistic. He'd done his best to support me through a tough time when the equipment wasn't up for the job and I valued that. Now he turned his attention towards trying to find me a more competitive ride and team for me.

He said it was time to stop chasing my tail in Grand Prix racing and take a different tack. Maybe with the right equipment and tyres I could have competed with the very best riders. Unfortunately the chance never came – and by mid-year I was deep into plans for 1995 and excited about the opportunity to race in World Superbikes in a factory-backed team.

To make it even better, the team was going to be owned by my mate Ben Atkins.

Chapter 12

WORLD SUPERBIKES

I can understand why people could be cynical about my friendship with Ben Atkins. He paid my mortgage through the Grand Prix years and then, when I was destitute and at the end of my tether without a competitive ride, he created a team for me and gave me a well-paid job. Looking at it from the outside, it smacks of me being an opportunist, but there's nothing further from the truth. If at any time I'd thought our friendship would suffer because of our professional relationship, then I'd have walked away. That's the honest-to-God truth.

It wasn't one-way traffic, with me sponging up anything I could get my hands on – this was a partnership and together we made it work. When Ben and June first told me they were thinking of setting up a team to go racing in World Superbikes I didn't believe them. But they seemed determined, and I knew them well enough by then to accept that if they set their minds on something, they tended to achieve it. I thought they were crazy to start off going straight into World Superbikes, but there was no point arguing with them.

We'd already proved ourselves to be a good team. At the end of 1993 Ben had decided to enter me in a national race at the Brands Hatch Powerbikes meeting. We didn't have a bike so we asked Rob McElnea if we could race one of his Yamahas. Jamie Whitham had just won the British Superbike title with him and I was the returning former champion. Having the old and the new champions on the same machinery would be a great head-to-head, we said, and should grab plenty of media attention. This was traditionally a good meeting, and I'm not ashamed to admit that the chance of earning some decent prize money was a big motivator. Rob rejected our suggestion and I guess that was understandable. He'd invested in Jamie, who'd done a great job for him, so why would he want to put the pressure on his golden boy?

Instead, Ben asked if I knew the whereabouts of my 1992 championship-winning Kawasaki ZX-R750? I hadn't a clue where it was but managed to track it down, and it was still genuine and in fair condition. By now it was a year out of date compared with the competition, but I had happy memories of the bike and thought it could do the job. Ben bought it there and then.

Logic told me I wouldn't be able to keep up with the latest machinery, but something inside me was desperate not just to race, but to get back to winning again. On top of that, Brands Hatch had already ingrained itself in me and I adored the place. The secret with Brands is to set up the bike properly for the fast, flowing corners, and I already knew a base setting for my old bike.

We took the ZX-R750 to Mallory Park and it felt OK. But when we took it to Brands the front end felt like a pig. I was distraught, but we took the forks apart and found the seals had rotted and were leaking oil. That's what happens when a bike's mothballed for a year. We fixed this and went out in the first race – and won. When I say I loved the feeling, I really mean it. I could only compare it to a man dying of thirst in a desert and coming across a reservoir. I'd beaten the best riders in the UK, including the reigning champion, and was ecstatic. It was also a splendid bench-marker for Ben's first ever race as a team owner.

As I was sitting on the start line for the second race, someone told me that my bike would be stripped by the scrutineers if I were to win again. I wasn't bothered and was going to do my best to win. I won the second race as well and, after spraying the champagne, I sat back in the garage and allowed myself the satisfaction of a genuine smile for the first time in as long as I could remember. I wasn't there to rub Jamie's nose in anything, but I had a point to prove to myself and Ben, and I'd done that. There was a decent prize purse as well. I was already planning on how to spend this when I was told the bike needed to be stripped.

I didn't think there'd be any problem with our bike but, as it turned out, Ben had a huge issue with it. He'd arranged to take the bike to a prospective sponsor's premises the next day with a view to gaining financial backing for his own new team. When the officials said they needed to confiscate the bike and strip the engine, he told them they couldn't. He'd just bought it and was trying to arrange sponsorship – he didn't want anyone taking it apart and giving it back in a box. He had no spares for the bike and no way of rebuilding it.

I stayed in the background grinding my teeth and praying that Ben would allow them to strip the bike. Not only was my pride at stake but I was dead keen to keep the prize money – it was just what we needed after a year on the breadline. In fairness to Ben, he relented and said they could strip the bike, but it had to be after he'd presented it to the potential sponsors. He suggested that they seal the engine so it couldn't be tampered with in the meantime. I think that was a fair compromise and, in the context of the sport, it was forward-thinking and reasonable. The officials disagreed, though, and gave him no option. He packed the bike in the van and I gave back the prize money and trophy.

We were both furious at the intransigence of the officials and their petty politics towards someone trying to start a team and bring money into the sport. I told Shelley we'd be eating in instead of having the meal out I promised her, and we went home.

Motorcycle racing nearly lost Ben Atkins that day.

Later Ben and I talked about it, however, and agreed to put the whole thing behind us. Luckily Ben could see through the problems and was chasing a vision. We'd won our first race meeting together and we knew it was fair and square. So did most of the paddock. I was happy and couldn't wait to get racing again. The two wins were just what I'd needed.

ABOVE: *Aged 17 months, perched on dad's Velocette Venom. I was born for this. (Family Collection)*

BELOW LEFT: *My dad, Jack Reynolds, on his Rudge-framed JAP-engined racer, 1951. (Family Collection)*

BELOW RIGHT: *Uncle Tom with his works Dot and trophies, 1964. (Family Collection)*

ABOVE LEFT: *At my first motocross race, aged eight, at Kniveton on an 80cc Suzuki that dad built. (Family Collection)*

ABOVE RIGHT: *The teenage motocross racer, with mum and dad, 1977. (Family Collection)*

BELOW: *Meeting my all-time hero Barry Sheene with my mates Steve and Dave Hogg. I'm the one on the right. (Family Collection)*

ABOVE: *On holiday in Lindos, Rhodes, in 1985 with Shelley. I'd given up motocross and hadn't found road racing yet. (Family Collection)*

BELOW: *Mallory Park, 1987, on the way to my first road race victory on dad's Velocette. (Family Collection)*

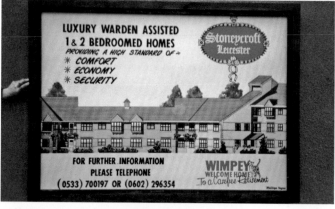

Opposite top: *My first ride with Team Green Kawasaki, at Cadwell Park in 1988, wearing leathers donated by Ron Haslam. (Double Red)*

Opposite centre: *This is an example of my sign-writing work, from 1988. It started life as a plain piece of wood. (Family Collection)*

Opposite bottom: *I was best man for Tony Brown at his wedding in 1989. He would later be my best man when I married his sister. (Family Collection)*

Above: *Cadwell Park, 1992. A youthful Colin Wright (team boss) carries the King of Cadwell trophy I'd just won. (Double Red)*

Below: *In 1992 at Brands Hatch, the year I won both the Supercup and ACU British Championships with Kawasaki. I'm seen leading Jamie Whitham, Brian Morrison and Ray Stringer. (Double Red)*

ABOVE: *The day Shelley and I got married, 28 February 1993 and, on our honeymoon in Australia, she keeps busy opening fins on the radiator before my first Grand Prix. (both Family Collection)*

BELOW: *On the Padgetts 500 GP bike, Laguna Seca, 1993. Ben Atkins designed the helmet…he liked fish. (Double Red)*

ABOVE: *Sea trials – me at the controls of a yacht that I was about to take into Sydney harbour and race against Mick Doohan and the rest of the GP stars. (Family Collection)*

BELOW: *Relaxing with Shelley and friends Ben and June Atkins, and Colin Barnes, at Monterey, in California, before the 1994 Laguna Seca GP. (Family Collection)*

ABOVE: *Assen, 1995, talking with Carl Fogarty and Aaron Slight. (Double Red)*

RIGHT: *On the hard-to-tame 1996 factory Suzuki GSX-R750. (Double Red)*

Below: *Back in Britain in 1997 and enjoying racing again. I'm chasing my hero and friend, the British Champion Niall Mackenzie. (Double Red)*

ABOVE: *With Sean Emmett in 1999. After riling me in my early years as a racer, he later became a good friend. (Double Red)*

BELOW: *Chatting with one of the hardest racers in the business, Troy Bayliss, 1999. (Double Red)*

TOP: *Front row of the 2000 British Superbike round at Brands Hatch, and what a line-up. Hodgson, JR (no. 3), Walker and Mackenzie are ready for battle. (Double Red)*

ABOVE: *The start of the 2000 WSB round at Brands. JR (no. 47) getting away with the leaders ... (Double Red)*

LEFT: *... I was happy to win the WSB race at Brands and this was just before I managed to slip on champagne. (Double Red)*

ABOVE: *Big rivals in 2002, and good mates. Giving Steve Hislop a lift back to the pits at Oulton Park. (Double Red)*

BELOW: *I received the 2003 Prince Michael International Road Safety Award for my work with Shiny Side Up, an Eastern Region road safety campaign aimed at motorcyclists and therefore very dear to my heart. Here I am with (from left) HRH Prince Michael of Kent, Patron of the Prince Michael International Road Safety Awards, Sheila Ormerod, campaign originator and Shiny Side Up Partnership facilitator, and Heidi Duffy, Nottinghamshire Police representative. (Shiny Side Up)*

ABOVE: *Cadwell Park, 2003. This is one of my favourite pictures, taken by friend and Double Red photographer James Wright. (Double Red)*

Below: Thruxton, 2004. I'd just clashed with my team-mate Gregorio Lavilla and was in the process of breaking my collarbone while leading the British Superbike Championship. (Double Red)

ABOVE: *Donington Park, 2004. Mission accomplished. Celebrating the BSB title with team boss Paul Denning… (Double Red)*

BELOW LEFT: *…doing a rare wheelie to mark the occasion… (Double Red)*

BELOW RIGHT: *…and taking to the podium with my son Ben. He pretended at home and now he got to celebrate with his dad for real. (Double Red)*

ABOVE: *Ben looking for a lift at Donington BSB, 2005. (Double Red)*

OPPOSITE, TOP LEFT: *Fighting back to fitness after my pre-season crash in 2005. (Double Red)*

OPPOSITE, TOP RIGHT: *My dad came to almost every race I started, with a few exceptions when I was competing abroad in World Superbike and Grand Prix Championships. (Double Red)*

OPPOSITE BOTTOM LEFT: *Ben with a trike that's just the same as the one I had as a child and made by the same person – my dad. (Family Collection)*

LEFT: *Like father, like son. Ben and I are racing each other and neither wants to lose. (Family Collection)*

RIGHT: *Adjusting Ben's JR80 scrambler. (Double Red)*

ABOVE: *Relaxing at home in Nottinghamshire. (Double Red)*

RIGHT: *I've made good friends with the Red Arrows over the years and love flying. (Double Red)*

BELOW: *The Reynolds family, 2006. (Cathy-Marie Robinson – The Photographer)*

You probably couldn't get two people more opposite than Ben and myself. I'm normally a placid character and it takes a lot to fire me up when I'm not racing a bike. Ben, on the other hand, is a loaded gun ready to go off at the slightest provocation and, just like a gun, once he explodes he's straight back to his old self as if nothing had ever happened. We have a completely different angle on life and the chemistry worked between us.

By the end of the 1994 season Ben and I had made our plans and I walked away from Padgett's, despite them offering to pay me to stay with the team in 1995. It was the first time they'd given me the chance of earning, but that wasn't important to me any more. After two years of being beaten, I'd have given anything to get on a competitive bike. I'd sacrificed earnings for the chance to race in Grands Prix and now I was saying 'no' to a salary that would keep me there. I wanted to go somewhere I could race again. I needed to rediscover my joy in the sport and that was in World Superbikes with Ben.

Shelley, mum and dad were my support network through the grim Grand Prix years, and when I mentioned to them that Ben was thinking of setting up a World Superbike team and that I'd be a rider, they were all thrilled. The fact that Shelley and June Atkins were good friends was a bonus. The pair of them schemed about what a great time they could have together while Ben and I got down to the business of racing.

Ben is a fantastic businessman and, in creating the World Superbike team, he was contemplating something I hadn't even dreamed about. It would save my career, because he wanted me to ride for him, but even then I took a step back. I wasn't sure he should be jumping in at the deep end. I could see him getting burned and losing a lot of money. Racing in World Superbikes is a massive financial commitment and a huge undertaking. It's not something that Ben knew much about so I advised him as best I could. I told him what difficulties to expect, and the impact it might have on his own home and business life. In truth he'd served an apprenticeship of sorts by following the Padgett's team round the world. He'd also been quietly watching Kenny Roberts run his Marlboro Yamaha Grand Prix team, and he'd come to the conclusion that he could create the perception of a large well-funded team for a fraction of the cost of the big operations.

That would work, providing he had a good rider on board – and that's where I came in. He might not be able to provide the very latest bike or technology, but motorcycle racing isn't dependent solely on machinery: performance might be split as 60 per cent based on rider ability and 40 per cent on the bike. You just need to look at Valentino Rossi in MotoGP. The Yamaha he races is a good bike but, while he's winning, the next best Yamaha rider on the same machinery could be anywhere between fifth and tenth, and a second a lap slower than him. The difference is the rider. Of course, if the bike is too far off the pace then no amount of talent will help. Staying with a MotoGP example, just look at the efforts of the WCM squad. Even with a Rossi on board the bike probably wouldn't win because it's just too slow compared with the competition – we're talking maybe 15mph slower on the straights and that's too much to give away.

So, Ben asked me to ride for him – and then told me he didn't have any bikes, mechanics or infrastructure in place to make it happen. Luckily I could help there, thanks to my relationship with Kawasaki.

If I was named as a rider, then there was a chance Kawasaki would support with bikes. I called Gin Inui, a boss at Kawasaki UK who I'd worked with in 1992 when I'd won the British Superbike Championship, and who'd then gone back to Japan and been promoted. He was pleased to hear from me and, when I explained our plans to go racing in World Superbikes with a new team, he was genuinely excited. He agreed to meet Ben and discuss the supply of bikes, so Ben visited him in Japan and paved the way for us to obtain factory backing for the coming year. It was more than I could have hoped for and I was a very happy man that winter, looking forward to the 1995 season.

We knew the bikes were good, thanks to the performances of the Muzzy team based in the US. Even with two volatile riders like Scott Russell and Anthony Gobert, the team was competitive and that gave us hope we could pull off a strong first year. The fact it was an on-the-edge set-up also helped us because, after Ben and I'd met the Japanese racing bosses, he knew they liked dealing with straight-talking, easy-to-work-with people, and that's exactly what he was.

It was at about this time that Ben mentioned the team name. He really liked Reve as it's French for 'dream' and the connection with racing and revving engines was obvious. I liked it as well and the team Reve Racing was born. Once the bikes were in place Ben arranged a team around them. That winter he put together the mechanics, support staff, drivers and all the components needed – and he did it properly. He selected the people he wanted and head-hunted them. We ended up with an outfit that had real strength.

A young David Jefferies was my team-mate. He was a big lad back then and, while he had talent on a bike, he was probably just a little too tall to make it at the very top. He would go on to be a champion in Superstock and at the Isle of Man TT.

During the season I'd go running round the circuits with Chris Anderson, one of my mechanics. He's ten years younger than me and immensely strong. I made it my mission to try to beat him at anything we did. If we were in the gym together I'd tell him I could do more sit-ups than him. I'd give it my best but more often than not he'd do ten more. But I got satisfaction from seeing just how hard he had to try to do them. Neither of us would ever give up. It kept me fit and sharp, with the physical capabilities of someone a lot younger than I was.

At Monza, David Jefferies decided to join us for a run round the track. He got about a mile and a half out and was completely knackered. He walked back and Chris and I kept on going. It always ended in a sprint finish and I just edged him across the line. He'll contest that he beat me, but he didn't…

At some stage you might have expected the friendship between

Ben and me to have been compromised, but even on that count Ben had it covered. He put a manager in place between himself and the team. He accepted someone might have more experience and skills at the job and gave the responsibility to Stuart Hicken. That put a layer between Ben and me that we never crossed. If I had an issue I took it up with Stuart, and Ben did likewise. I guess if you spoke to Stuart he might have had a different viewpoint. From an operational point of view it must have been a nightmare to have a rider who's best friends with the team owner, and Stuart did a good job.

But, as I've said before, if the friendship had been compromised I'd have seen the year out and then resigned. Shelley and I discussed this and we both agreed we had few enough real friends as it stood, and we weren't prepared to lose Ben and June.

With a new team, new bikes and a new championship, I can only describe 1995 as another learning year. We started in the UK with the Spring Cups: I won and finished third at Mallory Park, then went on to win at Oulton Park, and followed that up with two more podiums at Donington Park. Then it was off to Hockenheim for the opening round of World Superbikes, and straight in at the deep end. We were up against the factory Muzzy Kawasakis and it was our first real test.

I was struggling through practice and felt that the engine in the bike I favoured was down on power. The Japanese staff with Muzzy had a look, found the timing was slightly off and fixed it. I ended up putting the bike on the front row in fourth place. All through the weekend, though, we had a problem with the brakes. When they were consistently warm or cold they were strong and gave excellent feedback. The problem came when they cooled off after being warm. The brake disc was expanding when warm and knocking the pads back in the callipers, and then as the disc cooled, on the long straights, it would contract and leave the pads out of position. When I pulled the brake lever, that meant I had to squeeze to the bar to get any response, and on more than one occasion I had to pump the lever to apply braking force. At 180mph that's scary and it robs you of confidence in the brakes. It had a notable effect on my lap times. I had no idea where to start braking and lost myself a couple of tenths through almost every corner.

In the first race I came to the end of the straight, pulled the front brake and nothing happened. I dived up the slip road, pumping the lever, before rejoining well down the field. I ended up 17th, which was better than the second race as I had to retire with no feeling whatsoever in the brakes. It was a hard start to the World Superbike Championship, but our qualifying position had hinted at the potential. When we went to Misano we did rather better, taking home a seventh and a ninth.

At the time Scott Russell knew the Kawasaki and was able to compete for race wins with Carl Fogarty on the Ducati. I felt our bike was good enough to run with those guys but, as we had to learn everything from scratch, we were at a slight disadvantage and more often than not ended up in the middle of the top ten. But I knew I could win and kept my head down and the team did the same. I'd been beating Foggy only a couple of years earlier in British Superbikes, so to come to the World Championship and be struggling to stay with him was a bit of a surprise. I could complain that he had a machine advantage with the Ducati, but the truth is I don't think did – all the bikes were pretty similar.

What happened with Foggy and Ducati was something unique. Carl had a good bike and was riding out of his skin, but it was more than that. Carl and the Ducati gelled and together they were world-class, and he won World Championships. I take my hat off to Carl as a fantastic rider. I raced and beat him, and he returned the compliment. I've a lot of respect for him as one of the best riders England has ever produced.

At Laguna Seca in 1995 I crashed out of qualifying. It was a big one – I went into the tyre wall at a rapid pace and knocked myself clean out. Five minutes later I was sitting on the fence, watching the riders go past and recognising their colours and helmets, but I couldn't have told you any names. I was desperately trying to guess where I was and what was happening. Slowly it came back to me and I made my way back to the tents that served as our makeshift garages.

I walked into the medical centre, dazed and confused. Ben took my leathers away and I changed into some casual clothes. When I returned to my tent I found my leathers and every other stitch of clothing had been stolen – my whole kit bag. I even had to borrow a pair of trousers from Ben to go and buy some new clothes for the flight home.

When we got to Brands Hatch in 1995 I felt as though I was coming home. I took a fourth in the opening race and then went one better with third place in the next race. However, I didn't get to stand on the podium. On the last lap I was third but another rider passed me under waved yellow flags, just before the chequered flag. The team contested the result and after the race I was reinstated to third. I'm not terribly proud of that and never had the pleasure of spraying the champagne. The rider who was demoted to fourth for passing me under yellow flags was Yasi Nagai from Japan. I'm sure he simply hadn't seen the flags.

Perhaps more important, though, the result marked my return to racing at the front. I was a contender again. I'd come back to life. As I drove home from Brands I felt as though I really belonged in World Superbikes. I was no longer the sideshow – I was back in the main event and contributing to the racing and entertainment. To be in the top three or four riders was exactly where I wanted to be.

I actually got to stand on the podium for the first time at Assen, a couple of rounds later, and heads were turning in our direction. A new team with a has-been privateer Grand Prix rider was competing and threatening to win. I loved it, Ben loved it and the whole team lapped it up. There wasn't a man on the squad who didn't enjoy the season.

Going into the winter I think Ben realised what a huge commitment racing was and how hard it would be to succeed. We'd had a good season, but for him that wasn't enough. He'd been working in the background to try to sort me a full factory World Superbike ride. He thought his own team wasn't giving me an equal chance to compete for wins and, as much as I wanted to do well, I think he wanted it more. He had heard there was a ride for the factory Suzuki team coming up, and put me forward for this, not as a team boss trying to get rid of a lame rider but as a friend looking to help his mate. That was a strange feeling and it took me a long time to get my head round why he wanted me to leave his team, and I didn't ask too many questions.

At the time the Suzuki team was being run by Harris in the UK, so we all spoke the same language and knew each other pretty well. Ben took me along for a meeting with them and was my manager. We agreed terms there and then and the job was sorted. For the first time in my life I was going to be a factory rider. One of the upshots, I think, was both June and Karen, Ben's daughter, were upset that they wouldn't be racing with Shelley and me in 1996. They enjoyed the lifestyle and there were floods of tears. But we all accepted it was the best move for my racing career.

For 1996 Suzuki had a new GSX-R750, which was being heralded as the next big thing. I could hardly wait to get my hands on it. The deal with Suzuki was for very good money – it was easily my best payday. Compared with 1994, when I was barely scraping enough together for the mortgage, suddenly I was flush and being treated as a real star.

Ben wanted to be involved in 1996 but there was no need for him to sponsor me on the wages I was earning, so he disbanded the Reve Racing team and bought a motorhome instead in order to travel with us round Europe. We had some comical moments doing that. Ben may be good at many things, but driving a motorhome isn't one of them. He'd follow our motorhome and if ever we had to make a three-point turn or go round a tight corner, I'd always be watching in the mirrors and cringing as he tried to make the manoeuvre without bashing into something. June says she assumes the crash position every time she gets in a car with her husband.

If he was bad driving the motorhome, then he was even worse at parking it. We'd normally arrive at the circuit and save a space for Ben to park beside us. That meant finding the easiest parking space and reserving it for him. Even then he'd swap paint with any nearby walls or stationary objects. He was just a nightmare driver.

We had a brilliant year together travelling as friends. What was really awesome about the experience was that we had exactly the same good relationship as the previous years when he'd been a sponsor and team owner.

In 1995 I'd probably said things as the team rider that made him take a step back. If there was fault to be pinned on a mechanic, for instance, I'd tend to stick up for him because the mechanics were working for me. I probably went above my station a couple of times with my comments. Ben could have grabbed me round the throat and rattled me, but he didn't. I guess a true friend is one who can accept different opinions and still get on with you.

By 1996 I was 33. My age was becoming a big factor and I knew it. Teams wanted young, hungry riders, and I was viewed as being in the twilight of my career. I was very defensive about my age and worked hard to be as fit as, or fitter than, any of the other riders. I wasn't thinking about the future but was aware that I was an ageing force in what most people considered a young man's sport. I come up against that mentality a lot and today I can only hope that my record of winning one British Superbike Championship just before I was 40 and another one just after might have gone some way to proving that age isn't a restraint when you have talent and determination.

I started the 1996 season feeling young and optimistic, and was lifted by the news that Shelley was pregnant. We hadn't planned to become parents, but then again we hadn't planned not to, and when we got the news we were delighted.

The first time I tested the GSX-R750 was at Daytona and within a couple of laps I was only just over a second away from the lap record. I came into the pits, took off my helmet and smiled. This was a proper weapon. It was a brand-new bike, only just launched, and it was living up to the hype.

My team-mate, Kirk McCarthy, was a real character. After winning the 1995 Australian Superbike Championship, he'd gone out celebrating and got disqualified for drink-driving. Now, when he joined our team in Daytona, the first thing he did was introduce us to the triple challenge, which was a single spirit, then a double spirit, then a pint of lager, all to be downed in succession. After that, Kirk thought it would be a good idea for us all to go out for a drive. I declined, and next morning I heard Kirk was in prison. Apparently, during the drive someone had pulled on the handbrake while Kirk was driving, and the car had spun. Unluckily for Kirk, he was being followed by Officer Hemming, who turned on his lights, jumped out of his patrol car and pointed his gun at them. They were spread-eagled on the bonnet, searched for drugs, and then Kirk was taken to jail for being over the limit. Lester Harris, the team boss, wasn't there at the time, and the senior technicians spent a while trying to work out how to tell him. Eventually Kirk was bailed for several thousand dollars and we could get on with testing.

I crashed the GSX-R750 later in the test and went to hospital, had stitches in my elbow and came back to the track. Lester reckoned it had been a good day and I agreed, apart from the hole in my elbow. Despite the accident I left upbeat and optimistic for the season. When we returned to Daytona it was to race and when I went out on race tyres for the first time there was immediately a problem. I couldn't get within 20 seconds of the lap record.

The GSX-R750 had developed a wobble at speed. I thought of it more as a death weave. When I complained, the team pointed out that Kirk didn't have any trouble. The night before the race a tornado blew in and I lay in bed praying this would mean the races were cancelled – which eventually happened. That saved me a lot of embarrassment.

The wobble was a bewildering problem. We tried everything to cure it, even to the point of me trying Kirk's helmet to see if it was anything to do with the aerodynamics. It seemed that the problem was only with me and only showed itself at fast circuits. I'd be going from upright to a slight lean for a high-speed corner and the bike would start bucking like a bronco. The GSX-R750 has a reputation for being an animal and that year proved this – it was on a very short leash and ready to bite me any time I wasn't giving it maximum concentration. I never made friends with that Suzuki and when I looked at it in the garage I'd swear it was snarling at me.

I felt that 1996 was the longest year in my career. It put the Grand Prix years into perspective because I was now a factory rider and under immensely more pressure than when I'd been a privateer. The entire year was hard work and embarrassing because a factory rider shouldn't be running round the middle of the pack.

The GSX-R750 needed to be developed in 1996. This was its first season and it had to be refined, which is what we ended up doing. I think by the end of the year we knew what we had to do for 1997 and I was keen to stay with the team and launch a championship challenge. My self-belief was strong.

I spoke to Lester and Steve Harris about riding for the team again in 1997 and told them I didn't want to give up on the job. There was potential, we'd learned a considerable amount, and the next season was promising to be much better. They kept me hanging on, though, and couldn't commit to anything. I knew Frankie Chili, the popular Italian, was on the radar for the ride. He wasn't giving them an answer, so they couldn't give me an answer. It was frustrating. Kirk had been released a lot earlier and in many ways I envied his position – at least he could plan and go forward.

By now Ben Atkins was racing again, this time in the British

Superbike Championship. Late in 1996 he'd been invited to run the Nemesis Kawasaki team when it ran into financial difficulty. Red Bull was one of the team sponsors and he kept its logo on the fairings although all the money had been spent. As a result, for 1997 he had the promise of a lot more commitment from Red Bull and was fired up to run his own team again. He liked the idea of me riding in the team with him and so did I, especially when he said he was going to have competitive Ducati Superbikes for us to race. He told me if Suzuki didn't want me then I had a ride.

From my point of view that was a brilliant position to be in. I was no longer waiting on Suzuki and could push Harris for a decision. I told Lester and Steve I wanted an answer and they told me they couldn't give me one. I then signed for Ben to race in the British Superbike Championship and it lifted a weight off my mind. I've always been loyal to people, for better or worse. If I was offered a job and it looked right I'd go for it and give it my best shot. I wouldn't argue down to the last penny but would come to an agreement and as long as I felt we were moving forward we'd be a partnership, trying to win races. That was what counted. I never played one team off against another when it came to contract negotiations. I'm a straight bloke who simply wanted a straight answer.

Racing in World Superbikes for a factory team had not been a pleasure at all. There was so much responsibility and pressure that it turned out to be one of the worst experiences of my career. Whenever any of the Japanese bosses came over to visit you'd be grilled and left questioning your own ability.

The windows on our house needed replacing that winter and by the time I added up how much it was going to cost, I told Shelley we might as well move home as it would be cheaper. Fresh from a season as a factory rider and buoyed by having a salary for the coming year in British Superbikes, we took the plunge. Our new house, a four-bedroom detached, was right across the road from our old home in Kimberley. It was ideal as our family grew with the birth of our son, Ben, and we needed the extra space for him and his toys.

You could never accuse Shelley and me of being anything but home birds. Moving away from the area didn't occur to us. We love where we are – our families, friends, neighbours, the weather, everything.

Looking at 1997, I suspected I was stepping back in quality from Grands Prix and World Superbikes into British national racing, but I remained optimistic. We were going to have Ducati Superbikes, I was with a team I knew and at circuits I'd cut my teeth on early in my racing career. I had a chance to win races again and that kept me looking forward.

The chance to test ride the Ducati came late in 1996 and I loved it. Instantly the bike was my friend. I harboured aspirations that if I could win again in Britain, then perhaps I could return to World Superbikes. I had no thoughts of returning to Grands Prix.

Moving from a factory World Superbike team to a semi-factory British Superbike team meant a cut in wages, but it wasn't something that unduly bothered me. I'm not extravagant. I was much happier to have a deal done and the carrot of competing for race wins dangling in front of me. I was ready to taste the podium champagne again.

Chapter 13

FATHERHOOD

O ne day not long after returning home from hospital in November 2005, I got up and had to spend two hours just having a shower and getting dressed. Every movement was agony. I eventually I crept downstairs, back brace in place and sweat on my brow from my exertions. I sat down in the living room and thought again about whether this really was the right time to retire. My body was healing after all. If I retired, what was I going to do and how could I earn money? Then Ben, my eight-year-old son, came over. He was careful not to touch me – he knew how much pain I was in. Ben said he was glad I'd retired from bike racing because he didn't need to be scared now. He loved the fact I wasn't racing any more.

I was astounded by his comment. It slammed home the impact my life as a racer had had on him. Then, with the innocence of childhood, he was gone again, looking for one of his toys before I had a chance to react. I hope in years to come he'll read this book and understand how profoundly his words affected me. It reinforced my decision to retire and how important my family was to me.

I always wanted to be a father but never had any concrete plans. When my racing career started to accelerate, the idea of having children wasn't really practical. Shelley and I were so focused on travelling round the UK with Kawasaki that it just didn't seem possible or relevant at the time. Then when I was racing in Grands Prix and World Superbikes, it was an even more distant thought. When you're away from home for well over half the year, desires to nest-build and start a family are the last thing on your mind.

At the start of 1996 I realised that time was ticking by and I wasn't getting any younger. Shelley and I decided that if we were going to be parents we needed to let things happen. I had by then secured the factory Suzuki World Superbike ride and, as seems common in the bike racing world, it was early in the year when Shelley told me she was pregnant. I'd just returned from a test abroad and was having breakfast with her one morning when she said, 'Guess what?'

'What?'

'We're having a baby.'

I laughed and was immediately overcome with emotion. It was the best news ever and a complete surprise to me. We were waiting on nature to take its course but, even knowing that, the news of a baby on the way was just fantastic. We hadn't been forcing the issue, eating special foods or setting our clocks to try to conceive, but we were quietly hoping. We both felt very happy. It didn't matter to either of us if we had a boy or a girl as we were open-minded, but a bit of me deep down thought a little girl would end up breaking my heart and a little boy would want to ride and race motorcycles. Either way I didn't care as long as our child was healthy and we could be a family together. The news that I was going to be a dad had absolutely no impact on my racing career at all. I don't know whether or not that's because I can be incredibly selfish, but it simply didn't register on my professional radar.

I'd had an incredible opportunity to become a factory rider for 1996 and my entire motivation was to make that work and to win races. I got my head down and carried on racing and, as the months ticked by, Shelley travelled to fewer races and eventually stopped coming altogether. For the first time since we'd been together she was no longer at the events with me – but even then I used it positively to focus on the job.

The same day Shelley told me about her pregnancy we told our parents. They were delighted for us. I then called Ben and June

Atkins. We told a lot of people, and some may have thought a child would get in the way of my career, but it never occurred to me. I could shut everything out of my head and concentrate on racing. That was critical to my success. When I pulled my helmet on, I didn't think about my wife, my son or any repercussions that might happen if I was racing or injured. If you're thinking of anything else, then your concentration is compromised and that's when trouble occurs or when you struggle to make the results.

We decided to wait until the birth to find out for certain if we were having a boy or girl, although we'd been given a clue during one of Shelley's scheduled scans. The nurse asked us if we'd like to know but we'd already agreed that we wanted it to be a surprise. The nurse said that was fine, before explaining a few of the photographs for us. She pointed to the feet and said the baby had 'a footballer's feet'. In my book, that means a boy. I know there are many girls playing football now but it's not the sort of comment you make about a baby girl!

Ben was eventually born on 14 December 1996 after a long-drawn-out labour. Shelley had got up on Friday the 13th and told me her waters had broken. I was used to controlling Superbikes at 200mph and making decisions on braking and accelerating in fractions of a second, but that morning I felt everything was moving too fast and I could barely keep up. I quickly worked out, however, that it was eight o'clock in the morning, Shelley could have the baby by noon and I'd make it to the pub to celebrate at five o'clock that evening. But it didn't happen like that. As soon as I realised the date I felt worried. By six o'clock that evening there was little sign of our baby being born quickly. We were watching *Only Fools and Horses* – it was the episode about the birth of Damian and the music from *The Omen* was being played. I hoped this wasn't a real omen for us.

Just before two o'clock the next morning the hospital staff sent me home. I didn't want to go but they insisted and I drove home alone. Two hours later the phone rang and it was the same staff asking me to come back to support my wife. I was knackered but couldn't imagine how much harder it was for Shelley, and it was my mission to be there for her.

Shelley gave birth at midday on Saturday. In true male style I was there giving her support all the way. By that I mean staying out of the way of the midwives and handing her the gas mask whenever she wanted it. I didn't know what to say or do so guessed the best thing would be to keep a low profile and hold her hand. I wouldn't like to give birth myself, I can tell you that. It looks impossibly painful.

The whole birth experience was a miracle. As soon as our baby was born I was filled with the strongest feeling of unconditional love. I cried. We decided to call our son Ben because Shelley liked the name. I was comfortable with that as well. If it was a boy it was always going to be Ben, and for a girl we'd picked Megan.

Ben was born with glorious golden hair and was perfect in every way. When I held him it was an indescribable feeling. It was a magical day and all I wanted to do was spend time with my wife and son. Ben was a part of me. I'm no philosopher but you do some hard thinking when you become a father and it blows you away. I've never loved anything or anyone in my life as much as my son.

But even so, after Ben was born my attitude to my career didn't change. I was looking at 1997 as a new opportunity with a team capable of winning races in the British Superbike Championship. My family may have been concerned about me, but I just concentrated on the job. Motorcycle racing is extremely dangerous. When you are going round a circuit at well over 100mph, you can't allow doubts about safety and mortality to enter your head. You'd be paralysed with fear.

It was more difficult for Shelley. She never once let on to me that she was anything other than completely supportive, but I knew she worried every time I went out to compete. This was the hardest thing for me. I knew that becoming parents had altered what she thought of me racing. If I'd packed it in she wouldn't have been bothered at all, in fact she probably would have been happy. But, despite knowing this, at no time did I entertain the thought of ending my racing career. That's what I mean about it being such a selfish job: there's no room for other people's opinions, even when they belong to the people you love most in the world. You have to think about what you want to do and get on and do it. There can be no distractions.

Shelley knew my thoughts on racing and that's exactly why she never asked me to stop. She knew in my heart a building block of my personality was being a racer. If she'd given me an ultimatum it would have put me in an impossible position – would I choose racing or my family? I like to think I'd have chosen my family but I'm sincerely grateful I was never asked. We both treated racing like a job and, just like anyone else, I needed to work to pay the bills. The danger of my job was reflected in a decent salary and we knew that.

My aspirations as a rider never changed. I went out wanting to dominate every session. I also raced to maintain the standard of living that my family was used to.

But some things changed. They had to. With a young baby in the house it was impossible for Shelley to come to as many races as before. Looking after Ben, she was busier than I was. We did try at Brands Hatch in 1997 but it didn't work out very well. I hardly slept the night before the race. We decided between us that until Ben settled down it would be best if Shelley stayed at home when I was at the tracks. Again, it was my selfishness and determination to succeed coming to the fore, but there's no substitute for this level of commitment. Every advantage you can give yourself is needed if you want to win, and if that means leaving your family at home so you can get a good night's sleep, then it must be done.

It took Ben a long time to sleep well at night. There were many times when Shelley would stay with her mum and dad and leave me at home to rest. I think when she was with her parents they were able to reassure and support her in ways that I couldn't. When you have your first child I think most parents are shocked by just how much their lives have to change. No matter how hard you prepare for it there's no way you can be ready for the sleepless nights and on-call demands all day long. To get Ben to sleep you had to carry him, and then when he woke he'd call for your attention immediately. This lasted for 16 months non-stop. It was a difficult time for all three of us – but there was a very simple explanation.

One day I was testing at Pembrey trying to find the solution to a handling problem and was getting ready for the day ahead when I called home. There was no answer. Worried, I called Shelley's dad and he told me everything was OK but Ben was in hospital. He'd been diagnosed as having diabetes. My stomach dropped. I immediately picked my car keys out of my pocket and got ready to drive home but he told me everything was under control. I knew nothing about diabetes above the need for daily injections, and didn't know how to react. Do I go home or do I stay?

Shelley's dad told me to complete the test because there was nothing I could do at the hospital. I just wanted to be there with Shelley and Ben but, in a numb state of mind, I ended up staying at the circuit and we eventually found out that the handling problem was being caused by the steering damper. As soon as I was allowed, I drove back to Nottingham and straight to the hospital. Seeing my little son in a sorry state and my wife upset was one of the hardest moments of my life. I'll never forget the terrible fear and emotions – to think of them now causes immense pain. Suffice to say that, once diagnosed, the diabetes could be controlled and Ben was able to come home with us shortly afterwards.

When I was less than a year old my dad had built me my trike. When Ben was a similar age I asked my dad to build him one just like mine. The trike was Ben's first proper toy and when we gave it to him he loved it. Just like me, he was riding it before he could walk. He was bashing into tables, walls and doors in the house and laughing all the time.

When Ben was first born I harboured hopes that perhaps one day he might win a World Championship and beat his old man's record. He still might, but now I'm not bothered. I don't care what he does with his life as long as he's happy. That's all I can wish for. It's as simple as that.

As a racer you could very easily be hypocritical and say you'd never want your son or daughter to try motorcycle racing. We all know people who've been killed or seriously injured in the sport. I've broken just about every bone I can think of at least once, so I know the pain and sacrifices you have to be prepared to make if you want to succeed. But I'd never say 'no' to any child of mine who was interested in racing bikes, simply because of the lifestyle and experiences it has given me.

What I wouldn't do is push him into racing or any situation where he wasn't comfortable. My dad never pushed me into racing, despite his own interest. He gave me advice. He supported me financially when I was struggling. And I think he liked watching me enjoy myself racing and building a career.

As he has grown up it has been wonderful to see Ben acting out real life and I enjoy playing with him. There aren't enough hours in the day for spending time with him. One of the things he loves doing – whether it's on his bicycle, trike or the PlayStation – is to pretend he's on the podium and spraying champagne. On the PlayStation when he's racing me he tends to win most of the time and gets to spray a lot of champagne. More than once when I came back from a race weekend and had won, Ben would be waiting for me and asking for the champagne. I'd have to find a cheap bottle from somewhere and then we'd cheer him on as he stood on top of the table and sprayed us. His innocent flattery and imitation touched me more than you'd imagine and I loved to watch him pretending he'd just won a race.

When I won the British Superbike Championship for Rizla Suzuki in 2004 at Donington Park, Ben and Shelley were in the garage waiting for me. After I'd hugged and kissed them, my team-mates brought out a championship-winning T-shirt. I put it on and was then asked by the race organisation to make my way to the podium for the celebrations. I asked Ben if he'd like to join his dad on the podium and his face lit up. It was a wonderful feeling to have my son up alongside me. After I sprayed the champagne I started waving to the crowd and, when I looked beside me, there was Ben doing the same thing. I was just so happy to see him enjoying himself doing it properly. He'd seen his dad on TV and now he was getting to do it for real. What a fantastic experience for him – and I was immensely proud.

In 2001 he'd been with me when I celebrated my second British Superbike title, but he was younger and maybe a little bit shy. He wore a T-shirt with 'My dad is the Champion' written on it.

I'm very grateful for the joy and happiness being a father to Ben has brought to me. The modern Superbike racing paddock, however, isn't really the place for a child. In reality racing is a business and you need to treat it like a professional. I liken the paddock to a corporate boardroom. You just wouldn't bring your young children into that environment. From the outside it looks glamorous and exciting, but the reality is that racing a motorcycle is hard graft. Taking yourself to the edge lap after lap after lap is demanding work. It's even more difficult when you're not winning and off the pace, because then you have to search for the extra tenths of a second to shave from your lap times. That means putting your neck on the line and pushing outside your comfort zone. Failure is something that's not tolerated by teams, the public or myself. That puts the pressure on and takes the pleasure out of it.

Another factor in having children in the paddock is that it affects how you communicate with your team. When there were children around I was conscious of their presence and things I'd say or do would be tempered for the young audience. That's all very admirable, but there are times when you need to say things in harder terms and it's difficult to do that when young and impressionable ears and eyes are listening and observing. It's not that I'd be swearing all the time, but you couldn't come into the garage and react openly and make the point you wanted to.

Shelley brought Ben to a couple of races when he was young,

and it would affect me deeply. I'd be pulling on my helmet and I'd see my son beside me, and it would be distracting. I'd slap his hand in a high five and say 'see you mate' but it would raise doubts in my mind. The question 'will I ever see him again?' is one I needed to quash instantly. I couldn't compete in that frame of mind. It just wasn't right. I thought it was unfair on both of us, so I talked with Shelley and she stopped bringing him into the garage before the races. To get the job done I needed my family in the right place at the right time.

If I'd watched my dad racing when I was a child, I think I'd have been frightened for him, and I didn't want Ben to be frightened for me. My gut feeling was right as it turned out. Once I'd retired Shelley told me that when Ben was at home watching the racing on TV he'd hide behind the door, peeking at the screen. He was worried for me. I guess all riders are different and some may take inspiration from their children being beside them in the paddock. One of the things I really enjoyed was coming back to the garage after the final race of the day and seeing Shelley and Ben waiting there. It meant everything to me.

We'd considered having more children but decided against it. We love Ben with all our hearts and with him we found contentment. I was an only child and I don't subscribe to the view that only children are lonely. If you don't have any brothers or sisters it's not something you miss. Besides, you have all the attention of your entire family and that can be a very good thing.

Now I've retired I'm enjoying myself immensely with my family. I feel I'm a changed person. I'm no longer the selfish race winner, I'm simply dad, and I've settled into that job more quickly and easily than I could have guessed. When I was still racing, the shutters would start to come down around Christmas time and I'd become preoccupied with the coming season. The focused JR would take over and I don't think I was a good person to spend time with. Now that I'm relaxed and the shutters are wide open all the time, showing me a whole new world I can access with my family, it's the best thing ever.

I still get worked up about racing as I'm an advisor to Suzuki and the Rizla Suzuki Superbike team, but it's very different. I join them at trackside and do what I can to help, but it's not me putting my neck on the line any more. Afterwards, when I go home, Ben hasn't been hiding behind the door worried for me, he's been looking for his dad when the camera pans through the garage. One of these days I might just wave to him…

I've had a long career and been racing in one form or another for most of my life. I don't feel guilty to have retired and moved on. Now it's time to spend time with my family. I'd hoped that I could make up for a lot of missed weekends with Ben and Shelley but the paradox is that now I'm busier than ever. If I'm not advising Rizla Suzuki then I'm making appearances at dealerships or for BikeSafe. I've less time at weekends now than when I was racing, but that's OK because during the week I can make up for it.

Being a racer and a father wasn't easy. There were lots of conflicting emotions. I was 'Dad, the British Superbike Champion'. Now I'm just 'Dad' and I like that even better.

Chapter 14

Return to British Superbikes

When I knew I was going to be racing in British Superbikes in 1997, it was initially quite difficult to accept. After four years in Grands Prix and World Superbikes, I viewed the return to the UK as a bit of a step backwards and, deep down, I was thinking to myself that British Superbikes wasn't the championship I wanted to be racing in. Also, compared with the very best circuits around the world, the British tracks seemed much less appealing. For a start, they were generally narrower and shorter than top circuits abroad, and I'd need to alter my approach to riding to suit. The facilities at British tracks also lagged behind the venues I'd been racing at in the World Championships. But perhaps the biggest concern I had about returning to British Superbikes was the depth of quality in the field. I was concerned the competition might not be credible and it would be easy to get into the top ten. The last time I raced in British Superbikes, in 1992, I'd won the championship and now I was the hotshot coming back. I had a huge target on my back. Every racer wanted to beat me. So I knew I'd have to dig deep if I was going to win races, and there was pressure on me as the season approached.

The Reve Racing team had disbanded when I went to Suzuki at the start of 1996, but Ben Atkins had re-formed it mid-way through the season when the Nemesis Kawasaki team went out of business. I really wanted to race competitively again and the opportunity in British Superbikes was my best chance. I harboured thoughts that if I could win again then perhaps other opportunities would open up for me.

After my experiences with a factory team, the Reve Racing team could have been a disappointment, but it wasn't. Ben had built an exceptional professional team for 1997 and each member of the squad was solid gold – a match for any factory team. Roger Marshall was the team manager and his pedigree was beyond question. Then there was big Stuie Smith, one of the best mechanics in the business. His loyalty to Reve and me was complete – when I moved to Rizla Suzuki later in my career he came too. Steve Thompson went on to join Foggy Petronas, helped design the bike and is one of the best engineers in the business. Chris Anderson was a team technician and he has worked for the factory Suzuki and Honda teams since his Reve days, as well as Foggy Petronas. It was a dream team. If you brought the same crew together today they could do a lot of damage with a good rider in whatever championship you cared to choose.

Reve Racing raised the standard of presentation and professionalism in the British paddock, for example by introducing sponsors like Red Bull, Rizla and Aiwa to the sport. While the other teams chased sponsors from the bike industry, Ben looked elsewhere and lifted the profile of the team and, by default, the championship. He was applying his intuitive commercial skills to the job and it worked. Having Red Bull as a sponsor was a real bonus for us all. The company and its staff were into anything as long as it was extreme, from aviation to rock climbing and mountain biking. If it was dangerous, edgy and exciting, then it tickled Red Bull and was great fun – but there was also a professional side. Red Bull wanted results. The pressure was on.

I started the season with Steve Hislop as my team-mate. I could remember watching him on TV years earlier, in awe of his skills. I got to know Steve quite well through the years and had massive respect for him. In the same team and on the same bike he was a very serious threat to me. When he was on song he was impossible to beat, but he could go from brilliance to despair in the blink of an eye. When everything was just right, Steve was unstoppable, but if there was even a seed of doubt in his mind then it could be disastrous. The conditions had to be just right.

After Ben Atkins had stepped in to help Steve in 1996 when the Nemesis Kawasaki squad had folded, he kept him on and I was the new rider coming to the team. But you wouldn't have thought that from either the inside or the outside. My friendship with Ben meant it was hard to think there was parity within the team. Even I could understand that I might be thought of as the teacher's pet, so it must have been obvious to my team-mates through the years. I didn't see this as anyone's fault and there were times I was sure Ben was busting my balls to try to over-compensate and help my team-mates. And to back it up, I'm absolutely sure there was no favouritism with bikes or resources – we were both given the same. The team was too professional for it to be anything else.

With Steve, though, that just wasn't going to cut it. His brilliance demanded complete support and I'm sure he wasn't happy with what he thought of as an imbalance in support within the team. He ended up leaving, disappointed in the team and in the results he was achieving. The entire team was disappointed for him as well because we all knew his talent. I'd been beating him but if he'd switched on the Hislop magic on the same machinery then it would have been a lot harder for me. When Steve left, Ian Simpson replaced him. Ian was the natural successor as he was already riding for the team in the Production Powerbike Championship and the TT. He was quick and an asset to the squad.

At the end of 1996 I'd spoken with Ben about the bikes we should be using in 1997. After years on Kawasakis I told him it would be great if we could have Ducatis for the British Superbike Championship. Ben agreed and, in typical fashion, he went straight to the Italian factory looking for support. They invited us to a test at Misano and we knew the purpose was to see if we were good enough to race the bikes.

I'd raced against the Ducatis in World Superbikes for the previous two years and they looked special. They had the power, handling, looks and even the World Championship trophies to back them up. I desperately wanted to race a Ducati to see how good they were and to give myself the best shot I could for winning the British title again. After watching the factory riders test for a day and a half, I got my chance. Carl Fogarty wasn't there but the rest of the names were, so it was a proper test and I was under pressure.

There were some enormous differences between the Ducati 996cc V-twin and the 750cc in-line four-cylinder bikes I was used to riding. The Ducati was really grunty. It had a lot more torque than the bikes I'd ridden before, plus top-end power and precise handling as well. This was the complete package. It felt tiny and agile.

At Misano, turns four through to six are a long series of bends that I hadn't been able to piece together the previous year on the Suzuki. But after a couple of laps on the Ducati, I found I could go through the bends flat-out, thanks to the bike's confidence-inspiring stability. Even riding cautiously, knowing a lot of eyes were on me at the test, I found the Ducati lightning quick.

After the sessions I told Ben the 996 had lots of potential. Looking back I'm embarrassed I said that. We all knew it had bags of potential: it had just won umpteen championships and was clearly the kit to be racing on. There's no doubt the Ducati had a performance edge with extra capacity over the competition at the time and I wanted any advantage I could get. Ever since watching Raymond Roche on a Ducati World Superbike in the early 1990s I'd dreamed of riding one. Ben made another trip to Bologna shortly after and secured factory support for the team in British Superbikes. It meant we had the dream start to 1997.

The season opened at Mallory Park, where I finished second, and then it was on to Donington Park, then Oulton Park. Immediately my concern that the British Championship might have lacked strength was dispelled. I was getting on the podium – but winning races was another story. The Yamahas and Kawasakis were factory race bikes and I was up against riders like Niall Mackenzie, Terry Rymer, Steve Hislop, Iain MacPherson, Chris Walker, Sean Emmett, Brian Morrison and Matt Llewellyn. These were world-class riders and there wasn't an inch of give in any of them. I might have been on the best machinery with the best chance of winning for years, but the field was ultra-strong and it was going to be a tough season.

Niall Mackenzie had scored podiums in Grands Prix and finished fourth in the 1990 World Championship. He was a legend and I honestly believe he left some of the best riding of his career until he returned to the UK to race in British Superbikes. He was on fire – fit, determined and the consummate professional. I'm proud to have been on the same track competing with him while he won three consecutive British Superbike Championships on the Cadbury's Boost Yamahas. I'm even happier to say I got the better of him on a few occasions. That reinforced my own self-belief and he was a constant target for me to aim for.

The first time I beat him was at the second round of the 1997 championship at Oulton Park, where I took my first win of the year. I'd started the season well enough but was realistic: I was on a new bike with a new team and we were all learning. I'm an eternal optimist about racing and knew a win would come eventually. I can be very impatient but had developed a sort of understanding with racing. I could wait for a couple of races before winning because I knew I had a lot to learn.

Oulton Park has always been kind to me. It's tight and technical, and suits my riding style. Circuits like this were my hunting grounds. I was ecstatic to have won a race again. The last championship race I won had been in 1992, five years earlier. I was glad the drought was at an end and drank the champagne deep and for a lot longer than normal on the top step of the podium. I savoured the moment. Just like in the earlier days, going home from a race meeting knowing you'd bettered every single rider was a feeling I craved.

As the 1997 season progressed I approached racing as professionally as possible. I didn't go all-out to win every race, because that was unrealistic. If I binned the bike and injured myself early on, then it would wreck the season for the team and sponsors. Instead, I grew accustomed to the Ducati, learned its foibles and concentrated on scoring strong points when I could. I was looking on 1997 as an investment season, with the payback to come later.

Brands Hatch, the fourth round of the season, was the first time my son Ben came to a race meeting. Brands was my favourite circuit and the short Indy circuit had just been resurfaced and was a joy to be riding on. I was quickest in all the sessions and felt incredibly strong, almost invincible. I was in tune with everything on race day and went out in the first race from pole position, determined to put on a good show for my infant son, my family and the fans.

The circuit was wet and drying so I was using intermediate tyres, and on the opening lap I took nearly three seconds out of the rest of the competition. I could feel the grip and was on a song, but it didn't last. Going into the left-hander at Graham Hill the tyre wasn't quite at temperature, I lost the front end and crashed. I was devastated. It was my chance for a second victory of the season and, instead of cruising to the win, I'd thrown it away.

I made up for this in the second race with an emphatic win in the dry and left the circuit a happy man. For a rider, if you're going to crash, then it's much better for this to be in the opening race and then to score a good result in the second race. In a way you've made amends and reaffirmed your own ability. If you crash in the second race it's always a nightmare and you brood on it for longer and can't wait to get back on track again.

Round seven of the championship at Mallory Park was to prove a critical point of the season when I crashed out at 120mph in a practice session at the entrance to Gerard's. It seemed innocuous enough and I slid along the Tarmac and grass before going shoulder-first into the gravel trap. I catapulted into the air and landed heavily. After taking a moment to collect my thoughts, I walked over to the barrier with a couple of marshals. I wasn't in a great deal of pain but it felt like my back protector had slid round my leathers and was poking me in the ribs. I sat down and decided to wait until I got to the pits before sorting out my leathers. As the minutes ticked by I began to feel sick and there was a pain building where my back protector was sticking into me.

'I think you might need to stop the session,' I told a marshal. 'I don't feel very well.'

He looked me up and down and said I was fine, that there wasn't long left before I could cross the track. A couple of minutes later I said it again and got the same reply. Eventually I asked him for a third time and the pain must have shown in my eyes, along with the sweat on my brow. By now I was in agony. I couldn't make it across the track to the pits by myself so an ambulance was dispatched to pick me up.

The doctors in the circuit medical facility took my leathers off and that's when we found it wasn't my back protector digging into my ribs, rather it was my arm. I had dislocated my shoulder. The doctor told me he was going to try and pull it back into place, which might sting. Boy, did it ever. In the end there were three doctors heaving on my arm and shoulder. After three attempts I told them if they were to try again then it would kill me. I meant it. I hadn't experienced pain like this before.

I'd been doing quite a lot of weight training as part of my race preparation and the muscles were fighting the efforts to put my arm back in place. The doctors told me I needed to go to hospital. The doctors at the hospital tried putting it back in place again and when I told them I was about to die of pain they said they'd need to knock me out. I smiled for the first time in hours. When I woke up I was dazed and there was a doctor standing above me. 'Is my arm back in place?' I asked. He nodded and the relief was immense.

As it turned out, though, for a crash that didn't involve any broken bones, it couldn't have been much worse. Damage to ligaments and muscle tissue was immense. Three weeks later I was in the team garage but wasn't competing. I climbed on the bike and stretched my right arm to the handlebar. It was sheer hell and there was no way I could have raced. Recovery took a total of six weeks and I missed six races in the championship, which scuppered my chances for the season.

I felt disheartened that I was no longer a contender for the title. I'd come back to Britain to race for victories and was stopped because of injury. I ended up fourth overall in the series, which was a good result, and my abiding memory of the season was happiness at being back on a competitive bike, able to fight at the front of the field. I'd tasted a lot of champagne in 1997. I'd won two races and they were very satisfying victories. I'd gone up against some of the best Superbike riders in the world and been forced to work my heart out to beat them. When you really earn your wins, that's when they're most valuable and I treasured those two.

It was a straightforward discussion to stay on with Ben Atkins at Reve Racing for the following season. We were both enjoying the team atmosphere and felt we were building for success. We didn't know when this would come but it was on order and we were determined to achieve it.

It was the same every season until the end of 2001. I'd visit Ben at his home on bonfire night and, over a beer, we'd talk terms for the coming year. It was always a verbal agreement as we trusted each other. The negotiations would be over in minutes and then we'd get down to the business of emptying beer cans for the rest of the evening. They were great nights. Most riders probably look forward to contract negotiations with dread but I actually enjoyed mine in those years.

Before the start of the new season, when Ben had told me Sean Emmett was to be my team-mate I'd wondered how I could work with him. It's funny how things turn around. When we went to

Italy for our first test I thought he was the enemy. After a week we came back the best of friends, and have been mates ever since. I understand him now and really like his sense of humour.

For 1998 we stayed with Ducati but now had the latest Superbikes to race. It was a difficult start to the season for me, though, and at the end of the opening round at Brands Hatch, when I'd only just scraped inside the top ten, I sat on the steps at the back of the garage with team manager Roger Marshall and Ben Atkins, my head in my hands. I was distraught. I couldn't figure out what had gone wrong that weekend. The bike and team were good and the fault was coming from me. I raced to win and be the best, but all I'd done was get soundly beaten – without any excuse. It was the worst weekend of racing ever.

We made a plan and booked Mallory Park for a private test shortly after that. I was determined to start afresh and the test was going fantastically well until, at 120mph, the rear end slid out slightly on the exit of Gerard's. The bike shifted a foot to the left and just touched the grass. Normally you'd get away with that but during the spring there'd been a lot of rain, the grass was waterlogged and my new Michelins, despite being great on Tarmac, didn't stand a chance off-road. I was sent flying over the bars in a monumental crash and ended up breaking my heel bone.

I spent the next two weeks in hospital and missed my chance to ride as a wild card at a World Superbike race. Sean Emmett rode at the event and broke his elbow. In a strange twist of fate he ended up in the bed beside mine, and that made for an awful picture for Ben Atkins and Reve Racing. Both his riders were injured and in the same hospital.

The doctors told me the heel bone wasn't like a normal bone. When you break a leg or arm, the two bits of bone can be set and will grow together again. If a normal break was like snapping a Kit-Kat, then breaking your heel was like crushing an Aero bar. In the hospital all I could think of was healing as fast as possible and getting back on a bike, but the news was grim. The professor in charge of my case was quite aloof. One morning he peered over the rim of his glasses and told me that if I'd been a window cleaner then my career would be over. The implication was obvious – he was saying I had no future on a Superbike. It was the last thing I wanted to hear. As a racer you need nurturing and encouragement, not doom and gloom. I told him it was just as well I wasn't a window cleaner.

Luckily my surgeon was much more positive. He fixed my heel with a lot of help from some metal pins and then sent me on my way, with the warning that if I was to crash again there might be nothing more that could be done and I could lose my right foot. When a doctor gives you that sort of warning you take it very seriously. It didn't for an instant stop me from racing – but it certainly focused my mind. I weighed up the physical risk against the demands of my job. I had sponsors and a team of people relying on me, not to mention my family to support. The pressure was immense. In the end it was my own desire to race that was the deciding factor. I wanted to go for the victories.

The fear of failure was a motivating factor as well. If ever I was beaten, injured or disconsolate, I'd stare fear in the face, grit my teeth and be determined to vanquish it. That's what I said to myself. The injury was serious and I had to respect it. A special boot was made with a carbon-fibre insert that took the pressure off my heel and allowed me to race. Without it I'd have been in too much pain.

I made a deal with myself that I'd race within my own comfort zone. I'd compete within my limits, even if that meant forfeiting the chance to be at the very front. To go for the victory you need to be on the limit through every corner and be prepared to ask more of the bike and yourself than you can realistically expect. I knew I couldn't bring that to the track just then. But I felt I could minimise the risk. My fellow competitors were going to be the biggest worry. I might be comfortable and in control, but if one of them crashed into me then it wouldn't matter whose fault it was, I'd be the one paying for it.

I eased myself back into the competition. Top-ten positions

were good results and, as my injury healed, I was able to improve. By the end of the season I was winning races and on the podium regularly, and I notched the year down to experience – very painful experience.

For other reasons, the 1998 season also had its painful moments. Embarrassing ones. One was at Silverstone when Ben was turning Reve Racing into a serious player in the championship. I'd crashed in the rain and was desperately angry with myself for making a stupid mistake. To make it worse, Sean Emmett had beaten me on the day. After getting changed in my motorhome I stormed into the garage with my wet, dirty and ripped leathers. Without looking, I flung them across the garage into the panels, kicked a helmet or two nearby and slumped down into a chair, scowling at anyone who dared look at me.

Ben was in the garage at the time and he wasn't alone. After pumping his own money into the team he'd secured some new sponsors and was busy introducing them to the squad and telling them how approachable, friendly and marketable Superbikes was. The sponsors raised their eyebrows while watching JR's 'angry, spoiled racer show', and Ben made a quip about it being a tough day and then tried his best to rescue the situation. Sitting in my chair glowering at people I realised that maybe I'd just stuck my foot in it – I felt exactly the same way I did the day I broke my next-door neighbour's window when I was a kid. There was an unnatural calm and I knew a storm was coming.

That was the day my good friend and technician, Stuart Smith, gave me the nickname 'Mardy Little Bastard' – MLB. It stuck with me until the end of my career and summed me up pretty accurately when I was racing. Ben called me in to his truck office. He told me in no uncertain terms that if I didn't like the job then I could take a hike. His exact words were, 'Tosspot, sort yourself out or you'll be out on your ear.' Ben could understand why I'd got angry but was shocked by my actions. He'd never seen me like that in front of anyone. I'd shown him a new side of me at exactly the wrong moment. After that, if I ever felt like letting loose with my thoughts in the garage, I always had a quick look round first to make sure there was no-one who shouldn't be there. I could vent my anger and frustration with my team, but if there were sponsors or media in attendance then I'd keep my mouth shut until they left.

I nearly got fingered for being bad-tempered one other time. It was at Albacete during practice. The bike felt fine for the first four or five laps and I came into the garage to make a couple of changes. But as I tried to make the turn into the garage I found the bike just wouldn't do it and I ended up throwing it down pitlane rather than crashing into a wall. I picked myself up, bemused, and June Atkins was staring at me in horror. She thought I was so angry with the bike that I'd deliberately chucked it down. It turned out the steering lock was minimal, just about enough to do a lap without showing, but nowhere near enough to make a tight turn. I was mortified and nearly had a bollocking because of it.

In 1999 Troy Bayliss came to the British Superbike Championship and won it. He's an incredibly nice chap and a really hard racer. He'd miss his apexes and corners but still be lightning fast. He never seemed to ride at anything less than maximum attack and full aggression. I'm proud to have raced against him and able to call him a friend. Troy went on to become World Superbike Champion and to win the 'Rookie of the Year' award in MotoGP. Those results show the quality of rider the British Superbike Championship could attract and how hard it was to race in the domestic series and win.

Troy is a bit younger than me and he made the most of his chances and breaks after winning the British Superbike Championship. If I'd been offered the same opportunities, I often wonder, would I have taken them? In 1999 I was quite happy living and working in the UK, having my family close to hand all the time. But saying that, if I'd been given the same opportunities as Troy I'd have taken them with both hands. I wouldn't have been able to resist the chance of racing a factory Ducati in World Superbikes.

I was in contention for the title in 1999 and there are two defining moments that stand out and maybe prove that what goes around comes around. At Silverstone, battling hard with Chris Walker, I rammed into the side of him while overtaking and knocked him off. I only just held onto my bike and think it was by shunting him I had the extra grip to stay upright. Then, at Donington Park in the very final race of the season, I was up against Chris fighting for second place in the championship. I overtook him on the straight and immediately, at the Fogarty Esses, he T-boned me, leaving me in the gravel and having to settle for third in the series. We're good friends now and there are no hard feelings about those clashes, but I'm sure revenge was sweet.

For 2000 it was more of the same, with a three-way battle for the championship between myself, Chris Walker and Neil Hodgson. I enjoyed the season and was a proper contender for the title, but not many people will remember that. Although I led for the first six rounds of the series and eventually finished third, only 17 points behind the champion, Hodgson, the story for the season was the Walker v Hodgson rivalry. Walker and Hodgson overwhelmed everyone with their personal battle and ended up tearing chunks out of each other. It was a vintage season and it was great to be part of it but in the end I think those boys pushed themselves way beyond anything they'd previously achieved. For the record, Neil had exactly the same bike as me that season, except for perhaps a couple of races when he benefited from full factory engines. That may have given him a slight advantage but I'll not take anything away from him – he won the title and I didn't.

Like Troy Bayliss before him, and riding for the same GSE team, Neil Hodgson showed he had world-class potential. Neil had raced for the factory Ducati team in the 1990s and was lucky to get a second chance at the World Superbike Championship after winning the BSB title. Not many people would ever be given a second attempt but Neil had the right people around advising and pushing him to the big teams. He went on to be a worthy World Champion and I believe he did well in MotoGP, given the level of non-factory machinery he was racing on. I'm proud to have raced Neil in British Superbikes and very happy when you look at the number of World Superbike Champions I can now count as friends.

Looking back on the season's result, I'd say, if life was fair, that perhaps Chris Walker should have won the championship. He went into the final round at Donington with a 21-point lead and only needed to finish the second race, but his bike broke and he ended up walking to the pits in tears. I maintain that the 1000cc Ducatis had a slight advantage over the 750cc race bikes that season and the fact that Chris came so close just underlines his achievements and how well he was riding. If he'd won the title then very possibly he could have gone on to be a World Champion the way Neil did.

Chris is a good friend and I'm a big fan of his as he continues to race. It was no fluke in 2000, he's immensely talented, perhaps the best rider never to have won a major championship. When I was in hospital at the end of my career, pondering my future, Chris came to visit and it meant a lot to me. I had a lot of visitors but he stands out as one of a few riders, including Michael Rutter and James Haydon, to come and see me. Thanks guys, it helped a lot!

For me, the lesson from that season was clear: a rider has to take his chances if he wants to win and I was ready to take mine in 2001.

Once again, on the Red Bull Ducati within the Reve Racing team, I came out of the blocks strongly at the start of 2001 and easily won the opening race at Donington Park. In a perverse way I was disappointed. I don't like winning easily: it reduces the value and effort in my own eyes, and I think the general public think a race is boring if it looks too easy. I felt the fans wouldn't be enjoying themselves and, because I hadn't dug deep into my own reserves, I felt a bit cheated as well. How stupid was I to think like that? 'Very stupid' is the answer, because the second race was extremely tough and I had to work hard to win it.

After the Walker and Hodgson season in 2000, it turned into the Reynolds and Hislop year in 2001. We enjoyed some epic tussles. We were on the same bikes, with paintwork and teams being the only difference. By the eighth round Steve was leading me by six points and that season we shared all the victories between us, except for the two races at Rockingham, a new circuit to the calendar.

I relished every race and, far from finding it too easy, I was in the fight of my life with a rival I respected above all others and who was a hero of mine. I knew exactly how good Steve Hislop was on a bike: he was one of the fastest men in the world on a motorcycle and untouchable on his day. He was sensitive to his surroundings and team and needed to be happy to perform, and that season he was always smiling and confident. For me to compete with him was brilliant. I felt people could mention my name in the same breath as Steve's and I wouldn't be embarrassed or feel second best.

Steve and I were friends as well. We wouldn't give an inch on the track, but off it we both were going through our helicopter flying lessons and were like two children every time we met, chatting about the exams and flying. We were having a race on that front as well – which one of us was going to pass the exams first.

In 2001 we visited Mallory Park and, during practice, I suffered a major crash at the Devil's Elbow and thought I'd broken my right ankle. I qualified well down the field but still managed to win a race and score decent points. The problem was I slipped to 25 points behind Steve as we went to Rockingham and the penultimate round of the championship.

The circuit at Rockingham is great for spectators, but for a rider it has some serious flaws. The run-off areas are short and that's never ideal. No matter what air fencing you put up, a Superbike is just so fast now that you can do serious damage if you crash without a lot of space around you to reduce the energy and slow you down safely.

In the opening race I was racing hard when I went into a fast corner with very little run-off. I missed a gear and before I could select another one someone thumped into the back of me. I knew there was someone behind me but didn't know who. Oblivious to the moment, I kept on racing – you get used to people touching and colliding with you, that's just part of racing. A little later in the lap the red flag came out and my stomach sank. I realised there'd been a crash behind me. I came back to the pits fully aware it had been my fault, as I'd missed a gear. My worst nightmare came true when I found out it was Steve who'd been so close behind and had crashed out. It looked like he'd slid under the Rectocele fence and hit a concrete wall and was very badly injured. It was clear his season was over.

We'd traded 22 race wins between us up to that point and were nearly inseparable on the track and in the championship. It was my mistake that saw him lose his lead in the championship to me and, with only one round to go, no-one else was close enough to be able to challenge. I was the British Superbike Champion.

That day at Rockingham was truly horrible. If Steve had crashed for any other reason then it would have been different. I'd have been able to accept it. But he crashed out and, despite this being a genuine mistake, it handed me the title. I may have been smiling on the outside to the TV cameras and media, but my 2001 championship title was hollow in my own eyes. I've never come to terms with this and, although my name goes down in the history books, I don't feel I won the title fair and square and it still haunts me to think about it.

Ben Atkins told me no-one else had worked as hard that year or deserved it more than me. My team celebrated and the fans cheered. I sprayed the champagne, waved and smiled, but actually I wanted to go home. But I couldn't. Despite what had happened I was a professional racer and had duties to my sponsors, team and fans. They'd won a championship and I needed to conduct myself professionally and according to what they needed. I did.

As soon as I got home from Rockingham, I picked up the 'phone to the hospital where Steve was admitted and we spoke. I asked him if he'd see me and was prepared for him to slam the 'phone down, but he didn't. He said 'yes' and I jumped in my car straight away. When I got to the hospital Steve was in bed. His team boss Paul Bird was there as well and as soon as I walked into the room I knew it wasn't going to be an easy meeting. I was the bad guy. I was there to admit that and to tell Steve myself that it was a mistake and I'd do anything to take it back. Thankfully they put me at ease as soon as I walked through the door. They were great.

I felt utterly awful. Despite having just won my second British Superbike title, it was one of the worst moments in my career. As I left the room Steve's parting words were, 'Win both races at Donington for me, show them who the boss is.'

I went to Donington Park two weeks later and won both races for Steve, just as he'd asked. I dedicated them to him. Would I have won the championship if Steve hadn't suffered the crash at Rockingham? I honestly don't know. He went to Rockingham with a 25-point advantage and only four races to go. He could have managed the situation and followed me around and still won the championship. I'd have preferred to be in his position with a points lead rather than chasing.

One thing is for sure: I wouldn't have given up until the chequered flag for the last race of the season. But the reality is that if he hadn't crashed I probably wouldn't have beaten him.

As I stood on the podium at Donington Park to accept the championship trophy I had a terrible thought: 'What will Steve's mum think of me?' I was getting the applause and spraying the champagne while her son was in hospital with a broken leg and collarbone. She's such a lovely lady that I didn't want to do anything to offend her and I knew she wouldn't like to watch the victory ceremony, in just the same way my mum wouldn't have enjoyed it if the situation had been reversed. It wasn't the party celebration I wanted. I was satisfied with the job I'd done for the team and happy to give Ben Atkins a title he deserved for the efforts and finance he'd invested in the team. But I wasn't jumping on the tables. It just didn't feel right.

I can remember waking up one morning in mid-summer of 2003 while staying in Dorset with John Denning, father of Paul Denning, the British Superbike team boss. I went outside his house, switched on my mobile 'phone and it started bleeping at me with message after message. They kept flooding in and I called my voicemail to hear person after person telling me they were sad to hear the news about Steve.

At first I hadn't a clue which Steve they were talking about or what had happened, but a couple of messages later it became clear. Steve had been killed in a helicopter accident. I sat down hard. I didn't know what to think or say. Steve had been one of my best friends in the paddock. We were a similar age, shared the same love of flying and enjoyed a great rivalry. I can't express how much I miss him as a friend and competitor. He was without a doubt one of the best motorcycle racers of all time.

After I'd dominated the British Superbike Championship in 1992, nine years passed before I won it again. To win a championship a lot of factors must fall into place: the team, riders, bikes and luck must all be with you under the same umbrella. That doesn't happen very often and that's why winning a title is so special and so difficult to achieve, unless you're lucky to find yourself with a machine or tyre advantage.

It takes a whole year of effort to win a title, thousands of miles in testing and riding on the edge of your performance abilities at every corner for every lap without crashing and hurting yourself.

After I'd spent the season living on the edge and putting it all on the line for the team and sponsors, Red Bull invited us to Austria as a big 'thank you'. My biggest fears are climbing and heights, so naturally they'd put on a scaling event at a 500ft sheer rock face that was around 3,000ft up a mountain. As clear as day I thought I wasn't going to make it home from the climb. I was petrified and couldn't stop thinking how I'd risked my life for them all season and this was how they repaid me. Once you got to the top you had to unclip yourself, and then attach to a line, before letting yourself free-fall down to the base camp, flying down a wire 3,500ft above the ground. My hands were sweating and shaking so much that I only just got myself clipped in and by then I was so scared I simply did as I was told and leaped off the mountain.

It was an exhilarating ride to the bottom and was a typical Red Bull extreme adventure. Despite my absolute terror, once I completed it and downed a few swift drinks, I started to enjoy the experience. The guys at Red Bull know how to enjoy themselves and the company is without doubt one of the best sponsors I've ever had. I still count many of them as my friends – and I hope I get the opportunity to repay them by taking them on high-speed pillion rides. I'd do anything to scare them as much as they did me.

The difference between winning the championship in 1992 and 2001 was immense. While both had been great achievements against brilliant riders, the difference came in the professional approach of the teams and championship organisation in 2001. The Motor Cycle Race Control Board (MCRCB) had lifted the profile and professionalism of the racing in Britain and, with big-name sponsors and TV coverage, the pressure to perform was enormous.

I think the British Superbike Championship has increased in credibility year after year and is now a shop window for riders to show their ability on a world level, with the Japanese factories taking notice. Recently British Superbike racers like Troy Bayliss, Neil Hodgson and James Toseland have all won World Superbike Championships. Troy, Neil, Shane 'Shakey' Byrne, James Haydon and James Ellison have all tasted life at the very top in MotoGP. The British Superbike format has also helped Casey Stoner into

MotoGP and, although he's Australian, he can at least partially trace his rise to stardom back to the British 125cc Championship.

I think you could take Gregorio Lavilla or Leon Haslam to World Superbikes and both would be hot contenders for the title, especially if they were part of the GSE squad that's in BSB at the time of writing. The championship is strong and growing in esteem for the factories and I can see it continuing to improve in stature. It's great that Honda's mighty HRC is racing in BSB, and even better that it isn't dominating. The level is very high indeed.

In 2000 we were permitted to race as wild-card entries at the UK rounds of WSB, regardless of tyres, and I'm very grateful. That's the year I won my only World Superbike Championship race and it was one of the best days of my life.

Chapter 15

WORLD SUPERBIKE VICTORY

In 2000 the World Superbike Championship visited Britain three times. It was the height of Foggy-mania and Superbike racing was attracting lots of interest in this country. When the Italian Imola round dropped off the calendar in 2000 it was an easy decision for the series organisers to come back to the UK. Brands Hatch was attracting 60,000-plus fans on race day, the biggest crowd of the entire year, so they decided another race at the venue wouldn't be a bad idea.

In 2000 Colin Edwards won the championship and Troy Bayliss was becoming a force to be reckoned with. Bayliss was popular in the UK after winning the British Championship the year before and there was a groundswell of support for him and all of the British riders who were entered into the home rounds.

Red Bull Ducati entered all three British World Superbike races. I got a tenth and retirement at Donington and followed that with a fourth and retirement at Brands Hatch. When another round was announced at Brands Hatch I was itching to race. I had been in the shadow of the feud between Chris Walker and Neil Hodgson for most of the season and had a point to prove.

It was October and the weather was both changeable and cool. It didn't keep the crowd at bay though and, with names like Neil Hodgson, Chris Walker, Colin Edwards, Troy Corser, Troy Bayliss, Pier Francesco Chili, Aaron Slight and Akira Yanagawa in the races, this was a mouth-watering prospect.

After dry practice I ended up second in a wet Superpole behind Neil Hodgson who was riding on the crest of a wave after winning the British title only a week earlier. I was happy though, I had a good set up on the number 47 Ducati and was sure I could race with the front runners.

Standing on the podium in a World Superbike event is something most riders only dream of doing. Winning a World Championship points-scoring race is difficult to achieve but I had always wanted to add that to my CV. In 2000 I was riding well and on race morning I dared to think I might actually win a race – but then quickly locked the thought away.

It was a typical stressful race weekend. The domestic British Superbike season was over but that didn't matter to the World Superbike boys. They were mugging each other for championship points and were racing harder and faster as the season drew to an end and contracts were up for negotiation and renewal. There was no room for complacency from any of the wild-card entries.

I went through all of my normal pre-race routines and as the crowd was winding up to the first race the rain started to fall. The crowd didn't care and on the sighting lap I could hear the chants and cheers, despite wearing a helmet with ear plugs and a very loud Ducati revving under me. It was almost a surreal experience and one I enjoyed: I knew I was in the middle of a proper event and it meant something.

By the time we took to the grid the rain had stopped falling. The circuit was damp and drying, which is probably one of the worst conditions to race in. I've always dreaded racing on a damp but drying track as it's difficult to know the limits of grip available, or even what tyres to select. I won't pretend to have had any idea what tyres to use as the weather looked as though it could get worse or better at any moment, so we parked on the grid and scanned the tyres everyone else was using. Most were on full wet tyres so we put our wets on and waited for the race to start.

The lights turned to green and I got a great start. After a lap I had a couple of seconds gap and was leading a World Championship race again, something I hadn't done for years. As the race wore on, the track started to dry out and my Ducati started to move around a lot as the tyres overheated. I kept my eyes on the pit boards and rode as smoothly as I could but Troy Bayliss was catching up. He must have conserved his tyres exceptionally well because he latched on to my tail and then made a strong pass to take the lead.

Inside my helmet I was oblivious to everything else; the crowd that had been vocal earlier wasn't even on my radar, I was concentrating so hard. When you are thinking as hard as I was, you may as well have been on an empty track at a private test. You are completely focused on the job in hand.

I was able to keep with Troy's pace and noticed he was struggling with tyres as well. I was on a mission, I wanted to win the race and was desperate to make my dream come true. There were no thoughts of the past or the opportunities I might get in the future: I just had a driving need to win the race.

I passed Troy and made it stick this time, pulling a small gap and extending it as I counted the laps down. Then my pit board started to tell me Colin Edwards, the Texan World Champion elect, was on a charge and catching up fast. He had gone out with intermediate tyres and had paid the price early in the race when the circuit was wet. Now, with the track drying fast, his tyres were working much better and he was clawing me back in at around four seconds a lap. I didn't have time to do the maths in my head but suddenly it wasn't Troy who concerned me any more, it was Colin.

I pushed my Ducati on its ruined tyres as hard as I possibly could, going into corners knowing I had to go faster than comfortable and could possibly crash. If I was any slower then I'd be caught and the race lost and I wasn't prepared to do that. I was close to winning a race and not just any race, it was at my favourite circuit in front of my home fans.

Going into the penultimate lap I knew the gap had reduced and, after glancing at my board, I knew he would catch me by the chequered flag. I buried my head and kept going, coaxing the last performance out of the Dunlops and hoping Colin might hit traffic and I might still make the chequered flag first.

Colin crashed, unhurt, later in the lap and when I came round to start the last lap my pit board no longer had him hounding me.

It's difficult when you are trying so hard on a motorcycle to assimilate all the information you read, especially when you are on wet tyres on a dry circuit and on the last lap before winning a World Superbike race.

I got round the last lap and, as I passed Clearways on to the start/finish straight, the jubilation began and I crossed the finish line in a state of semi disbelief mingled with ecstasy. After so many years of trying, I had at last won a World Championship race and I was stunned. My crew had been waving and cheering wildly as I took the chequered flag and all of a sudden I could hear the crowd again. They were going ballistic and my name was on their lips.

There's nothing like winning in front of your home crowd and beating the rest of the world at the same time. On my cooling down lap I was numb with shock and joy. All I wanted to do was get back to my team in the pits and share the moment with them. It's at times like that when being on a motorcycle can be really lonely, even when there are thousands of people shouting your name. It was one of the fastest cool down laps of my life. I needed to get back to the garage to make sure the result was real. I didn't mean to speed past the cheering fans, I just couldn't believe I had won.

Winning a championship race against such quality riders was something I wasn't going to forget in a long time. It was one of the best races of my career, I felt I had earned the win. I climbed off the bike and Ben Atkins gave me a huge bear hug. He's a lot bigger than me and I thought at one point he might just squash me but I gave it back as hard as I could, at last really coming to terms with winning the race.

After getting my helmet off and kissing and hugging anyone within arms reach, I was led to the podium and that's when I suffered my only crash of the day. As I mounted the steps there was that much champagne on the metal, I slipped and landed on my backside. After 45 minutes of staying upright at high speed in damp drying conditions, I was caught out by spilt champagne. It can be dangerous stuff.

I picked myself up to a cheer and then climbed up and on to the top step and waved to the crowd. The noise was deafening. It was so loud I couldn't hear it, there was just a wall of sound that couldn't be differentiated from anything else. Above all else I felt complete pride in what I had achieved and for the Reve Racing team who had helped me. You cannot achieve winning results in World or British championship events without a team of highly skilled professionals backing you every step of the way. The Ducati had been prepared and set up brilliantly by my team. They had kept me away from any undue pressure and allowed me to go to the race in the right frame of mind. They had even made the right tyre choice under changeable weather conditions. I had ridden the bike and delivered what every man in the team deserved, a win.

If I was excited by the victory then I hardly had time to put my feet on the ground before the second race of the day. Normally I'd go back to my motorhome and relax in preparation but that wasn't an option. The race organisers took me to a tent to give a rider briefing and, in the middle of that, an RAF Tornado flew overhead. It mustn't have been very high because it deafened most of us and I could have swore the tent nearly blew away.

After that I was pulled from pillar to post and didn't have a moment to myself. If it wasn't the media wanting an interview then it was a fan or competitor wishing me well. The gap between the races vanished in the blink of an eye and the next thing I knew I was back on the bike lining up on the grid for the second race, utterly exhausted and head still spinning.

It was a dry second race and, although I was in contention for all of it, I finished fourth and relieved to have the day come to an end. I was completely spent, with nothing left to give. It had been a dream day and I was emotionally and physically drained. As the team got down to the serious job of celebrating I packed my kit away and drove the motorhome back to Kimberley. Shelley was waiting for me and we raised a glass of champagne to the results. It was a brilliant way to finish the 2000 season and I was overjoyed. It was the crowning moment of my career.

I think the World Superbike Championship peaked around 2000 and was at the height of its attraction to the British audience. Carl Fogarty had won his titles and built the series up to the point where it was getting serious recognition in the UK from the tabloids and television. In turn that put the racing on the map for the general public and it sort of built itself up as the main race of the year for bikers, easily rivalling and pulling much bigger crowds than MotoGP before the Rossi era.

Carl Fogarty is a fantastic character in the world of bike racing, but he never really set the scene alight in British racing and I can remember soundly beating him when we raced against each other in the early 1990s.

Jamie Whitham was another rider who ran with, and beat, Carl in the early 1990s and I spoke with him about Carl's transformation from a good rider into a truly great rider in the mid to late 1990s when he took four world titles. Jamie told me the Carl Fogarty in World Superbikes was a much different rider. He was aggressive, confident and a winner through and through.

I watched Carl race at Sugo in Japan one year when he suffered a massive knock in the first race. It was a big crash, enough to call into question your reasons to race again the same day, but Carl shrugged it off and got on his bike to win the second race of the day. To win in Sugo was special, thanks to the strength of the local Japanese riders, but to do it after a huge crash was just plain impressive.

Carl has had his detractors but in my eyes he is simply a bike racing phenomenon. You can't argue against the fact that the man can ride a bike. There has been a lot of debate on whether he might have been successful in Grand Prix, given the opportunity. I think a good rider can make it no matter what the series and he would've made an impact in Grand Prix. I watched him ride the

Cagiva at the 1993 British GP and cruelly miss the podium on the last lap due to bike problems. That sort of performance isn't something an ordinary rider could ever achieve.

If Carl had been able to go to Grand Prix with the same sort of Ducati support that's available today, then there's every likelihood he might have been a World Champion. That's not taking anything away from Mick Doohan or any of the other great riders, but reflects Carl's riding ability.

The main contribution Carl has made in my eyes is how he brought Superbike racing to the forefront in the UK. He is a team boss now in World Superbikes. I always enjoy reading stories about him and his Petronas squad and, thankfully, have never registered on his radar for comment. I'm happy with that.

I had no regrets about coming back to British Superbikes and competing in the UK during the late 1990s. Racing as a wild-card in the British rounds of World Superbikes in many ways was giving the best of both worlds. I could race every weekend in the UK and then return to my own house, family and bed. Then, when the World Superbike series came to the UK, we could enter as wild-cards and enjoy the big-time feeling without having to go through the pain of living out of a suitcase. Because we weren't putting together a championship challenge, we could race a bit more for the glory on the day rather than thinking of points and the overall picture. It was a great set up and I loved it.

I think since around 2001 the crowds started to dwindle at the British rounds. They certainly haven't become small crowds but the mass appeal has drifted away despite both Neil Hodgson and James Toseland claiming World Championships in the intervening years.

Compared to World Superbikes, I now think quite favourably of British Superbikes. In both series the best bikes and manufacturers are attracting world-class riders. In British Superbikes the difference is open competition between tyre suppliers, with Michelin, Dunlop and Pirelli constantly fighting for supremacy. In World Superbikes there's a Pirelli control tyre. With everything else being almost equal, the control tyre is the limiting factor and on the same tracks as the British Superbike racers, the World Championship stars can be anything from a second to two seconds a lap slower. For me that isn't right for a higher level of racing.

The slightly slower lap times are easier to achieve by more riders and that was exactly what the control tyre rule was designed to achieve – close racing for spectators. There's no doubting the racing in World Superbikes is exciting to watch. But it's easier to ride at two seconds away from the fastest pace. In British Superbikes the limit is a bit higher, and lap times faster, thanks to the tyres. When you get down to deciphering the information and riding a bike right at the very limit it's a very difficult thing to do. You are trying to coax out the last tenth of a second and are right on the edge of grip and adhesion, only a fraction away from crashing.

On a set of modern Dunlop slicks it's hard to describe the incredible amount of grip you have on offer. To make the most of it takes a whole lot of courage and skill at very high speed. But if you fit a bike with tyres that bring that limit a little lower, even by just a couple of miles per hour, then your brain has more time to figure out what is going on and it's easier to ride. The lower the speed means there are more riders who can ride at that pace and it's easier to race at the front for the wins.

I love both British and World Superbike Championships and if you can win in one series then you can be a winner in the other. It's just a shame you cannot ride as a wild-card in World Superbikes any more unless you use Pirelli tyres. I'm not decrying any skill from the World Superbike riders as they're still world-class, but the tyre rule does appear to slow them down a bit and that's not in line with my thoughts that the World Championship should be the fastest and best.

There's some talk currently of British Superbikes going to a control tyre like World Superbikes, but I'm not a fan at all. Open competition is much more attractive and would keep British Superbikes at a very high level, producing riders that can compete for World Championships if they get the breaks.

The current debate on moving to new rules and regulations for Superbike racing across the world can be viewed as a good and a bad thing. Personally I think the series at 1000cc is very open, with good close competition and no single manufacturer having any machinery advantage. To lift that to 1200cc for V-twins seems to hearken back to the old days when the Ducatis had a definite advantage over the other bikes and that doesn't make sense. It's perhaps a little more complicated, with other rules being touted to make sure there's parity, but they would take developing and watching to make sure they work.

I guess every series needs a shake-up every now and then to stay on top of its game but whenever it's thriving and producing entertaining racing, why change it? If it isn't broke, don't fix it. If I view British Superbikes as slightly higher than World Superbikes right at this minute because of the limiting tyre factor, then there's no such confusion when you compare Superbikes to MotoGP.

Put simply, MotoGP is the blue riband class – the absolute highest level of racing in the world. A modern MotoGP bike is a prototype racer designed to go around a circuit as fast as possible. Compared to a Superbike at Donington Park they're about four seconds a lap faster and that's astonishing. What really amazes me about the MotoGP class is the complexity of the bikes and how difficult it is to get the absolute performance out of them. You can change and alter just about anything on these bikes and to be a leading rider you need to have the skills to turn up on a Friday morning and, in three practice and one qualifying sessions, make the bike competitive before the race. There aren't many riders in the world who can take on that challenge. No matter how gifted and talented you are as a rider, you need to understand the dynamics and limits of a MotoGP bike if you want to succeed in this class. This means you need immense application and understanding on top of world-class bike control.

To be the best in MotoGP is really an accolade. The series features the best bikes, tyres, teams and riders in the world and the limits are so far in excess of what a production Superbike can achieve, it's like night and day. That's why when you win in MotoGP you really are special.

To get into MotoGP isn't easy. It's more like Formula One car racing than anything else: an exclusive club. I firmly believe a grounding in Superbikes can be a stepping stone into MotoGP though. Neil Hodgson, Troy Bayliss and Colin Edwards all showed they could cut it in MotoGP after winning World Superbike titles. Edwards is still there and chasing his 2006 team-mate Valentino Rossi hard. Bayliss was rookie of the year and then, after a disastrous season, was dropped. That's hard but shows just how competitive MotoGP is: there's no room for weakness. Hodgson suffered with poor machinery and it was no surprise he moved on but at least he showed the stepping stone still exists from World Superbikes to MotoGP.

I think if you want a career in MotoGP then the natural path is from World Superbikes. You get to know a lot of the circuits the two series share and, importantly, you learn how to live out of a suitcase and cope with jet lag, and those are two lessons British Superbikes isn't able to teach.

The young Australian Casey Stoner used the British Superbike set-up well to advance to MotoGP, perhaps more successfully than anyone else in recent years. He won the 125cc British Championship before progressing to 125cc Grands Prix. He made the most of the British racing set-up and took his opportunity to join the Grand Prix circus and is proving a real contender in MotoGP now. Well done to him.

Shakey Byrne came through from British Superbikes to MotoGP, but unfortunately he didn't know many of the circuits and was never blessed with the best machinery. It's a shame. I really rate him as a rider and don't think he got the time to learn.

Just as he was coming to terms with the series he was forced to come back to the UK.

I think between British Superbikes, World Superbikes and MotoGP there are three fantastic race series with the best riders in the world littering them all. There's a hierarchy between them but to win any of these championships is a major achievement and sets you out as one of the best riders on the planet.

If I was 20 years old and could cherry pick my way in motorcycle racing then I'd start off with claiming the British Superbike Championship. After that I'd go to World Superbikes and, as important as winning the title would be, so is learning the tracks. After that it's the final step to MotoGP and the fastest and most difficult race championship of them all. A pre-requisite for all is the need for a good factory team backing you in all three championships. You can't win any of those titles without factory support.

After winning a World Superbike race and then the British Championship in 2001, the next step for me was to change teams within the British paddock. I never got another chance in Grand Prix which is a real shame, I'd love to have competed on a factory-backed machine against Rossi et al but I really think I was too old to even warrant a consideration by the end of 2001.

Instead, I moved to the factory-backed Rizla Suzuki squad and knew I had my work cut out with the introduction of the new GSX-R1000 and a hot young team-mate called Karl Harris who'd just won the British Supersport Championship.

Chapter 16

RIZLA SUZUKI

At the end of 2001 I'd won the British Superbike Championship but wasn't sure if I had a ride with Reve Racing in 2002. It was a worry for me and I spoke to Ben Atkins about his plans but there were no concrete answers coming from my friend and boss. One of the great stresses of being a motorcycle racer is working on an annual contract without any guarantee of employment the following year. The years with Ben had been easy as he was a friend. Now, though, I had the feeling he'd had enough of racing and was seriously considering his involvement in the paddock for 2002.

The Ducati fitted me perfectly and the Reve team was great, I couldn't have wished for anything more or better, but the time had come to make a decision. Ben hadn't told me he wanted to retire from racing but I could sense the tension within him. He desperately didn't want to let me down and that was one of the main reasons he was hanging on and considering racing again in 2002.

Time dragged by at the end of 2001 and, while Ben was deciding what to do, I was approached by several other teams. The best opportunity lay with Rizla Suzuki and I was in discussions with Paul Denning, the team owner, over a contract for 2002. One evening I made the decision to call Paul and said I'd be riding for Rizla Suzuki. Regardless of my friendship with Ben, I still had a mortgage to pay and a family to support and couldn't wait any longer. If I did wait then I risked not having a job the following year.

I called Ben and told him what I'd done and he said he'd come and see me the next day. I think he was relieved I was racing for another team as it lifted the responsibility from him. He was great about my decision and he folded the Reve Racing team shortly afterwards, wanting to spend more time developing his growing business. The last thing he asked me to do for the team was to test the Red Bull Ducati at Rockingham for a magazine. It was a brisk but dry day and I thoroughly enjoyed my laps on the Ducati. It was an old friend, a well-worn glove that fitted me perfectly and we knew each other inside-out. After I climbed off the bike it was packed away and that was the last time I rode a Ducati.

By design, Crescent Racing had attended the same track day and brought along the new Rizla Suzuki GSX-R1000 race bike I'd be riding the following season. It was meant to be a comparison ride between the two bikes. This was an exciting moment for me as I climbed aboard the bike and took off around the circuit. It wasn't a brand new machine – it had been developed by John Crawford and Crescent to some extent, so it wasn't straight out of the crate. It felt physically bigger than my Ducati and the seating position was all wrong for my size and style of riding, but that could easily be fixed.

During those opening couple of laps I couldn't believe the difference between the Suzuki and Ducati. It came home to me very quickly that this was a new motorcycle, never raced before and needing a lot of development if it was ever going to win. Compared to my well-honed Ducati it was fairly basic.

I pulled in to the pits and smiled for the cameras but was reeling from the difference between the two bikes. I went home and in my own mind started work on developing the GSX-R1000. The first thing was to change the handlebar, seat and footrest position to my size. Those were simple to fix. After that we could discuss the engine and chassis characteristics.

I wasn't bothered by the differences between the bikes because the team I was joining was one of the best in the world. We all knew we were developing a bike from scratch and there was hard work ahead. I was enthused by the opportunity to be at the leading edge of development and looking forward to getting the bike performing the way I wanted it to. If we achieved that, then I was going to win races, no doubt. When I had first heard about 1000cc four-cylinder bikes being allowed to compete in British Superbikes I was on a Ducati and worried. If you get a four-cylinder bike working well, it would be tough to beat even with the various rule changes brought in to try and make the racing fair.

Compared to the Ducati though, the limits imposed on the Suzuki were quite stringent and it was much more production-based. With those controls in place it was clear the Ducatis were still going to be the bikes to beat in 2002 and, more than most, I knew the mountain we had to climb.

Overall though, the move to 1000cc production-based bikes was a key moment in Superbike racing and a step in the right direction. The cost of racing was reduced compared to the old 750cc four-cylinder race bikes that needed enormous tuning. The differences between Reve Racing and Crescent's Rizla Suzuki weren't so big when it came to technical know-how and will to win. They were both professional teams, well run with highly experienced staff who knew their stuff.

The major difference was that the workload at Rizla Suzuki went through the roof and was completely relentless. Rizla, as a sponsor, was very demanding and results-driven, both on and off the track. It meant that if I wasn't racing then I could expect to be spending my time making appearances or attending sponsor functions. That wasn't new to me, but the sheer volume was. I was thankful I enjoyed that line of work. I'd guess that all of the public relations and marketing work at Red Bull Ducati was less than half of what Rizla Suzuki planned in the first year.

The new Rizla Suzuki GSX-R1000 was going to go through a massive test programme before the season started and our first trip was to Valencia, in Spain, in January. I knew there was a lot of testing ahead and that gave me great heart and hope for the bike. No expense was being spared in developing it into a winner.

By the end of the first day we'd fitted the bike to my size and found the suspension was just too hard for the circuit. Once we got those things right the lap times started to tumble and we started to make progress. Stuart Smith, my mechanic at Reve Racing, had joined Rizla Suzuki and it was great to have him with me as a bit of continuity and someone I could speak with. I never told him that though, I just commented that he was following me around wherever I went...

The deal with Rizla Suzuki was I had to develop the bike. That wasn't new to me because when I had joined Kawasaki at the start of my career, every bike I had been given was new and had to be developed. I took pleasure in developing a bike into a racer and as my career progressed I think I was getting better at it.

For 2002 I had Karl Harris as a team-mate and that felt a big threat. He had just won the British Supersport Championship for Crescent Suzuki and was one of the best and most natural motorcycle racers in the world. On the first day's test at Valencia, while I was struggling to get the bike set up and fitting me, I expected Karl to struggle with the increase in power and amount of settings that could be altered on a Superbike compared to a 600cc Supersport machine. He didn't. He was playing with the GSX-R1000 like it was a toy and was a lot faster than me.

I was sitting in the pits and he had just put in a couple of storming laps with the bike working well for him. He then came in to the pit lane and, at about 80mph and 150 yards from the garage, he put the bike onto the front wheel and rolled it to a stop right outside his garage in one of the biggest stoppies I've ever watched. The bike control he had was unbelievable and from that moment I knew I had a team-mate capable of pushing me to my limits.

In my own head I turned the tables on Karl. I knew he was going to be tough to beat but I was ready to do everything in my power and ability for it to be as hard as possible for him to beat me. The first race you need to win is against your own team-mate and I think the pair of us were a good match, we could push each other.

After a couple more tests I began to find a comfortable setting on the GSX-R1000 and accustomed myself to riding a four-cylinder bike again and my times came down to match Karl's. During the first two days I followed Karl around and watched how he got the power down out of the turns and, despite all of my experience and success, I was the one learning from him. I'm not shy about that, it had been a long time since I'd ridden anything apart from a Ducati and every pointer I could get I used.

There were big differences between the Suzuki and Ducati. The main problem at the outset with the Suzuki was that, while it had the horsepower, it also had a big hole in the power delivery. On the Ducati you had tractable power everywhere from 2,000rpm to 12,000rpm, while on the Suzuki there was a lack of drive at around 7,000rpm. It meant I had to ride the bike differently. The technique was to commit into the turn and, as you approached the apex, start to wind the power on so you'd be past the hole in the rev range by the time you were through the corner and able to drive out. As the bike developed it all came together pretty quickly and by the time the season started I'd acclimatised myself to the engine power delivery and the bike was handling as well as anything else I'd ever ridden.

It was during one of the first tests with the team in Spain that I first tasted the fun we were going to have together as a team. We got in six hire cars to go from the airport to the track and, in convoy, headed off down the coastal route. I didn't think I was going to make it to the circuit in one piece. Paul Denning is a part-time rally driver and he took off like a scalded cat, and the other drivers decided to try and follow. The road from the airport to Almeria is a stunning bit of Tarmac made for driving. It was late at night and dark, and the cars were driven flat-out.

It was a 90-minute journey and after about 30 minutes we pulled into a village. Someone must have told the local law enforcement that a convoy of cars was racing along the road as two cop cars were waiting. The police were convinced this was a drugs-running operation and let the dogs loose on the cars. Cyril, the junior technician, was the front passenger in our car and one dog bounded in and leaped on him, licking and sniffing – thankfully I was in the back!

Eventually they let us go and, as soon as everyone was round the next corner, the race restarted, only this time I think the drivers went even faster because they wanted to make up for the hour that had been lost. By the end of the journey I was laughing, more from nerves than anything else. I don't know how everyone got away with it.

On the way back to the airport, after the test, the race continued. We came into a village after screaming down a hill flat-out before a tight right-hander. None of us knew there were traffic lights just ahead, and as we came round the corner there were three cars in front, stopped. We skidded to a halt. So did the other cars – we were all only inches from each other's bumpers.

Relieved at not being shunted from behind we thought it would be a laugh to tap the car in front. We crept forward and nudged the bumper. The driver was Paul Denning and he whipped his head around and stared at us. Would we be in trouble? He was the boss after all. He slammed his car into first and drove forwards a few yards before stopping. Then his reversing lights came on and you could hear the revs rising. With a puff of tyre smoke he hurtled back into our car with an enormous bang. He turned round and laughed. I'd signed responsibility for the car and any damage was down to me to cover. It cost me a few Pesetas but I didn't mind. Not only was my new team serious about winning and prepared to put the time, effort and resource into achieving success, but they knew how to have a laugh as well. It was the start of a fantastic relationship and even though it was hard work, we always managed to have fun. When there's a bit of downtime it's important that the team and rider can relax a bit and enjoy themselves. I guess when you work hard you feel justified in partying hard as well.

The first round at Silverstone threw us a curve ball when we found the bike moving and shaking enormously. It was something we hadn't encountered at the tests but because it was a new bike we had no reference data to fall back on and had to fix it during the race weekend.

I crashed a few times early in the season and every time it was for the same reason: the bike would slide predictably enough but then crash viciously immediately after the slide. Once the slide finished the bike would tie itself up in knots and I'd be sent over the handlebars. We ended up tracing it back to the bike being set up too hard. It was a painful way of learning how to set the bike up but, once this was sorted, we found the chassis on the GSX-R1000 was a good package and capable of running with the Ducatis and anything else on the day.

The engine on the GSX-R1000 evolved quickly into a powerful and flexible unit, but there were teething problems as you'd expect with a brand new power plant that's being tuned for maximum performance.

There was only one engine failure that caused any problems and that was mid-season at Oulton Park. It was catastrophic and you don't realise how fast you are going until you have a problem like that. I was flat-out in fourth gear just touching the rev limiter at Cascades when the engine failed and oil went everywhere. I was aware of it because the bike slid and I picked it up and went straight on into the gravel trap.

Unfortunately the next rider down the road was my own team-mate Karl Harris and he got tangled up with the oil and suffered a heavy crash that broke his wrist severely and forced him to miss the next couple of rounds, scuppering his season.

Karl really had the worst of luck that season – only a few rounds earlier, at Donington Park, he had been T-boned by Simon Crafar at McLeans and seriously hurt. He showed real determination to come back and race as hard as he did but he never got the chance to show his true talent because of injury. At the end of the year he parted company with the team and went back to the British Supersport Championship. I wasn't in the least surprised when he dominated and won the next year.

When I joined the team I knew that regaining the championship I'd won in 2001 wasn't going to be easy. The bike would take time to evolve into a winning package. My first target was the podium, and that was going to be hard enough to achieve against the quality of field and riders in the championship – including a renewed and motivated Steve Hislop on a Ducati.

As the races ticked by, it was apparent the Rizla Suzuki was improving on an almost daily basis. We were climbing the results sheets as the bike made leaps forward every weekend. The whole team put in an enormous amount of effort and it all came good at the sixth round, at my favourite Brands Hatch circuit.

We'd been securing good results and podiums before this, but when the win came, it was one of the best feelings you could imagine, not just for me but for the entire team. When you have invested as much time and effort into a project as we had, the victory was a very sweet and just reward. For me it felt like the first win I ever had. Coming into pit lane I saw my chief mechanic Oz's face, and then Paul Denning's, and they were ecstatic. It was a fantastic moment. We'd gone through a lot of pain and dug deep – as deep as I ever had to – and really deserved the triumph. The victory was needed by us all.

After the win we continued to develop the bike but, as the season progressed, our competitors upped their games and it was difficult fighting for the podium. Steve Hislop was a man on a mission and deservedly won the title, but there were a raft of other quality riders in contention for the next places such as Shakey Byrne, Michael Rutter, Steve Plater and Glen Richards.

I finished sixth in the championship. Despite the race win and podium finishes I was never really in the running for the title. My contract with Crescent and Rizla Suzuki was for a single year and I desperately wanted it to continue into 2003. After all the effort invested I felt there was unfinished business with the bike and the team. By the end of 2002 I was sure we'd made enough progress that, if we backed it with a solid winter test programme, we could compete for the title in 2003 and I wanted to be part of that.

I spoke with Paul Denning and we agreed terms early on for 2003. He told me how he wanted to continue. He chucked in a figure that he wanted to pay me, I responded with a figure I'd like to earn. We negotiated and ended up shaking hands on a figure in the middle.

I was getting to know the team now and had found my place within the squad. At the start of 2002 the team and mechanics had a sense of humour and personalities that were new to me. Karl Harris was an established rider and he shared in the jokes with the mechanics when I couldn't. I'd laugh politely with them but wasn't really part of the fun. By the end of the season I had established myself and really liked the atmosphere within the team and was proud to be part of it.

The first year with Rizla Suzuki marked an important time in my career. Paul Denning and his dad John were great through the season but I knew if I didn't perform then they would place another rider on the bike. There was no team owner and friend to put his arm around me and tell me it was all okay, like Ben Atkins had done. After spending so many years in the Reve Racing team I was on my own now and felt extremely vulnerable. Paul Denning was a very different manager and proposition to Ben Atkins and at the end of the season I was delighted to have secured his trust and a ride in his team for the next season. That was achieved purely on merit. I was standing alone for myself. It felt important to have achieved that support from one of the leading managers and it made me even more determined to repay him with success in 2003.

Ben Atkins remained a good friend in 2002, but I think he found it hard to come and watch the racing, especially with me on a bike other than his. The nature of the job, working for Rizla Suzuki, was full on and due to my full diary I had very few opportunities to socialise with Ben and June that year, which was a shame. If ever Ben was in the area for work he would call in at our house for a cup of tea and a chat. It was hard for all of us I think.

The importance of working for the sponsors and corporate

clients of the team was something I was always aware of but, as my time with Rizla Suzuki progressed, I noticed that aspect of the job climbing in importance. You cannot go racing nowadays without delivering to the sponsors above and beyond racing. The fact is, to be racing for victories and the championship takes a lot of financial commitment and you cannot do it without the corporate sponsors backing the team. As a rider you are their biggest promotional tool and they will rightly use you to maximise the return on their investment. It took me a long time to get my head around the importance of the sponsors and meeting them on race day, shaking hands and smiling when all I wanted to do was to concentrate on the racing. I used to think anything other than 100 per cent concentration for the racing was a distraction but I had to adapt if I was going to survive in the team and the paddock. That also meant speaking to the television cameras on the grid and going through interviews with journalists on race day. The media exposure is one of the key benefits for any sponsor as it puts their brand name in front of the masses. It meant understanding the power and value of the media to the sponsor and doing as much as possible to return value to them.

I was smart enough to notice the change in requirements and went with them. I could have stamped my feet like a spoilt rider and demanded to be left alone but if I had then I think my career would have finished a lot earlier than the end of 2005. Getting the balance of on- and off-track success is a real challenge for any modern rider. You could be the best rider in the world but if you aren't marketable by a corporate sponsor then the ride will go elsewhere. Racing a bike is now only part of the job.

I was content with Rizla Suzuki at the end of 2002 and desperately wanted to win a championship on the GSX-R1000. Our pre-season tests for 2003 were very positive. We were fast everywhere and I wanted to start the year as the pace setter and the man everyone had to beat. We had developed a bike and package that was awesome and, I believed, a real challenge to the dominant Ducatis.

Japanese factory Suzuki rider Yukio Kagayama was my new team-mate for 2003. This showed the commitment the Suzuki factory was prepared to make to the team and its success. For the factory in Japan to send an employee to work with us was a huge compliment and boost. Yuki is a very intelligent rider and great to work with. At the outset his English wasn't great but he learnt quickly, despite our best efforts to teach him nothing but slang language. The first words he learnt had nothing to do with bikes and he played along like a real professional. His English was fine but he allowed us to teach him the finer points of insulting someone or getting your opinion across and he revelled in it. We laughed a lot in 2003 and Yuki played a big part in that.

I remember going to his birthday party in May. Typically, Yuki had rocked up to the UK with nowhere to live but had landed a gorgeous apartment at Sandbanks, in Poole, the most expensive real estate in Europe. This suited him right down to the ground and – with his big hair, laid back lifestyle and cutting sense of humour – he fitted right in. The whole team turned up for the party and Yuki was really happy. I thought I'd give him an expensive bottle of Scottish malt whisky as a present. I told him he should take a sip of it every year at his birthday for the next decade or so and hopefully remember his old mate JR in the UK. He bowed a bit, thanked me and unscrewed the cap. He drank the entire bottle in under five minutes. Apparently it's Japanese etiquette to show appreciation and they must use or consume their gifts in front of the provider. Yuki, who I'd never seen touch a drop of alcohol, was now blind drunk. He started demonstrating some form of martial arts, stripped to the waist, with a rollerblade helmet on his head. Once he got hold of an ice hockey stick we all dived for cover. It was a brilliant party and Yuki's open, honest and infectious personality continued to touch us all for the whole season.

Yuki is also one of the best riders in the world and one of the fastest team-mates I've ever ridden alongside. His technical understanding and feedback to the technicians was second to none. He helped me enormously with bike set up and moved the team a step forward. After each test he would speak on a direct line to the Suzuki factory and tell them his thoughts. If Yuki thought something needed sorting he wasn't shy about picking up the phone and telling them. He was dealing with the people who actually made the bikes. He commanded real influence with the factory and that ended up helping me because my bike was being developed at a rate of knots faster than I could have hoped for. It was as good as a factory team.

Going to the 2003 opening round at Silverstone, the Rizla Suzuki team had pretty much set the pace everywhere in testing, as I had hoped. During practice and qualification I was right at the top of the timesheets and then we had our first Superpole of the season. Despite being fast and on top of our game, we made a mistake on the approach to Superpole. I'd ridden on race tyres all weekend and not even tried a qualifying tyre. We were that intent on finding a winning race pace we hadn't got around to trying a qualifier before the critical one-lap winner-takes-all Superpole session. It was completely my fault for not requesting a qualifying tyre earlier in the weekend. Normally I'd have tried one in practice but on this occasion we'd bypassed it and my first time on the super-sticky qualifier was for Superpole.

There's enormous pressure on you when it comes to Superpole. A mistake could wreck your starting position and make winning the race much more difficult. As I went out on the track all I could think of was the amount of grip I could expect from the rear qualifying tyre. This is designed to last one or two laps and gives more grip than anything you could ever get in a race. In effect it needs you to re-evaluate your riding and approach to get the most out of it. I was figuring that out on my sighting lap before my single qualifying lap, which was simply too late in the day. I should have practised earlier.

Superpole was going exceptionally well for the first half of the lap. I was in complete control and the tyre was doing everything I expected. Then it all went wrong when I came under Bridge and the fast left-hander into the complex section in front of the grandstands.

Coming out of Brooklands in third gear I was asking a lot from the qualifying tyre, I knew I was on a blistering fast lap. I asked too much and the bike slid and then flipped me over the bars onto the Tarmac before bouncing into the gravel trap. I knew instantly I had broken my left collarbone and sat there for a long moment going through the accident and what it meant. I had made a stupid mistake and broken a bone the day before the green flag dropped and the racing started.

It couldn't have been much worse. I could see the season stretching out in front of me and having to miss several rounds due to injury. That would make winning the title virtually impossible. I was injured, gutted and demoralised all at once. What made it worse was knowing the Rizla Suzuki was such a good bike and ready to go for the championship.

Paul Denning was brilliant about it though. His ability to take the positives from any situation is one of his real strengths and he didn't allow me to be negative. He sent me to Brian Simpson's clinic in Ipswich the next day for treatment and an assessment on how long I'd be out of racing. He told me to get sorted and back on a bike as soon as I could.

Usually a broken bone has a pretty standard healing process and it takes time before you can climb back on a bike again. When I went to see Brian Simpson I had an open mind and was utterly determined to do everything I could to get back on my bike as soon as possible. Yuki, fresh to the UK and to Silverstone, had put the Rizla Suzuki on the podium and that reinforced my beliefs that here was a motorcycle capable of taking the championship. I didn't want to miss my chance at the title or winning races.

There's a lot of debate over the merits of laser treatment on broken bones. Many of the doctors I've spoken to aren't great believers, but I went into Brian's clinic with my arm in a sling and very little movement and I came out without the sling and able to lift my arm above my head. What that told me was my broken collarbone didn't have to be a problem. It was painful but I had movement and ever since then I haven't considered a sling to be the best way to deal with a broken collarbone.

Paul Denning's drive to get me fit to race was inspirational. He identified the problem as my injury and put a lot of energy and enthusiasm into getting it fixed. It was support and pressure all at once. He didn't do it because he liked me; rather, he wanted me on a bike, winning races for his team. Two weeks after breaking my collarbone I raced at Snetterton in Norfolk. I rode the races riding mostly one-handed. The bike was working fantastically well and with most of the corners being smooth right-handers, it reduced the load on my left arm and shoulder. There were only two corners I had to muscle the bike into; where I'd lift the bike, settle it and then make the turn. I could cope with that workload on my body and came away with two third places. Without Toby and Ali, the series doctors, spending hours strapping my shoulder up with just the right mix of support and movement, I couldn't have raced at all. And if it had been any circuit other than Snetterton I don't think the results would have been as strong. I'm not sure I could have even taken to the circuit if it had been Donington with its fast corners, chicanes and tight corners.

I had less than a week after Snetterton before visiting Thruxton. The Hampshire circuit is much more demanding and famously bumpy. Despite the extra time to heal, I was riding in agony and at one point came into the garage convinced my collarbone, which had been knitting together, had re-broken and must be sticking out through the skin. I asked one of the team to check for me but it came to nothing and illustrated just how much pain I was going through.

As my collarbone healed I was able to compete for the podium, but it wasn't until round six at Brands Hatch before full movement came back and I was ready to go for victory.

Up until the second race at Brands Hatch GP circuit, Shane 'Shakey' Byrne had won every race on his Ducati and was looking unbeatable. In the second race I took the first non-Shakey win of the season and it marked my comeback to form. It was a magic feeling and fired me up for the second half of the season.

After that, I scored another three wins and lots of podium places in the final six rounds of the year. I wasn't looking back on the injury but looking forward and taking each race as it came. I was giving 100 per cent to win and, with the bike performing as well as it was, it meant for the rest of the season I was always knocking on the door. If the season had started with round six at Brands Hatch, then I'd have won the championship. I was the rider to beat in the second half of the season but, unfortunately for me, Shakey had been the rider to beat in the first half and no-one had been able to touch him.

As I've said before, to win a championship is something special and it takes everything to go right for you. It did for Shakey in 2003 and he deserved the title.

I like Shakey. He was always fair on the track and great to ride against. He is natural, quick on a bike and stylish as well. I have utmost respect for him and he never gave me any problems while racing against him and I hope he could say the same about me.

It was Shakey who denied me another World Superbike win at Brands Hatch in 2003, but I take my hat off to him for the effort he put in. In the first race we broke away from the pack but I ended up suffering a problem and had to pull in.

In the second race Shakey and I were well ahead of the pack and it was between us on the last lap. He led across the start/finish line and we both broke the lap record on that last circulation in our efforts to win, which is an amazing feat when you consider our tyres were spent.

We both wanted it as much as each other and I think the only difference between us was a difference in the power delivery of the Suzuki and Ducati. I'd overtake him on the entry into a corner and then, because I'd have missed my apex, my exit from the corner wasn't perfect and he would use the extra grunt of the Ducati to overtake me right back.

If ever we sat up together coming out of a corner he would take a couple of bike lengths on the mid-range power before my Suzuki got into its power zone and clawed him back. It was a fascinating contest between two different but very evenly matched bikes and I ended the day frustrated for not winning but content I had been beaten fair and square.

As the year progressed I told Paul Denning I wanted to stay with Rizla Suzuki. I've always been loyal and wanted to repay the team with a championship title after all the hard work we'd put in together. I also knew there was a new GSX-R1000 coming in 2004 that was an evolution rather than a revolution. It was going to help us in the areas we needed and allow us to maximise the existing strengths of the bike. It was looking very promising and to put it bluntly I knew Rizla Suzuki was the best team in the championship and had a bike that could get the job done. Why would I have wanted to go elsewhere? I'd have been mad.

The British Superbike crowd was very knowledgeable and knew the difficulties, trials and tribulations that both Rizla Suzuki and I were going through to try to win the British crown. The support of the fans for what we were doing was immense. They'd watched us fall down, get back up again, get kicked in the teeth, get back up again and so on, for two years. I think they really wanted to see us do well and get some reward for our efforts. The team's popularity was growing fast – we had earned respect from the fans for our 'never say die' attitude.

Paul said he wanted to keep working with me in 2004. We shuffled a few figures about but I never thought the agreement was in doubt until the afternoon when the contract was being sent to me. Paul called and asked me if I was by my fax machine as he had something he needed to send me. A couple of minutes later a fax started coming through and by now I was paranoid so I was standing over the machine reading the message as it appeared. It was addressed to me on official team paper. The first line started with: 'Unfortunately'. My heart started beating faster and I read on: 'due to budget restrictions, cut backs are required and we have not been able to meet the agreed terms.'

I was sweating and my stomach sank through the floor.

The fax continued and I was looking everywhere in a mild panic wondering what had gone wrong. I picked it up and re-read the bad news and that's when I noticed towards the bottom of the fax another line. I can't remember exactly what it said but was something along the lines of: 'GOT YOU TOSSER!!! Looking forward to working with you in 2004 and winning the championship, full contract to follow.'

I slumped back into my seat and said: 'Thank God for that.'

I told you I knew the team's sense of humour, and I shouldn't have been fooled on the first sentence, but Paul had read me like a book and when I called him back he could hardly speak for laughing. That was fairly typical of Paul and another of his strengths. No matter how serious the situation – and to me contract negotiations were very serious – he could always find a nugget of humour. He did it when I suffered injury and in many ways it was vital to keep us all sane and going forward.

I've had many different team managers during my time, starting off with Colin Wright, then Clive Padgett, Ben Atkins, Stuart Hicken, Roger Marshall, Nigel Bosworth, Paul Denning and finally Robert Wicks. Every one of those managers had their own style and was very different.

Colin got the best out of me as a younger rider using a no-nonsense approach. He isn't out there to make friends but to win races and championships and his record speaks for itself; he's one of the best in the business and has won titles with every team he's managed, as well as developing riders into World Champions themselves.

Ben Atkins was never really a manager for me. He was a friend and that was always the important factor between us and work wasn't going to get in the way of it. That's why he employed Roger Marshall and then Nigel Bosworth as team managers.

Roger Marshall, just like Paul Denning, is an ex-rider and that brought another aspect to the job. He knew the score as he had been out there competing himself, and that could help or hinder depending on the situation. He could see from a rider's point of view and could sympathise or criticise accordingly, so there was no real hiding place.

Paul Denning tries not to upset you and is always looking at the best things on a bad day. Like Colin though, he leaves nothing to chance and behind the scenes will work harder than anyone to get the job right and to win. Paul has something special as a character and is an inspiration to his riders. He thoroughly deserved his call up to manage the factory Suzuki MotoGP team and if anyone can succeed in the class then it will be him. As a Brit in charge of one of the best teams in the world, there are worse people a young upcoming rider could get to know and try to impress.

Going into 2004, not even Paul knew it was going to be his final season as Rizla Suzuki's BSB Team Manager. All he was concerned about was winning the championship and, after two years on an ever-developing bike, we had the data and team to put together a proper challenge. I was excited looking into 2004 and thought it was going to be my best chance in years to win the championship. What we hadn't counted on was the mighty big-budget Honda Racing Corporation coming to the UK with its factory bikes and rider with a very public objective of winning the British Superbike Championship.

The bar had been raised again...

Chapter 17

BRITISH CHAMPION AT 41

At Cadwell Park on 25 August 2003 my team-mate Yukio Kagayama nearly lost his life in a horrific crash. It was morning warm-up for the races and, coming into the Mountain section, he was passing a slower rider who moved back onto the racing line and they collided. At around 70mph Yuki was sent across a short stretch of grass before hitting a banking head-on. He might as well have hit a brick wall.

Yuki suffered the most horrendous injuries, the worst of which was a double break to his pelvis that later led to internal poisoning, which was potentially fatal. I was one of the first riders past him and I saw him lying on the floor, his boot 15 yards away. I honestly thought he was dead and when I got back to the garage I walked out to the back and broke down sobbing.

That day I got on with the job and recorded two second-place podium finishes, but I was never as glad to leave a circuit behind me. Superbikes are now so fast they're outgrowing the facilities at some circuits, and in 2003 Cadwell Park just didn't have the safety built in. Thankfully, since the accident the circuit has been bought by MotorSport Vision (MSV) and improved considerably, including the addition of a new chicane where Yuki crashed.

Yuki spent six months in hospital but was adamant the entire time that he would be back racing in 2004. At our first pre-season test at Valencia he arrived at the hotel and had to be almost lifted from the car into the lobby. He was the same larger-than-life star he always was, but now he could hardly walk and, when he did, it was with great pain and effort. We went to the circuit the next day and Yuki had to be lifted on to the bike. It was troubling to watch but after the first session he joked it was easier to ride than to walk.

By the end of the test he didn't need helping on or off the bike and was walking with a limp but nothing more. He earned my respect and admiration for his determination to overcome his injuries. I wasn't the only one on the team who'd doubted his chances of making the start of the new season but he proved us wrong and showed astounding spirit on the way.

I had a good a working relationship with Yuki and was delighted to have him back. It meant the technical development and direction of the bike would continue to be as proactive as before, and that was a good thing. Now Yuki knew the circuits as well, it meant I had a seriously quick and determined team-mate to push me on and help in the championship chase.

There was no doubt in my mind that I could win the British Championship in 2004. I was as fit as ever and working hard on all aspects of the job, from gym training to diet and all the PR activities asked of me. If I didn't think I was up to the job I'd have retired: I wasn't in the game to pull the wool over anyone's eyes. My CV may have said 39 but I was 40 and the team knew this and still wanted to employ me. Rizla Suzuki had made a massive commitment to me as a rider and something inside me needed to repay that.

My age came up every now and then when speaking with journalists, and the reason for reducing it on my CV was simple. If they thought I was a bit younger then maybe they wouldn't be asking me about plans for retirement every time we met. I hated it when people asked if this was my last season. In my own mind and perceptions, I was as fit and hungry as ever before and just wanted to get on with racing. Retirement was a long way from my thoughts and I was sickened by the ageism in the sport I loved. Steve Hislop and Jeremy McWilliams had proved you could be at the top of your game well into middle age and now I was doing the same. Was I really too old to do the job of a Superbike racer? Some would argue yes but I never saw it that way. I simply worked harder and in the end I responded to all my critics on the track – with results.

Going into my third season with Rizla Suzuki I faced a lot of pressure to win the championship. And I wanted to be the man who won the title for Rizla Suzuki, after the hard work and graft we'd all put in. It was a do-or-die year. I was aware that if I didn't deliver then the chances of me staying with the team for 2005 were remote at best.

Honda's arrival in the championship, with its famous Honda Racing Corporation (HRC) backing, was one of the best things that could have happened to the British Superbike Championship in 2004. It lifted the whole series to another level and added value to the racing. The stakes were raised and Rizla Suzuki responded and put even more work and effort into the development of the GSX-R1000. There's no way HRC was going to come to the championship and settle for second best. If you could race and win against HRC then it really was an achievement, and that was our target.

Michelin came into the series to support HRC at the same time and helped to raise the bar even further. Dunlop had dominated in British Superbikes for years and now there was a serious challenge to its supremacy. Michelin had promised the best tyres possible to HRC and Dunlop was forced to dig deep and come up with tyres to match.

All in all, 2004 was shaping up to be a fantastic season with possibly the strongest line-up of riders and teams in years. BSB was now on the map with the Japanese Factories and the series was benefiting from big investment.

The difference between the old GSX-R1000K3 and the new K4 model was relatively small. The bike I had raced in 2003 was as good as anything else and I had proved that by out-pointing everybody in the second half of the season. What the slightly smaller 2004 K4 model did was take the strengths of the older bike and build on them. There wasn't any one area you could have pointed at and said it was so much better, but as an overall package the incremental changes led to a decent step forward in performance. It was just as well really. This season the race pace was going to be a second a lap or thereabouts faster at every circuit, something which showed the accelerated level of development needed if you wanted to win.

The K4 was spot-on for me, once the team had applied my own build specification to it. Everything – handlebars, clutch settings, gear lever position and footrests – was measured from my old bike and applied to the new one. When I got on it I felt as though I was climbing onboard a bike I had been riding for years, when in fact it was brand new.

My mechanics knew exactly the specifications to build to and always delivered a bike tailor-made just for me. If I crashed in a session, then the bike would be rebuilt and feel exactly the same an hour later, all the same sizes, angles and specifications dialled in. We had a strong pre-season test programme but nobody was feeling overly confident thanks to the arrival of HRC. It was a completely unknown entity, and alongside Michael Rutter was team-mate Ryuichi Kiyonari, a former MotoGP prodigy who was part of HRC and expected to show us all how to ride bikes. There were a lot of unknown values as we started the season.

Paul Denning had said to me that the championship could not be won at the opening round at Silverstone, but if I crashed and injured myself then it could be lost that day. I knew exactly where he was coming from, because all I could think about was the nightmare start to 2003 when I had broken my collarbone.

I wasn't relaxed going to Silverstone and wanted to get the round out of the way safely. I approached practice and qualification feeling slightly restrained and with safety paramount in my mind. It's difficult for a rider to do this because if you really want to win you must be prepared to put everything on the line – you need to attack. I certainly wasn't in attack mode. I was controlled though and knew exactly what I wanted to do. If I could come away from the season opener with solid points and no injuries then I could lay the ghost of 2003 to rest.

Starting the first race I was on the grid thinking I had all of the expectation of Rizla Suzuki, the team sponsors and the fans on my shoulders. It was my third year in the team, on a familiar and fast bike. If I didn't perform there was nowhere to hide. I gulped and just wished for the race to start as soon as possible. The red lights couldn't go out quick enough – all I wanted to do was lose myself in the concentration of racing.

The first race was held on a wet track drying and I finished third. In the wet the Dunlop tyres had an advantage over the Michelins but, as the race progressed and the circuit dried, the Dunlops started to overheat and lose grip to a far bigger degree than the Michelins. Two-thirds of the way into the race the Hondas took off and I couldn't keep up. There was nothing I could do about it and starting the season with a podium was fine.

The second race was dry and we reverted my Rizla Suzuki to its dry settings. I never liked to change the bikes too much between races. If the bike felt the same or similar to the way it did in the first race then at least I knew what to expect. I won the second race after a titanic struggle with the two HRC bikes of Rutter and Kiyonari. Both of them made small mistakes and allowed me through to take the victory.

No races are easy to win, but perhaps a dry second race after a wet first race is the most difficult in my book. In the wet race your braking markers, throttle control and aggression must all be perfectly timed and pin sharp. Everything happens at a slower speed, you may be nine seconds off the lap record, so you have a bit of time to control the situation. In the dry you need to be on the limit of everything and the world goes past at a much faster rate. You are piling into corners much faster than you were just an hour and a half previously in the wet race. Making the adjustment from wet to dry isn't easy and it takes a special discipline to get it right.

I earned the win at Silverstone and was jubilant when I came down pit lane. I left the track leading the championship which was a dream start, but we weren't resting on our laurels. What the opening round had shown the team was just how hard it was going to be to win and there was no time for complacency.

Kiyonari had been heralded by the media as a championship

challenger for 2004 but this never materialised. I think it was simply down to him being a young man a long way from home and missing his family. Add the quirky nature of many of the British circuits and the fact that he didn't know his way around, and you can see why it took him time to adapt to the UK. When you put him on circuits like Cadwell and Mallory Park for the first time, with riders like me who'd been racing them for years, it was a big ask. For sure, if I was to race in Japan on national circuits the tables would be turned and I'd have the same problems learning and keeping up with the locals. It would certainly take more than one weekend to get the job right. When you weigh it all up, Kiyo learnt a lot and was quick at most places in his first year, so he was doing well. Kiyo's team-mate for the season was Michael Rutter and I knew early on that he was going to be my main challenger for the title. He was a class act. He was on a factory-backed bike with factory Michelin tyres and all the motivation in the world to try and win his first British Superbike Championship.

Before 2004 I might not have given Michael the respect he deserved but, after dicing with him all year, that changed. He's a fast, consistent, stylish rider who isn't dirty in any way. I could ride fairing to fairing with him with complete trust. He was the ace in the Honda pack that season.

As well the HRC challenge, one of my main threats in 2004 came from within my own team – Yuki. He was a nightmare to race against. At the opening round he finished the first race in fourth place and was in floods of tears, the emotion of racing again overwhelming him. It was a great result and, after getting on the podium at the next round, he went to the third round at Snetterton and won the first race.

Despite his injuries he was a serious title contender. He won pretty easily from me at the opening race at Snetterton and I was wondering how I could beat him in the second race as I lined up on the grid. In the end he was off the podium in the second race and I won. It was typical Yuki really. He had the pace to win but hadn't fastened his boot up properly. At speed, the wind pressure was trying to rip the boot off and it was distracting him. There were often small dramas like that with Yuki.

At the next round at Oulton Park – the circuit he'd laughed at the first time he visited, saying it was too dangerous to race – he won both races. I was really hacked off after the first race when he beat me. He tailed me for lap after lap and then on the last circulation he did me at the end of the start-finish straight. He passed me easily. The race might as well have been only one lap long because he was always going to make that move. I'd have done exactly the same to him if our positions had been reversed, it was a legitimate overtake, but to lead a race for so long and then get duffed up by my team-mate was a real smack in the face. I had done all the work and he took the win.

In the second race he won fair and square. He deserved that win. He got his head down and it was all I could do to hang on to him. At one point I knew he had the beating of me for the day and I had to let him go. He was completely relentless.

After winning three of the last four races, Yuki's challenge was growing. His little mistakes, like not lacing his boots properly, held him back and so did his sensitive nature. If he got out of the bed the wrong way he wouldn't perform. If he got out of bed the right way then you had a helluva battle on your hands. Yuki was the hardest and strongest team-mate I ever had in my years of racing. We never had a cross word between us, he was a real gentleman, intelligent and knew exactly what he was doing with the bike.

I was delighted to see him go to World Superbikes in 2005. Not because I thought he was a threat to me in BSB but because we'd spoken many times and I knew how much he wanted to race on the world stage. He had dabbled at MotoGP before but never had a proper opportunity. He was a young lad wanting to make his mark and I respected that. I thought Yuki could win a World Championship and still think so. When he's at his best there are very few people who can match him, never mind beat him.

On the run up to Thruxton and the sixth round of the championship, Yuki was recalled to Japan to race in an endurance event and broke his collarbone. Rizla Suzuki drafted former Suzuki World Superbike star Gregorio Lavilla in as my team-mate. Paul Denning told me the news and that Gregorio would be there to help rather than hinder our championship challenge. I was leading Michael by 33 points so we were in a healthy position, but as a rider you can never really have enough points so we wanted to extend the lead. I knew Gregorio from years ago, and he tested at Mallory Park a few days before Thruxton. I watched him test and thought everything was great. He was riding well and gelled with the bike immediately.

This was his first race at Thruxton, a circuit that can really blow your mind. It's super fast and the bumps are like mini motocross jumps. He struggled through practice and qualification and that was less than ideal for me. I went out for my qualifying lap and Gregorio followed me. Normally, if I know an arch rival is behind me on a qualifying lap, I will back off and not give them a tow or any advantage. I knew Gregorio was behind me but he was my team-mate and there to help, so I kept going and he ended up on the front row of the grid. I really wanted him with me at the front, thinking he could steal points from the Hondas and keep the other riders away from me. He might look after me a bit.

I finished second in the opening race behind Michael Rutter but it was a tough race. It was also obvious from the opening lap that Gregorio wasn't going to help me in any way, and was there to prove himself. He was trying to revive his career and that's absolutely fine with me but I had been led up the garden path a bit and wished I'd known from the start. I only found out his intentions in the race when I passed him. The next corner he made a hard pass on me and I responded with a harder pass on him. He came past me again even stronger and I realised then I was racing by myself and without any help from him.

Knowing how he was racing, I went into the second race treating him like any other competitor on the track. If he passed me then I'd fight with him all the way. It was a simple and direct approach. In my mind he wasn't a team-mate and that was okay, I could deal with it. A couple of laps into the race I had been battling with Gregorio. We were on the same bikes so it was close between us but I was mindful I was racing for a championship and wanted to get in front of him and break away so I could get out of trouble.

Going into Club chicane after the 200mph straight I went to go round the outside of Gregorio so I could take the inside for the sharp left hander that followed and pass him. At the same time he had climbed alongside Michael Rutter, probably thinking to do the same move and we barrelled into the corner three abreast. Normally the rule is you never ride around the outside of another rider, but at Thruxton it's a legitimate move at that corner on the brakes and accepted.

Michael, on the inside, made a mistake and Gregorio lifted his bike just as I was on his outside. My front brake lever hit the back of his leg and compressed, locking the front wheel. The front gave way and chucked me on my side. I cannot blame Michael or Gregorio for the crash. It was simply a racing incident and I was the unlucky one on the outside who ended up crashing out. There was nothing rash or wrong about what any of us were doing: that corner at Thruxton allows that sort of pass and it was one I had performed many times in the past. This time it didn't work out.

As I was lying in the hay bales I knew I had hurt myself. I had banged my head and was slightly dazed. I got up, aching, and sat down. The doctors asked me if I was okay and I said yes. As the race progressed a team member collected me on a scooter and took me to the medical centre to see Toby Branfoot, the chief doctor. I told him my right shoulder was sore and he put his hand into my leathers. I've had broken collarbones before – this didn't feel like that but there was a nagging doubt at the back of my mind.

'Tell me it's not broken,' I asked him.

'Yes it is,' he replied. 'I can feel the bone fizzing and that means it's broken.'

My world collapsed around me and I fell into a pit of despair. I was nearly suicidal and it was Paul Denning who dragged me back to reality and banished my fears. He was solid gold that day.

No matter how bad things were, Paul wouldn't be negative. He gave all the support I needed and wouldn't allow it to get me down. He told me I had two weeks before I was racing again and, instead of putting his head in his hands, he told me to go and get the job sorted. He picked me up and packed me off to Brian Simpson in Ipswich, the same expert who'd treated me the year before when I had broken my collarbone.

Paul had taken control and, as ever when there was a problem, he gave it his full attention and solved it. Defeat is a word absent from his vocabulary and he turned me around. An hour later I left Thruxton knowing what had to be done, and how to get myself fixed and back racing in a fortnight's time at Brands Hatch. I was actually upbeat leaving the track. I was determined to beat the injury and keep my challenge alive. I was utterly focused on that thought and nothing else.

Once again Brian Simpson was a complete star and his treatments gave me movement and strength far sooner than I could possibly have imagined. I spent a week with Brian and I owe a lot to him for getting me back on a bike within two weeks. I also owe a thank you to Paul Denning's wife, Kate, for her help as well. I didn't know whether I believed in organic homeopathic remedies but she did and supplied me with what I should be eating and, between them all, I turned up at Brands Hatch feeling sore but able to race. It was a miraculous turn around. Yuki was also back in the team, complete with his broken but mending collarbone. Between us we were 'team walking wounded', but you wouldn't have found two more determined riders in the paddock that weekend.

Brands Hatch is a physical circuit but on race day it was raining and I had a tyre given to me by God, or in this case Dunlop, that was just fantastic. In the rain you are riding at a slower speed and you do not need to muscle the bike around as much, so it was the ideal conditions for a man racing with a broken collarbone. I got away, clawed my way through the pack and ended up winning by quite some margin. I was in pain but I had decided to ride through it and do what was needed to keep my title hopes alive and it worked…with a lot of help from that rear Dunlop tyre, it was simply awesome. I was very conscious while riding that I didn't want to crash again under any circumstances. If I did, then the damage I might do to the already broken bone could be catastrophic, or even fatal. I rode as hard and fast as I could, but well within my own safety margins, and was delighted with the result. It was the strongest way possible to respond to the previous DNF, crash and injury.

In the second race it was wet and I led until the last couple of laps. The track was drying so the wet tyre, which is designed to work by moving around and generating heat in the rain, was starting to overheat. If it had rained for another five minutes I'm sure it would have been fine for the entire race, but a drying line couldn't be avoided and the bike started to vibrate as the rear tyre fell apart and the wheel went out of balance.

After a couple of laps the vibration was so strong the dash was nearly jumping up at me. It was generating a violent shake through the bike and on the straights I was having to roll off the throttle and cruise, just to conserve my tyre and try to get the bike home. I was wheel-spinning everywhere and it ended up being a war of attrition. I had built up a large lead but it tumbled quickly and by the chequered flag I was seventh. I scored points, however, and luckily finished ahead of Michael Rutter in the process. With a broken collarbone I had extended my lead in the championship and I couldn't have asked for more.

Have I thanked Dunlop enough for the tyre they gave me? I don't think I ever can, and that race meeting just goes to show what a difference tyres can make in motorcycle racing. If you have the best tyres then it's like having an extra ace up your sleeve.

The next memorable meeting in 2004 was the ninth round, at Mallory Park. It was a critical point in the championship and I was starting to feel the pressure. There was a lot of talk about Rizla Suzuki dishing out team orders and Yuki was going to help me in the title hunt. Paul Denning had mentioned to Yuki that if he was to help me to win the championship then it would be a very good thing. It wasn't team orders, rather team suggestions. Yuki could understand English very well when he wanted to but I think the conversation with Paul hadn't really been clear enough and I had a feeling he would be attacking full on in the races. I started all of the races clear in my own mind that regardless of any suggestions, Yuki was another competitor wanting to win the race and it was just as well I did.

In the first race he followed me for many laps and it was between us. As I said before, he is a superb rider and he was turning out to be one of my main rivals for the season. It made my life very difficult. On the last lap, going into the hairpin I braked hard and Yuki's blue Rizla Suzuki pulled right alongside mine. Many of the press said it was just for show and wasn't a serious overtaking attempt, but I can put that to bed now. It was a very determined attempt to out-brake me into the hairpin and win the race. I had been expecting it though. I knew that was where he would attack because it's what I'd have done. I had taken the defensive inside line and he was trying to out brake and then ride round the outside of me into the bus stop. If it worked he'd win the race because I wouldn't have time to respond.

I could have let my brakes off to try and edge in front of him but I resisted. I knew if I overshot the hairpin then he could turn quicker and win the race. I matched him and kept him within sight, my front wheel inches in front of his. As he tipped in to the corner I kept upright and forced him wide. We didn't touch but you couldn't have got a Rizla paper between us.

I squared the corner off while he turned, and went on to win. It was a blocking move I never would have dreamed of having to pull on my own team-mate at that time of the year and with the championship up for grabs. Yuki would have won the race if he could have, and regardless of how many times team orders were mentioned he wasn't going to listen. I respect the racer in him for that and it made the win that bit more special because I had to earn it right to the last corner on the last lap.

Round 11, at Cadwell Park, was quite possibly the worst day of racing I can recall and the pressure from Michael Rutter was immense. For some reason, in the latter years of my career that was never a happy place for me. I desperately wanted to win to banish my recent ill luck at the circuit but the gremlins in my head were sowing seeds of doubt. No matter how many years I was racing, and all the experience I could bring to the job, I was nervous and susceptible to the pressure. I have no explanation for this other than I'm human, like everyone else.

The two Hondas and Yuki got away in front of me and early in the race I made a mistake coming out of the last corner onto the start-finish straight. I lost 30 yards to the rider in front and was furious with myself. I went along the straight to the first corner, a steep left-hander up a hill that's taken at around 130mph. I attacked the corner faster than ever before, simply because I was trying to make up for my mistake. The mistake started right at the bottom of the hill, but I ended up crashing at the top. I had gone in to too fast and as I pulled the bike back to change to the right-hander at Charlies, instead of shifting down to third gear it stayed in fourth. It was my fault, everything was happening much faster than normal. I panicked and instead of the bike holding a tight line in third gear, it ran six inches wider than normal in fourth gear. That was three inches onto the grass and down I went.

It was a long and embarrassing walk back to the pits, but I'll never forget how good the crowd was. The fans were applauding and cheering and they helped to lift my spirits. I think they could see how hard we were trying and maybe even empathised with the pressure I was under.

The points started to close up and Michael was catching me as he finished second in the race. The oppressive pressure was just horrible and couldn't be shaken off. There wasn't a single person in our garage smiling. It was businesslike. I had screwed up and now had to redeem myself in the second outing. That didn't go to plan though. It was a wet but drying race and I've won under the same conditions many times. I can race as well as anyone under those circumstances, but something wasn't right in the second race and I knew it from the start.

I was on an intermediate front tyre and it just failed to grip. It turned out the tyre had been on the warmers at a previous weekend and had cooked well beyond its temperature, robbing it of grip. I struggled to eighth in the race.

It was a truly awful day and, although I had been under that sort of pressure before, it wasn't any easier thanks to experience. I was glad to pack up and get home that night. I was also very happy for Yuki who won the second race and vanquished the demons of his own crash exactly a year earlier.

I relegated the day to the back of my mind and told myself to get on with it. I had been lucky because Michael Rutter had made the wrong tyre choice in the second race and I had only conceded a handful of points in the championship chase.

The next round was at Oulton Park, and all I could think of was that I couldn't afford to fall or make any more mistakes. It was a two-week gap between the races and I couldn't get the job out of my mind, whether awake or asleep. When you are racing the job is all consuming, that's why it's so hard to live with someone who races: they never stop thinking about it. I might have been gardening or driving or eating dinner with the family but for the two weeks, all the time, five or six per cent of my thoughts were on Oulton Park and what that meant.

It was almost a relief to arrive there and get on with the title fight. I was consumed and completely concentrating on the races. I do remember the start to the first race very well.

The three-minute board came out.

The generators powering the tyre warmers were switched off.

The tyre warmers were taken off.

The front stand was taken away.

The bike was started.

The rear stand was removed.

Someone patted me on the back and words of encouragement struggled to make it past my ear plugs.

Everyone walked off.

One man with a red flag stood in front of me and the 30 other riders behind me who were desperate to get past. Sitting there watching him, I wished he would just get off the circuit and let us get on with the race. I wondered just how much pressure and stress any human could be expected to take before going barking mad.

I was beside myself. The race couldn't start quick enough. I needed to immerse myself in the concentration and get on with doing what I did best – race motorcycles.

I won both races and dominated, but it wasn't easy, and to make it worse Michael Rutter took runner-up spot in both. The title would be decided two weeks later at Donington, the final round.

I had done a good day's work and only needed seventh place or better in either race at the next round to seal the championship. This gave me a cushion, and it's always better to start a race weekend like that rather than chasing the points.

Before the final round I was invited to a track day by a good friend of mine, Jez Murray at Stamford Superbikes. It was at Cadwell Park and Sean Emmett was there as another guest and we were signing autographs and giving advice to the riders. We all met up at a hotel the day before and went out to an Italian restaurant for a meal in the evening. Sean was riding for Ducati in 2004 and on the walk to the Italian he dropped a bombshell on me.

'John, there's something I've got to tell you,' he said.

'What?'

'I can't keep it from you any longer but I can't believe what I just heard. I've just had a phone call from Neil Tuxworth (Honda Team Manager) offering me a brand new FireBlade if I take you out at Donington Park.'

'You're joking,' I said.

'I'm not.'

As soon as we got to the restaurant I called Paul Denning but couldn't get a hold of him and spent a very uncomfortable and angry evening forcing myself to smile and eat food. Back at the hotel I struggled to sleep and the next morning the first thing I did was try Paul again and this time I got through.

'Paul, you won't believe it but there's a bounty on my head, Neil is offering bikes to people if they take me out of the racing,' I told him.

'Really,' he said.

I wanted him to get angry and upset but he just listened to me and I was left with the wind taken out of my sails a bit. I think he clocked me as paranoid and worrying about things I shouldn't be.

I didn't enjoy the track day and every minute dragged on for ever as I mulled over what Sean had told me. I was in a corner and wondered how many other riders Neil had spoken with and who I'd need to avoid at Donington Park. I was properly stressed. At the end of the day we were all having a burger before going home and Sean came over to me and said: 'Mate, I've got to tell you, I was taking the piss. It was a joke.'

I'm not a violent man but I could have punched him. Instead I said: 'What's funny about that then? Is that supposed to be a joke?'

There was an awkward silence. I called him a few choice names and walked off. I was angry at being strung along and simultaneously relieved it had been a joke all along. The funny thing is I can look back on that incident with Sean now and find it hilarious. It was genuinely a great joke and I had taken it hook, line and sinker. How I ever thought someone like Neil Tuxworth might resort to those sort of tactics can only be put down to the stress I was under clouding my judgment. Superbike racing is too dangerous, and our world too small, for anyone to try dirty tactics and hope to get away with it.

Anyone could pull my leg about anything during the days running up to Donington Park. I wasn't the best company in the world and the five or six per cent of thought that usually went into racing all the time was probably closer to 20 or 30 per cent by now. If you were speaking to me I could easily drift off thinking about a racing scenario and not hear a word being said. The stakes were high and I had no sense of humour about racing, or anything else for that matter. I couldn't afford the energy on anything that wasn't related to winning the championship.

To make it worse, I had witnessed what had happened to Chris Walker when he was with Suzuki in 2000 at Donington Park. He only had a couple of laps left before the chequered flag and all he had to do was finish the race and he'd have been crowned the Champion. He suffered a mechanical failure two laps from the end and, despite a 21-point advantage going into the round, he lost the title to Neil Hodgson. I remember watching him walk back to the pits with tears streaming down his face. It illustrated just how cruel the sport could be and served me as a reminder – as if I needed one – of how I still had points to score before taking the title. Anything could happen.

I couldn't just worry about my own performance either. Someone else could crash into me or suffer an accident at the first corner and take me out. I could get a bad tyre or, even worse, a flat tyre. Paranoia wasn't very far away but I couldn't help myself, the thoughts entered my head and wouldn't go away. I resolved to approach this weekend like any other. It was my only option – otherwise I'd expire in a heap of anxiety.

At the start of the first race, knowing I needed seventh or better, I made the decision not to ride for the position but to race for the win. It was what I did best and I reckoned it would be safer than running in sixth place where I hadn't been all season and didn't know the guys I was up against or what they would be prepared to do to try and put one over on the Champion elect.

I got past Sean Emmett into third place, with a small sigh of relief he didn't crash in to me, and then set off after the two Hondas. I was racing and enjoying myself and pushed as hard as I dared to try to catch and pass Michael. I dearly wanted to win the championship by finishing in front of my nearest rival but discretion was the better part of valour and I ended up settling for third. The two Hondas were absolutely the class of the field that weekend and Kiyonari won both races.

When I saw the last-lap board come out, I was mindful not to relax or drop off my pace in any way. You cannot allow your concentration to lapse for a millisecond or you could end up running off the track, missing a gear or corner, or even being caught by the riders still racing behind you. If your mind switches off to the job in hand then you could end up in real trouble.

I raced the last lap right up until the Melbourne Loop and, as I came out of the corner, I knew if need be I could push the bike over the finish line and win the championship. That's the first time I allowed myself to relax even a little bit. Going into Goddards, the final bumpy corner, I rode safely. I rode down the straight to take the chequered flag and the emotion and relief that washed over me was spectacular. I could breathe again. A huge weight had been lifted from my shoulders.

The whole Rizla Suzuki team was hanging over the side of the pit wall, cheering like mad men. I was so happy for Paul Denning and his dad John, the team owners who'd invested so much of their time, effort and money into the squad. It was the perfect reward for them and they deserved it – the whole team did.

Paul and John Denning are special figures to me. I've known them a long time and they earned my respect for how they conducted themselves and run their business: they're really good people I admire. They had worked a long time to achieve the British Championship and I was proud to be the rider who delivered it to them.

Race two at Donington Park and I'm ashamed to say that for me it was 'job done' and I could happily have missed it entirely. We had started celebrating in between the two races and the sense of relief was so strong I couldn't help but relax and soak up the atmosphere.

In the second race I rode hard but it's amazing how far off the pace you are if you take two per cent of the will to win away from a rider. The lap times I'd been running in the opening race were a distant memory.

Yuki was battling with Scott Smart for third place in the title stakes. My business was done so I pulled over and let him go for it and he managed to take third place on the championship podium, making it almost the perfect season for Rizla Suzuki. At the end of the first race Simon Green from Rizla Suzuki met me at the end of pit lane and put a number one sticker on the front of my bike. He handed me a Rizla Suzuki flag with a huge 'JR number one' logo on it.

My nature is fairly reserved but I had been briefed to do a couple of burnouts for the crowds of well-wishers and fans and had agreed. With the flag in my clutch hand I tried to do a burnout – and stalled the bike. Anytime I try to impress people with how good I am with bike control I always seem to fall flat on my face, that's the reason why I didn't normally celebrate extravagantly. The heavy flag had got caught up with my clutch.

The bike was restarted and within minutes the flag had been dropped and without it I was able to complete a few burnouts in front of the spectators. I struggled though. Another reason I don't like doing burnouts is because my feet only just touch the ground and it makes burnouts difficult. There was almost as much pressure on doing the burnouts as there had been on finishing the first race.

It was all good fun in the end though, and when I got back to the garage the celebrations started in earnest. Was it a good party? I can't remember a great deal about it so I think it must have been an epic. I remember Yuki dancing on tables half naked and Shelley holding me upright towards the end of the night. If she hadn't then I might have suffered another crash similar to the Lego incident years before when I won the Supersport Championship.

To say I was happy would be an understatement: I was ecstatic. When you have worked so hard and long to achieve something, it really does have value and I was so pleased to have won the championship.

Michael Rutter, to his credit, put up a great fight in 2004 and although I led from start to finish in the points standings, the job was a lot more difficult than it looked. Before 2004 I wasn't sure if Michael had the winnings of a championship in him but at the end of the year I knew he did. He's a fantastic rider and he kept me completely honest, there was no quarter asked or given and in the end I edged it but not by a great deal.

As a 'thank you' for the championship, Rizla put on a corporate day at the Bedford Autodrome, where we got the chance to race a lot of performance cars against each other. Paul Denning, Niall Mackenzie and I had been twice before on various corporate days and I cannot stress how competitive the three of us are when you give us four wheels and a helmet.

Of the three of us, Niall and I had previously won a day each. Not only had we beaten each other but we tended to be the top three on the day out of the 100 or so guests. Car racing is something a bike racer enjoys. At one stage I thought that when I retired from Superbikes a move to Touring Cars would be good. I had a couple of runs in cars and thought I had the pace to be competitive, but in the end that championship changed and the only way to get a drive was to bring money with you and that ruled me out. I'd spent my life trying to earn a crust from racing and wasn't about to throw it back to indulge a bit of four-wheel frivolity.

Former F1 star Jonathan Palmer had flown us in to Bedford Autodrome in his helicopter and given us the red carpet treatment. It was a fantastic day. I'd spent all season trying to win races for Rizla Suzuki but it seemed to me the most important race of the year was about to happen. The pressure was on to beat Paul and Niall in cars. We had a brilliant time and on all the disciplines the three of us were within a tenth of a second of each other. The lead see-sawed and it was a battle royal. We smiled, shook hands and then did everything we could to beat each other – it was a proper race meeting.

In the end Niall and I had to let Paul win or else he would have spat his dummy. He was the boss and we all had negotiations to make for the coming 2005 season.

At least that's our story…

It levelled the score at one win for each of us, so I'm looking forward to the final decider when we get round to doing it.

I hoped I hadn't done anything in the season to make Rizla Suzuki want to change me for another rider and was eager to race for the team again the following year. I knew the guys, enjoyed working with them and wanted to retain my championship if I could. I even entertained the thought that if I won the title in 2005 for an unprecedented fourth time, then it would be a good point to retire while still at the top of the sport. I always wanted to retire while sporting the number one plate. That was my first real thought on the end of my career and I quickly pushed it aside, I was enjoying my job too much to think about it for long. It seemed a ridiculous idea.

I was very optimistic for the future and I was sure Rizla Suzuki would want to wear the number one plate. Negotiations were harder than the year before though. I had delivered the goods and, rightly so, I asked for more money. I wasn't having a laugh but I knew what other riders in the paddock were getting paid, wanted parity with them and thought I deserved it. I was embarrassed in the negotiations as I'm not great at talking about money but Paul Denning made it easy for me. He didn't want to underpay me so we came to an agreement.

At the end of 2004 Paul made the move to manage the factory Suzuki MotoGP team. It was a fantastic accolade for him and he is the best person for the job. I wasn't concerned and knew Paul would remain overseeing the British Superbike team the following year. The core of the team remained the same and, after meeting the new manager, Robert Wicks, I was quite happy and ready to win the championship again knowing I had a good squad behind me wanting to taste glory again.

There was a new bike due for 2005 and I had a new team-mate, Scott Smart, who'd switched from Kawasaki after proving himself to be a race winner in 2004. I was one of the happiest riders you could have met in the winter of 2004/2005.

Little was I to know the following season would nearly kill me and be the end of my career.

Chapter 18

Memories of a
Racing Lifetime

Throughout my career I didn't have a single main rival – as the years went by, I moved from class to class and met new riders I needed to beat if I wanted to win. Steve Hislop perhaps came closest to being my arch-rival; he was certainly one of the riders I respected the most. I admired the way he rode and his sheer talent.

I raced against so many good riders. Troy Bayliss is a prime example. I raced against him in the British Championship and we enjoyed some close finishes. I beat him, he beat me. Ultimately he won the British Superbike Championship, moved on to win the World Superbike Championship and then went into MotoGP. He's a class rider, a fighter and a champion, but he wasn't my arch-rival. He was a good, possibly great, rider I had the privilege to race against.

Neil Hodgson and Chris Walker were of similar ilk. Great riders that for a few seasons I had to beat if I wanted to win the British title but none of them were really arch-rivals. Certainly not in the way Hodgson and Walker were arch-rivals for each other. In 2000 they tore strips off each other and in many ways their rivalry was more important than the racing itself.

When I was racing for the British Supersport Championship I was up against Phil Borley. In Grand Prix racing, Sean Emmett and perhaps Niall Mackenzie were my peers and my benchmarks. I never really beat Niall in Grands Prix as he was the established star and always had the edge on me. He was tidy, fast and the complete racer. I'd be on the edge just to keep up with Niall but I did finish in front of Sean most of the time, which was very satisfying as we were on similar, but not the same, privateer machinery.

Going back to 1993, or just before, Sean had come into my world of racing and made a splash. He was a talented rider who got my goat. He was my biggest rival in Grand Prix racing and, as time passed, he remained a great rival in Superbikes right up to the moment I retired. In the Grand Prix years I didn't see eye-to-eye with Sean and had a burning need within me to beat him every week. We're now good friends and I can look back with a great deal of affection at the races between us. Sean could jump on just about any bike and win. His natural ability is nothing short of breath-taking but he seems to have a self-destruct button that he presses every now and then.

Steve Hislop was my main rival in 2001 when I won the British Superbike Championship for a second time. By then he wasn't an arch-rival, more like a mate with whom I could talk helicopters at any time. I think between us we won every race bar two that year and it was a great head-on battle for the title. Steve was incredibly hard to beat. In many ways that made the championship a lot more meaningful because the person I had to beat was so damned strong.

I'm very happy to be mentioned in the same breath alongside the likes of Niall Mackenzie and Steve Hislop. They're two of the best riders ever, and to be linked close to them is special.

One of the biggest honours of my life was being asked by Steve's mother, Margaret Hislop, to unveil a memorial plaque in his honour in his home town of Hawick, on the Scottish Borders, in 2004. His children stood beside me as I went through the ceremony and it touched me very deep inside.

I knew Margaret for many years and, although we'd only met a handful of times, she knew I respected her son enormously. For any mother, I think, if your son has a friend then he's likely to become your friend as well, and that's what happened with Margaret. She 'phoned me out of the blue one day asking if I'd be involved with the ride-in to Hawick and the unveiling of the memorial, and it stunned me. I felt so honoured to be asked. I missed Steve and of course it was a very sad time for his family, his friends and the thousands of fans who'd admired him. He was a fantastic man.

In 2003 my main rival was Shane 'Shakey' Byrne and then in 2004 it was Michael Rutter. I'd watched Shakey come through the ranks, and Michael was a superb rider who for some strange reason hasn't won the British title to date. It's when you race these sorts of riders that there's real meaning in the results. There were times I raced against them and would be beaten, but that wasn't the most important outcome. Winning wasn't everything but being a worthy winner – or loser – was. I've often finished second or third but really enjoyed the race. I'll have worked very hard and in the end been beaten by another rider on the day, but as long as it was a fair scrap then it was worthy.

To explain it another way, a hollow victory – when you beat riders easily – isn't worth a thing in my eyes. It's empty of achievement and that's when riders like Steve Hislop, Michael Rutter, Neil Hodgson, Troy Bayliss, Carl Fogarty and Sean Emmett really help you to understand your achievement. If you beat those guys then it's something to be proud of and has true value and meaning. There aren't many people in the world who can run with these guys. I always wanted to be riding against the best riders I could, on the best bikes. My target was always to be the best and the only way to test yourself is to race the people who are the best.

Of all the races I ever started there are only a handful that stand out, and one in particular I shall never forget – the day I won a World Superbike Championship race at Brands Hatch in 2000. It will always be the top of my list, and next in line is the day at Donington Park in 2004 when, with Rizla Suzuki, I won the British Superbike Championship for the third time.

Those were two incredibly emotional days and perhaps mark two of the achievements I value most in racing. To win at World Championship level was something I dearly wanted to do and the sheer jubilation of ticking the box on one of my main goals in life was very special.

There were other highlights, like meeting and working with great people, and flying aeroplanes. Every time I experienced one of those moments I said it was the best thing ever, but I think best of all has been my World Superbike victory.

Third on my all-time list of races is one I didn't win but I enjoyed as a true competitor and every time I remember it I smile. It was in 2003 at Brands Hatch World Superbikes and I finished second to a rampant Shakey. After my early-season injury and the amount of effort we were all putting in to try to win, it was an epic race with both of us hungry for the win. On the last lap I think we swapped positions every corner and he crossed the line just in front of me, but we'd left our very best to last – both of us smashing the lap record on the final lap. That's an incredible achievement by itself. Pushing to the limit for so long was a brilliant feeling, spending three-quarters of an hour on a bike on the edge and finishing as close as I did to the win was satisfying. I think we were both prepared to die to win that race.

As well as the highs of racing, I remember a couple of races which I really didn't enjoy. There was Oulton Park in 2002 when my engine dropped oil all over the circuit. I crashed and so did many others; my team-mate Karl Harris ended up badly injured. It was compounded by the feeling all weekend that although I could go fast and run with the leaders, after half a dozen laps when the initial grip on the tyre faded, the bike started to become a handful to ride. I think the team thought I was partly the reason and wasn't giving it my all and that upset me enormously. I always gave my maximum effort. Those two incidents together made the weekend entirely awful.

It was a couple of meetings later when we discovered the reason for the bike's behaviour on used tyres. We simply had the set up too stiff. Once we softened the bike it was much easier to ride and could exploit the tyres for a full race distance. That, by contrast, was a real positive time because I knew I could win with the GSX-R1000 and was already looking to the next season and a championship challenge – it was a breakthrough moment.

The 2001 Rockingham race was grim. After Steve Hislop ran into the back of me and, when the red flags came out warning of a crash, it was pure misery for me. All I wanted to do was go to the hospital to apologise to Steve but instead I had to go out for another race and smile for the cameras as the new Champion elect.

Perhaps the most embarrassing memory was in 2004 at Mondello Park in Ireland. The Rizla Suzuki was fast and I was on top form trying to score as many points as possible. In the second race I built up a good two-second lead and managed it from the front. Kawasaki's Scott Smart caught and passed me on the last corner. My bike was quick, though, and I hunted him down the straight and in the end I thought I crossed the line first but the timesheets said it was Scott, by just two thousandths of a second. I rode back to the garage, got off the bike and told team manager Paul Denning he could sack me there and then, it was an unforgivable schoolboy error. He told me if I lost the championship by five points then he would sack me.

When people ask me what was the best motorcycle I ever rode then the answer is very easy: the 2005 Rizla Suzuki GSX-R1000. Every year the race bikes got better and faster. If you went back to 1995 then it was the Kawasaki I was racing in World Superbikes. Each season the technology would improve and the bikes would be quicker and faster just about everywhere. The lap times we could record at any given circuit in 1995 were a lot slower than what we could achieve in 2005 and a lot of that was down to bike and tyre technology.

I may not have won a championship or any races on the 2005 Rizla Suzuki GSX-R1000 but it was still the quickest motorcycle I ever rode. I set my fastest lap times at a lot of circuits on that bike and only wish I had been completely fit to see just how good it really was. The potential was amazing – I only scratched the surface. I went to the final meeting at Brands Hatch fitter than ever that year and really thought I could win but the practice crash put paid to that.

My dream would be to have all three bikes I won British Championships on in my garage. All of them were brilliant and the best at the time. My dream garage would have a 1992 Kawasaki ZX-R750, a 2001 Ducati 996 and a 2004 Suzuki GSX-R1000. If I had to select one, then it would be the Suzuki. Not only do I think it's the prettiest of the bikes but it's the one I started on at the beginning when it was first introduced to Superbikes and helped develop into a championship winner. My own personal character developed and progressed along with that bike. It started not being able to win and along with the dedication, determination and passion of the Rizla Suzuki team, I helped mould it into one of the best Superbikes on the planet. I'm proud of that achievement and relish the memories of the good and bad times that we went through to make it into a winner.

Out of the three British Superbike Championships I won, there's a pecking order in terms of my own personal satisfaction. No championship was easy to win but the first in 1992 is placed third. At the time the stress was enormous and I needed to win the title to progress my career so it wasn't easy by any stretch but, compared to 2001 and 2004, I managed to dominate and win most races despite competing against some of my greatest heroes.

The 2001 championship was more of a massive relief than a celebration. I wanted to win for Ben Atkins and the team and was glad when I did, but no matter which way I look at it, I can't help but feel it was a little hollow because, as I said earlier, Steve Hislop wasn't there to fight with me right down to the chequered flag in the final race. It wasn't his fault, it was mine and that took the shine off the trophy despite the epic season of trading race wins with each other.

If Steve had been at the final round at Donington Park and I'd won the championship fair and square then I'd think very differently I'm sure. I feel as though I'm betraying my team and the effort they put in to win in 2001 by considering the victory to be hollow, but that's no reflection on them or the championship. It's a reflection on my state of mind. While I thought my Reve team deserved to be Champions I continue to harbour doubts about my own worthiness, all because Steve Hislop wasn't there to contest the series to the very end. It ranks second.

The most pride in winning a championship was with Rizla Suzuki in 2004. Not only had I developed the bike into a title winner and beaten the mighty HRC, the best Michelin tyres and Michael Rutter, I had done it all at the ripe old age of 40 when things like that weren't supposed to be possible. I was getting older and faster rather than slower. At 40 most riders are well past their sell-by date and I was constantly bombarded by that message but didn't believe it. In my own head I was as fit as ever, more determined, and setting my own personal best lap times everywhere I visited. I was bucking the trend and beating some of the best riders and teams in the world in what was widely acknowledged as the premier national Superbike championship.

Perhaps because of my age I had to work harder than ever before to win, and that by itself makes it extra special. Looking from the outside you might have thought that Michael and I were trying to give each other the championship. I'd make a mistake and he would fail to capitalise and then he would make a mistake and I'd mess up at the same time. That was pure pressure, and to be able to absorb and overcome it was another big achievement for me, although a lot of credit must go to the superb team that was supporting me every step of the way.

If I hadn't won the title in 2004 it would have been a dreadful failure on my part. I'd have been embarrassed and more than likely have lost my job. Certainly if I was Rizla Suzuki I'd have thought: 'how many chances do you need to give John Reynolds before he wins for you?'

As a professional rider I was being paid in 2004, whether I won the championship or not. I like to think I give an honest account of myself, put in the hard graft and earned my pay. The only way

I was going to feel like that was if I won the championship, otherwise I'd have felt I shortchanged my employers in some way. Any rider can take money and turn up on a Sunday but that was never in my make-up. I wanted to justify my position and employment with the team. That approach kept me honest and focused on doing the best job I possibly could. In many ways my work ethic I'm sure helped me to stay in the sport long after most riders retired. I put in extra effort for the team, sponsors and fans and thoroughly enjoyed myself. I think it really is a case of what you put in you get out – I invested a lot of time and effort and got a lot of reward and enjoyment back.

Not every rider can win a championship, that's a simple fact. There are some who can beat anybody on their day but unfortunately they can't string enough days together to challenge for a title.

I'd love to have won a World Championship. It's not a regret that I didn't, but rather a missed opportunity that I refuse to dwell upon. I don't think I was ever in the position to win a World Championship in either Grands Prix or World Superbikes. I had reasonable machinery but it was never the best and you can't afford to give quality riders any sort of head start on you or they will skin you alive.

The one year I was with the factory Suzuki team in World Superbikes doesn't really qualify as it was a development period for a brand new bike. We got some results but in reality the season was used to turn the bike into a racer able to compete with Ducati. It would have taken another year in the saddle to reap the rewards, a year I didn't have unfortunately.

I think if the right opportunity had come my way I'd have been competitive within any World Championship – by that I mean if I'd been supplied with a factory Honda NSR500 on first-rate tyres in Grands Prix. I think my 2000 or 2001 Ducatis were pretty close to the mark in World Superbikes and I actually won a race as a wild-card. I can only believe if I had been given a factory Ducati then I could have challenged for the championship.

If I'd been offered the chance to race in World Superbikes after winning the British Championship in 2004 I'd have seriously considered it. What I said at the time was that if Rizla Suzuki decided to go to World Superbikes then I'd do it, but not for any other team. There was nothing I wouldn't do for Rizla Suzuki: they supported me wholeheartedly and deserved the same in return.

In my own mind, never winning a World Championship is okay. I rate the main motorcycle championships in the order of MotoGP followed by World Superbikes which in turn just edges British Superbikes (although at the minute the tyre control rule means British Superbikes is actually a more openly competitive series). To win any of those championships is an achievement so I'm quite content with three British titles.

The fastest I've ever been on a motorcycle is just over 200mph. It wasn't during a race but at Bruntingthorpe Proving Ground in Leicestershire for a magazine feature on top speed with Rizla Suzuki. I think we recorded 201mph at the end of the day and it was an incredible experience.

Bruntingthorpe boasts a straight that's nearly two miles long. I could reach 190mph in probably the first half mile. The last bit of speed was difficult to coax from the bike as the aerodynamics came into play. We were also pretty inexperienced at speeds over 200mph because it wasn't often we went to circuits where we could hit that, so on the day 201mph was good. It certainly felt very fast.

I was very nervous doing speed runs. Looking down the straight I was thinking far too much about the figures and I frightened myself a bit. If it had been a circuit with bends I wouldn't have been half as concerned.

Out of all the race tracks in the world I've two distinct favourites. In England it's Brands Hatch, both the Indy and the GP circuits. From the rest of the world it's Phillip Island, which is similar to Brands Hatch but with the most amazing views. There's no where else on earth you come out of a hairpin, accelerate along a short straight into a quick left-hander and have the Pacific Ocean to look at. It would be a hard call between those two circuits to say which one is my favourite…but if I had to give an answer I guess it would be Brands Hatch.

During my career I developed some bizarre superstitions. Every rider has them and, once they set in, they can be very powerful. The longer you race the more of them you get – so you can imagine how many I have. I had a white T-shirt that I always used when racing. In fact I had eight T-shirts exactly the same that would come with me, and they were used for nothing other than racing. On the one occasion I decided to try a black T-shirt because it looked better under my leathers, but I suffered a nightmare meeting and swore never to change from my trusty white ones again. Someone once remarked that it looked like a bin-man T-shirt and that was fine with me as long as I was wearing it. The black T-shirt went straight in the bin.

If I forgot something from the house on the way to a race meeting then I'd go back in, pick it up, and then sit down in a chair for a count of ten before leaving again.

I always started a race weekend with freshly cut nails. Perhaps that was less of a superstition than just plain good thinking. Once I had lost a nail in a crash and it was extremely painful and I didn't want it to happen again.

Putting on my racing gear always had to be the same routine. It would be right foot in the leathers before left, right arm before left, right boot and glove before left. I wouldn't dare deviate.

Perhaps my worst habit was the need to go to the toilet just before a race or session. When I turned up at a race track I'd go to the gents and the first urinal or cubicle I used was the one I had to stick with all weekend. Sometimes that was embarrassing. On more than one occasion, as a race has been about to start I was stuck in the toilets with a dozen free urinals and me hopping about behind the bloke using the one I had chosen, wishing he would hurry up. He must have thought I was mad and he would have been right.

At the end of the day, superstitions are about putting yourself into a mental state of preparation to race. Over my career I sometimes flirted with them. If things were going well then the superstitions didn't seem to matter as much. I knew they were stupid, and would maybe put my left boot on first just out of spite, but I could never maintain it. If anything went wrong then I'd never forgive myself so I'd always go back to my tried and tested routines.

If I won using a particular routine the previous week, then to go through the same procedure before the next race might set me up to win again. I'm no psychologist but I'm sure there's some sort of reasoning for all of this and why it works.

The best bikes I ever raced against were the factory Honda NSR500s. By that I mean comparing the bike I was riding with those of the competition. They were a league better than the Padgett's YZR500 I was riding at the time and I can remember one of them helping to cause one of the scariest crashes of my career, at Hockenheim. My YZR was hitting around 175mph on the curved straights, but the NSR could breeze past me at 200mph plus. I think it was Shinichi Ito who came past flat out, nearly 30mph faster than me. He backed off just out of sight around the right-hand bend and when I came round at full chat there was nothing I could do except avoid him. But by doing so I missed my braking point by thirty yards and that meant I was never going to make the next corner.

I lifted the bike up across the kerbing at the chicane and the suspension bottomed out before it flung me into the gravel and self-destructed. I wasn't knocked out but had taken a massive thump to the head and, as I walked to the ambulance, I realised I was blind in my left eye.

That'll get your attention every time. When I met the doctor I told him I couldn't see anything out of my eye and asked if this was a problem? The Germans aren't great for humour and he simply said 'yes'. I lay on the couch in the ambulance staring out of the window and shut my right eye. Thank God, small perforations of light started to come into focus in my left eye. Gradually everything came back into focus and ended one of the scariest moments in my life.

I've endured a lot of crashes in my time and when I list my injuries it's frightening. I've broken both ankles, my cocanium (heel) bone, left and right lower legs, back, neck, wrists (twice), four collarbones, a knuckle and four ribs. And I've dislocated a shoulder. That doesn't include the tissue damage, but it gives you an idea of what I've put my body through because of racing.

All of them were painful but quite surprisingly the broken neck and back weren't actually as bad as I suspected they would have been. The worst part of those breaks was the operation to rectify the damage: I've never experienced pain like that in my life, but it needed to be done.

My worst crash for damage was the last one, at Brands Hatch, and it finished my career. Another one that sticks in my mind, and always haunted me when I raced at Donington Park, was a 120mph highside at Craner Curves in 1996. Just as the track went from right to left my Suzuki sent me flying through the air and I slammed down hard. I was barrelling towards what I thought was a concrete barrier and believed I was a dead man. Luckily it turned out to be a polystyrene braking marker, which exploded on impact, adding a bit more drama to an already spectacular crash. The faster the crash the scarier it is and I always thought of that moment every time I returned to the circuit.

Despite the amount of injury I've sustained, I don't expect there to be a physical price to pay as I get older. I still have a slight limp from a crash many years ago that was almost healed but resurfaced again when I broke my leg again at the start of 2005. Overall, as time has gone on my injuries have healed and there's not much I can't do any more. However, I do get to set off metal detectors when I go through airports. The security staff are normally impressed when you explain you have a metal rod in your back or ankle.

If I'd sat down with a fortune teller before the start of my racing career and been told I'd win three British Superbike Championships, travel the world, meet brilliant people, build life-long friendships and earn enough for a decent standard of living, but in return I'd suffer several injuries, then I'd have taken the deal with both hands. The trade off was worth it for sure.

Formula One drivers and MotoGP riders get paid a fantastic amount of money. Knock about six zeros off their salaries and you'll be closer to what I took home for my efforts. But racing has still given me and my family a nice standard of living, certainly better than if I had remained a signwriter. I haven't made enough that I can afford to retire but that's okay as well. I enjoy work and if I can stay within the bike industry then I'll keep on going – it's still a long way to pension age for me.

I was realistic about my earnings compared with World Superbike and MotoGP stars. You are paid what a team can afford and that was always good enough for me. In those two race series today, the sponsors are international conglomerates and budgets have gone through the roof. So has the media attention and television coverage, along with the pressure to perform, so I fully expect those guys to earn more money than I did. If 200,000 people were turning up each weekend at British Superbikes, the same as for MotoGP, then I could have argued for more money, but that never happened.

After reviewing all the ups and downs of my racing career, none of them come close to the main highlight of my life, the birth of my son. It sounds soft but it was the most moving and emotional moment I can remember.

I count myself as a hard worker who got lucky. The harder I worked, the luckier I got. You make your own luck to a large extent, but there are other things out of your control.

Meeting Vic Lamb, who put me in touch with Kawasaki, was a stroke of luck.

I'm also lucky I've always been involved with great people. No one has ever promised to do something and then let me down, they have always pulled through. A lot of people in racing are promised the earth and never get it and thankfully I avoided that pitfall.

I count myself incredibly fortunate to have made the good friends I have through my career. When you are a winner it is easy to be waylaid by insincere people wanting a piece of you, and sometimes it is difficult to know who your true friends are. In 2005 I found out who my true friends were; the ones who were prepared to stand by me as my time in racing stuttered and then came to an abrupt and very painful end. I count myself blessed that the friends I had while racing remained with me and helped me through one of the darkest seasons in my career.

Chapter 19

THE FINAL CHAPTER

Before the start of 2005 I had no inkling at all that this would be my last season racing. Some people may be able to tell the future or say they have a feeling in their bones but I'm not one of them. As the season approached I was training and preparing myself to defend the number one plate. I was putting in as much effort, if not more than at any time in my career and was confident about the job ahead.

I knew that a new GSX-R1000 was coming and had heard stories from Yukio Kagayama and Troy Corser, who'd been testing it before Christmas. Yuki had called Paul Denning and told him I was going to love the bike, that it was built for me. Yuki had been my team-mate for two years and knew exactly how I liked a bike to be set up, so when he said that it gave me a real lift. The new bike was physically smaller, which meant it would fit me well, and in standard trim favoured the way I liked my set up as the steering geometry and chassis were neutral and self-centring. Yuki didn't like that sort of base setting, but he knew I did and was enthusiastic for me. It was the dream start to the year.

Yuki had been called by the factory to join the World Superbike team for 2005 and we were all sad to see him go. He was an honest, fun character as well as one of the best riders in the world. He was also a massive asset to the team thanks to his incisive insight to the way a bike should handle and perform; we were going to miss him for lots of reasons. He was replaced at Rizla Suzuki by Scott Smart, the upcoming rider of 2004. Scott had won a couple of races on the Kawasaki and shown a lot of determination, talent and guts to earn the berth. On the way he had beaten me at Mondello Park, which was a lesson that my new team-mate was a fighter. I liked Scott and his family but wasn't going to let that have any impact on me at all. I knew my job was to win another championship for Rizla Suzuki and that's what I was concentrating on, nothing else. Whoever my team-mate was it didn't matter, because I was going to have to beat him to win the title.

Oz (Dave Marton), my chief mechanic from 2004, had decided to move on and was replaced by Stewart Johnstone, the man who'd guided me to my first British Championship back in 1992. I relished the idea of working with Stewie again as I admired his methodology and approach to racing. He was the one of the brainiest, brightest and most professional technicians I had ever worked with and had plenty of experience to go with it. His temperament was laid back: he was cool and positive. He was also brilliant with engines, chassis and suspension. In short, he was the complete all-round package – and he was on my team, which was just what I wanted.

Approaching the first test at Valencia in February we'd heard a lot about the motorcycle but not actually got our hands on it. We were running a little behind schedule and were going to be racing a month later. I was set on getting there, and working hard and fast at developing the GSX-R. I wanted it dialled in as early as possible. I meant business and was very focused when approaching the first morning of testing.

The first sessions before lunch went really well. I got a feel for the bike and started pushing it to see what worked and what didn't. As I rode faster we started to unearth little problems, like a weave along the straight. We cured that and then it was out again and it felt like everything was doing what it should and working well.

Getting on the bike I felt at home right from the first session. The smaller dimensions fitted my 5ft 6in frame. It was comfortable, it was almost exactly as Yuki had predicted and it could easily have been tailor-made for me. At lunch I didn't have much to eat as I believe that makes you lethargic and tired in the afternoon while your body tries to digest food. I was sharp and, in the first stint out of the pits in the afternoon, I did ten laps tyre-testing. The bike felt good, we knew we had better tyres to test and when I came in to the pits I was ready to make a few strides forward. We were doing competitive lap times already and I felt that with some better Dunlops in the bike we could see how fast it could really go.

With hindsight I think I was pushing too fast too soon. After a five-month lay-off from riding a motorcycle I had taken just a single morning to get to know a brand-new bike and just wasn't ready to break lap records. I maintain that you start the first test of the season around ten feet 'behind' the bike. The speed and capability of the bike are ahead of your ability to control it. Ideally, after the first test you are more 'on' the bike, controlling things as they happen. By the first race you want to be ten feet ahead of the bike, predicting what will happen and controlling this before it becomes a drama.

After a single morning I was so confident and comfortable with the bike that I was ready to push myself.

We put on a softer tyre to see what times I could do. For four or five laps it was brilliant. The bike was doing everything I wanted and expected and I was enjoying myself. It was on my final quick lap before coming in to the pits when I found out I wasn't keeping up with the bike and was still a few feet behind it. I came out of turn five, a second gear left-hander where it is important to get on the gas early for a long straight. The red gearshift light on my dashboard came on earlier than before, which meant it was revving harder and earlier, which meant I was going faster. On the straight the red light came on again and I changed into fifth for the first time in the day. I was going faster by a decent margin.

I sat up and hit the brakes as previously – and without warning the front end washed away from me. The data logging said I was doing 150mph when I crashed, which is a very serious speed indeed. One thing I need to be clear about here is that there was absolutely nothing wrong with the bike, tyres or anything. I was simply going too fast too early in the test. I wasn't able to keep up with, or in front of, the bike as I would if I'd been riding regularly or had a few tests behind me. Also, there had been some Formula One cars testing prior to us and the track was still dusty, which contributed as well.

I slid on the floor, then hit the gravel trap and it bit me. I dug in and was flipped head over heels a few times. The second or third time I was cart-wheeling at 120mph – my right foot buried into the gravel and stopped while I carried on. I was knocked out and when I came round my visor was missing and I felt badly beaten up. I sat up and could feel stones in my right boot. I lifted my knee up and felt all the bones below the knee moving. I collapsed back into the gravel.

A marshal was watching and it quickly became apparent that he didn't speak English and I don't know any Spanish. I was trying to tell him my leg was broken while fighting a wave of despair at such a serious injury with just over a month to go to the start of the racing. The marshal got the idea in the end, stopped the session and the ambulance came round. When they lifted me onto the stretcher they held my feet upright vertically. The doctor let go of my right foot and it fell over sideways. I pointed to it and he pulled it back in for me. That was the start of an absolute nightmare. One silly slip-up left me with a huge problem.

Spain is a lovely warm country but, if you ever need hospital treatment, then think again. I was taken to the Valencia hospital and left in a corridor hooked up to a drip. There were people everywhere. The doctor took an X-ray and said the bones were out of line and needed to be pulled into place. I told them to get on with it. I had two doctors holding my shoulders and two pulling on my broken leg in the opposite direction. The pain was so intense I nearly passed out. They then took another X-ray and said they'd have to do it again. I was less than enthusiastic but thankfully it worked this time and they transferred me to a ward with an elderly couple who didn't understand English. This pair proceeded to shout and argue with each other non-stop and it really started to play havoc with my head. The nurse kept bringing me food but I couldn't stomach any of it. I piled the sickly offerings beside me but nobody took the old plates away.

Rizla Suzuki's Robert Wicks and Niall Mackenzie stayed with me throughout the whole hellish experience and I started to beg them to get me out of the hospital and back to the UK. I had insurance but the company didn't want to pay for me to be flown back, saying I was too badly injured to be moved. The nightmare continued and I suggested to Robert and Niall that the only person who I knew could help us was Jonathan Palmer, the owner of Brands Hatch. A chartered plane had been ruled out, as had road transport. I really needed someone with access to a private plane.

We called and Jonathan got back to us straight away. A heart surgeon friend of his was on holiday in Switzerland skiing but agreed to fly back to England, pick up his plane, collect me the next day and take me back to East Midlands airport. I owe everyone involved in getting me home so much gratitude that it's difficult to express. I was suffering my worst nightmare in Spain and when I got back to England there was an ambulance waiting for me and everything improved dramatically and instantly. Once I was moved to the Queen's Medical Centre I was delighted. People spoke my language, the hospital was clean and I could eat the food. If you want to knock the NHS then go and try a foreign hospital first. You'll soon change your tune and be thankful for the services we have in Britain.

There were four breaks to my tibia and one to my fibula, all below the right knee. It had shattered. As I'd lain in the gravel trap in Spain the first thought I had was 'I can't finish my career like this.' I'd crashed out on the first test when I had everything going in my favour – I had the number one plate, along with the team and the bike behind me to defend it, and I'd thrown it all away in a crash. In a split second my fortune had changed from being brilliant to career-threatening.

But when I got back to England I met Dr Hahn, the surgeon who was going to be taking care of me, and my thoughts changed. He was a nice guy who knew how important it was for me to race again. He did everything he could to help get me ready for the opening race, which was just 38 days after my crash.

All of a sudden I felt there was a chance of fixing my leg and getting back on a bike again.

I was in hospital for two weeks and had an operation that placed a metal nail from my knee to my ankle, screwed in at each end. When I woke up I expected to see scars everywhere but there was just a single small incision in the knee, two at the side of my leg and two more at my ankle. I don't know how he did it, but Dr Hahn is known for pioneering surgery with minimal tissue damage, and I was impressed.

He told me that, because I'd suffered a high-velocity break, the chances were it wouldn't heal with the nail in place and he might have to refresh it in six weeks' time. That struck home hard because I was due to be racing by then and the last thing I wanted was a major operation coinciding with that. There was nothing I could say, but I think in the next six weeks he learned how important it was for me and for Rizla Suzuki that I race at the opening round.

I believe Dr Hahn actually became a member of the Rizla Suzuki team in those weeks. He was in charge of getting me fit enough to race and he has my thanks for doing everything he could to support me. I think he too wanted me to race at the opening round.

After the hospital I went to Ipswich to see Brian Simpson, the specialist who'd helped me with my collarbone breaks in the previous two seasons. He put me in hyperbaric chambers and tried other remedies that I think helped as well. I couldn't have worked any harder to get myself ready to race.

Then one day I heard a rumour that Rizla Suzuki was going to allow Gregorio Lavilla to test the bike and sideline me. I felt shocked and very defensive. I pleaded with Paul Denning to keep me on the bike and assured him I'd be ready for the first round, come what may. I felt kicked in the stomach thinking of someone else on my bike. The only feeling it can compare to is when your first girlfriend leaves you and you see her in the arms of another bloke. That's how I felt.

I think Paul could see my determination and, rightly or wrongly, made the choice to keep me on the bike. Loyalty is another of Paul's strong points and I was immensely grateful to know the seat was there for me to start the season. As the first round approached, my objectives remained the same as before. I was going to defend my title. I aimed to ride at Brands Hatch and score as many points as possible, then move on from there and build my challenge as I grew stronger and fitter.

With hindsight it was the right decision for me to keep me on the bike, but perhaps it was wrong for Rizla Suzuki. I was being very selfish. I didn't want to lose my ride and actually thought I could race with such a serious injury.

About a week before the season started I went to Mallory Park for a test and completed ten laps. It was difficult but I could physically ride the bike and was touched when my 2004 rival for the championship, Michael Rutter, visited to wish me well. That was a nice gesture from him and it lifted my spirits.

Racing at Brands Hatch was tough. It's difficult enough to race a bike when you're fit, but it's much harder when you're injured. I'd get on the bike and then find I couldn't move. I was stuck in one position because my right leg wasn't strong enough to push me around the bike. I had a special boot on my right foot and, because it had a hard cast underneath, it was quite a bit thicker than a normal boot. When I leaned the bike over going into the right-handers it would hit the ground way before the bike came to the edge of its grip and I simply couldn't lean the bike any further to corner as quickly as I wanted.

I'd visited Dr Hahn for a private session in the week before the race and he was quite happy with the boot I was wearing. But there was a warning: he made sure I was acutely aware that if I did crash, there was a good possibility I'd lose my leg. That was a sobering thought. It was never far from my mind all weekend, despite my best efforts to blank it.

After the first practice I was down in 20th place. I came into the pits and told my crew I couldn't do the job, but they rallied round me and altered a few things to make the bike more comfortable. I ended up qualifying 13th and scored two ninth-place finishes, largely thanks to the incredible depths of support I was receiving from my team and crew. They kept me going when I was ready to quit. For probably the only time in my life I was happy with a pair of ninth-place finishes. The reality of the situation was that I couldn't walk and shouldn't have been there, but I'd managed two top tens for all our efforts. I had to be proud of those results. Against all the odds I was there and beating some good riders in the process.

I knew it was possible to win a championship after scoring no points in the first round. I'd done it myself. Two ninths was a lot better than nothing. I didn't walk away from Brands Hatch – I was carried away, tired but with a bit more optimism than when I arrived.

At the start of 2005, racing a motorcycle held no joy for me. It was just impossibly hard graft, and painful. Being in the top ten, 15 or 20 was absolutely not where I wanted to be. I needed to be at the sharp end, fighting for the podium. That was what I enjoyed, but it was impossible with my injury. Rizla Suzuki was a championship-winning team that wanted to be at the front, competing for victories as well. There weren't many smiling faces in the pits for the first few rounds.

I went to the second round at Thruxton, thinking it might be a better track for me as it's fast and flowing, without many abrupt changes in direction or stop-start sections. I'd forgotten that

Thruxton, because it's such a fast circuit, needs complete commitment, which was something I didn't have in my armoury when we got there.

Every corner, bar two, is over 120mph and that needs courage by the spadeful. Early in timed practice I was following another rider through the second corner, a left-hander, at 120mph. A gust of wind caught his bike and he went down hard. I came in the next lap shaken. He'd done nothing wrong but crashed at high speed because of the wind. If that had been me I could have lost my leg. My head was in my hands.

When you're scared it's very difficult to go out and give it 100 per cent, but nothing shy of that will do in the most competitive national Superbike championship in the world. It was hard and frustrating – a horrible time. I knew I could enjoy racing again when I was completely fit, but wasn't sure if I was going to last that long. I knew it wouldn't be long before the bike would be taken away from me.

Many years earlier, with Kawasaki, I'd pulled in from a race thinking there was a problem with my bike. I'd vowed then never to retire voluntarily again, but I broke that vow at Thruxton. Ostensibly the team saw me outside the top 20 in the second race and ordered me in on the pit board, but I'd already made the same decision myself. I was floundering out of the points and felt embarrassed. I'm not proud of that one little bit – it was a low point. My Rizla Suzuki team technicians simply took this in their stride and continued to give me unbelievable support and confidence. Nobody shouted or let me know their disappointment. None of them told me the truth, which was that the bike was great and the only problem was the rider.

I knew the bike was on the pace. It was doing everything I wanted. I was holding it back because my leg hurt so much. To ride a Superbike at 100 per cent you need to be utterly committed. The rev counter in your head must be touching the red zone all the time and mine was well below that. I was erring on the safe side of caution.

The next round, at Mallory Park, wasn't a step forward either. I was beside myself with anxiety and it was one of the lowest points in my career. I withdrew from the first race and didn't even start the second as I was in so much pain and consternation over the terrible ramifications if I crashed. The weeks of healing seemed to be going nowhere. My leg was getting better far slower than I needed.

I got home and a friend called to say he'd heard talk that Rizla Suzuki was going to take me off the bike for the next round. I didn't believe that and said nothing. I had to visit Dr Hahn in hospital on the following Tuesday for another assessment and I was pinning all my hopes on him telling me the leg was healing well and making super progress. His diagnosis was the exact opposite. There was no sign of bone growth: the leg wasn't healing. I was breathless when I left the surgery. As soon as I got out to the car park I called Robert Wicks to tell him the news. Robert had already spoken with Dr Hahn and knew the score. He said, 'John, I hate to say this but it looks like we're going to have to pull you off the bike for the next round.'

My world collapsed around me and I started to shake violently. 'No Robert, please don't. Please do not take me off the bike. I promise I will not pull in.' He told me to leave it with him and, as soon as I hung up, there was a small voice inside saying 'Thank God for that'. I was still shaking with fear, worry and anxiety, but that was all tinged with a drop of relief.

As I was being driven home I came round to the decision. It was right to take me off the bike and put someone else on it. I needed time to get back to fitness. Two hours later Robert called to tell me I'd lost my ride for the next two rounds and James Haydon would be drafted in to take my place. I said that was fine with me and asked what I needed to do now. Where should I go? How could I support the team? What was next? The answer was simple. I was still part of the team and I needed to do everything I could to get back on the bike in around four weeks' time. That was all the motivation I needed.

At the start of the season, before injuring myself, I'd briefly considered retirement. I always wanted to finish as the champion and, if I retained my title in 2005, then I would have retired on a high point. Unfortunately, after the injury the chance of winning the title was shot. I was determined to see the season out, but thoughts of retirement were now coming thick and fast for different, darker reasons. I realised, coming away from Mallory Park, that I might never race there again in anger. That was hard to swallow.

My leg never healed during 2005. The best it got to was about 70 per cent, and that was in October, when I was at Brands Hatch. Thankfully the season started to improve for me at Croft, the sixth round of 13. Croft was the first time I was able to race aggressively, so much so that I ended up riding into the back of Ben Wilson in my frustration to get past him. It was a move a club rider would have made but the space I wanted was full of him and I ran off the track and fell over unhurt. The big difference was the commitment within myself. I was fired up and enjoying the racing again after a torrid four months.

In the second race I was in the top ten, following Leon Haslam and Gregorio Lavilla. I was amazed by how quick they were and how easily I'd forgotten how to push to that level. I was biting the screen trying to stay with them, but not far behind when the race was stopped because of the rain. When it restarted it was drizzling, I was on slick tyres and I couldn't get my head round pushing hard. All I wanted was a dry couple of races to find my form safely without worrying about crashing because of water on the surface. Slick tyres on damp roads are a lottery, so I rode as comfortably as I could. I wasn't prepared to risk further injury under those conditions.

After Croft, Scott Smart parted company with the team and James Haydon took his place. Scott and the team weren't gelling and it was the best solution for both I think. I rate Scott as a very talented rider and in the right team he can be a challenger.

By the time the season finished I'd scored four podium

finishes. The first one was at Snetterton and it was completely mind-blowing. At the time it felt like my first ever win – it was so important to me. The first person to congratulate me was my own team-mate, James Haydon, who I'd narrowly beaten for the final podium place. The negative thoughts from the previous rounds were obliterated.

Standing on the podium was the moment when I fell back in love with the sport – I sprayed the champagne and adored it. I'd come out of the doldrums and was able to ride a bike hard and fast for the full race distance. To get on the podium against the quality of riders I was facing was a real achievement.

There were rumours going around that the 2005 Rizla Suzuki GSX-R1000 had handling problems. I know Scott experienced front-end problems but I hadn't noticed anything like that early in the season, largely because I wasn't riding fast enough. As I healed I started to explore the limits of the bike's performance. That's when you quickly discover any weak points in the bike. The first on-the-edge crash I'd had was at Silverstone when the front end washed away from me. It was a surprise and I told my mechanics the bike felt great but suddenly went wrong without any warning. The problem didn't really surface again until the penultimate round, at Donington Park, when I crashed going into Redgate. I was on the brakes, tipping in, and again the bike washed away. It was a crash that should never have happened. We looked at the data and made an alteration to the top-out spring. In the next session I found the problem was cured.

Out of all my years racing, 2005 was probably the hardest of them all just because of my injury. To put in so much effort and receive so little reward is soul-destroying. When you perform well, the team is buoyant. You come back to the garage and everyone's smiling and it's easy to talk about going even faster. When I was qualifying tenth and finishing in the lower part of the top ten, there was none of that. Faces were grim and businesslike and my wheel-man and friend Stuart Smith would be banging wheels, throwing spanners into the tool box and shaking his head. No-one was happy. It's not pleasurable for anyone under those conditions.

Three-quarters of the way through the year, when I was healing fast, my thoughts of retirement started to recede. At Donington Park the GSX-R1000 was absolutely brilliant and I recorded my fastest ever lap time at the circuit on the way to challenging for the podium. I was over the moon, thinking I had a bike that could win and for the first time in the year I was a rider capable of winning. I crashed out of the second race but made the trip to Brands Hatch thinking the top step of the rostrum was achievable.

As soon as I started dreaming of winning again, any ideas about retirement were banished. During the break between Donington and Brands Hatch, I called Paul Denning and asked him what the plans were for the team in 2006. I told him I wanted to be back on the bike to recapture the championship we'd just lost.

While driving the motorhome down to Brands Hatch, the final round, I received a call from Paul saying the ride was mine for 2006 if I wanted it, and we'd sort the detail out later. I was the happiest man alive that Wednesday – there was a spring in my step despite the broken leg. I had high hopes for winning a race at the weekend to cement my new deal for 2006.

I knew I could win races and wasn't ready to quit. I believed I could win the title again in 2006 with the Rizla Suzuki GSX-R1000 – it was a bike that was capable of winning in 2005 and had been let down by me. After Brands Hatch I'd have several months to totally sort out my injured leg and I'd be 100 per cent fit for the start of the new season. I think I was riding well at the end of 2005, certainly as good as my injured leg was allowing. If that was good enough for podiums then I was certain that, when completely fit, I'd be a championship contender again.

Exiting Druids hairpin at 70mph, on my third lap in Friday's practice, I opened the throttle hard against the stop and was accelerating down the hill, getting ready for the left-hander – but it never arrived. I ran off the track at well over 100mph and hit the Graham Hill Bend crash barrier hard – the 162kg bike also hitting me for good measure.

I was unconscious for a moment and I can clearly remember seeing myself lying motionless on the ground. I was very still. I don't dwell on life after death and those types of thoughts, so I'm sure this was just a dream. Saying that, when I regained consciousness a few moments later the medical staff told me they'd been worried they might have lost me.

I was transferred to the medical centre and I was away with the fairies. I didn't know what was going on. I was looking for reassurance that my injuries weren't severe. Toby Branfoot, the series doctor, was with me and I was firing questions at him. As I spoke, it became harder and harder to breathe. Toby looked at me and told me to shut up as he had to do something that would hurt. He plunged a knife into my chest and turned me over. I hadn't been expecting that. The pain was blinding. I had a collapsed lung and he had to push a pipe in to re-inflate it. That moment of blinding pain made me realise that I'd suffered a crash much bigger than I'd thought. It turned out that, as well as the punctured lung, I'd broken four ribs, my back, neck and collar bone.

Within minutes I was transferred to an ambulance. I've been in plenty before but you know it's serious when the sirens and lights are switched on and the driver's speeding. I was terrified. I knew it wasn't just another crash.

In the hospital I had an MRI scan to look for breakages and brain damage. By then I was on morphine and other strong drugs to combat the pain. Six hours passed very quickly indeed. When I came round I was lying on my back with my head between two blocks and strapped down to a table. I wasn't allowed to move my arms or legs. I realised immediately that there was no way I was going to come back to racing. I'd spent all year battling fitness and a broken leg and now was facing paralysis. This was catastrophic. It focuses your mind. I retired from racing right there and then.

I spent a week in the intensive care unit in Derant Valley Hospital, near the Dartford Tunnel, and it wasn't pleasant. The staff were fantastic but I was a long way from my family and support network. I was also not allowed to move and that meant I couldn't wash my hair, which was encased in a plastic brace – the stink was awful. I was staring at a point in the ceiling for 24 hours a day and just had to cope with it because there was no alternative. It took a terrible toll on me and I was quite depressed. Shelley came to see me the next day, with mum. Dad had been with me the whole time, from crashing at the circuit, and warned them I was hooked up to machines and it looked bad, but they were both still shocked.

Usually they'd greet me with a smile but not this time – they were knocked for six. As soon as Shelley walked in I said, 'That's it Shell, I'm not sure what I'm going to do, but I'm not going to race a motorbike any more.'

'OK,' she said.

All I wanted was to be transferred to Nottingham, closer to my family, but I had to wait for a bed to become available at the Queen's Medical Centre. Shelley and the nurses were constantly in contact trying to arrange the move. I was due to go there on the sixth day but when Shelley called she was told it wasn't going to happen. She was in tears. Then the 'phone rang again. It was her mum, to say her dad had collapsed and was in hospital. She had Ben to look after as well. I don't know how she managed. My heart goes out to her for the emotional trauma she experienced.

Eventually, after a week I was transferred by ambulance to Nottingham and that was the worst journey of my life. They wrapped a mattress tightly round me and then inflated it so I couldn't move an inch. I'm not claustrophobic but it tested my mettle. The sister from Derant Valley came with me. I'd hoped to get into the ambulance and onto the motorway at 70mph for the two-hour journey. I couldn't have been further from the truth. With back injuries it's 35mph maximum and it took us nearly five hours. I said I was fine and asked them to speed up but they refused. Just as we joined the M1 from the M25 I suffered a panic attack and asked them to pull over. I couldn't go on. I felt ill. They explained that there was nothing they could do. If they pulled over I'd be in my cocoon on the hard shoulder of the motorway, unable to move. It wasn't like I could get out and stretch my legs or anything. I had to grin and bear it. The relief at finally arriving at the Queen's Medical Centre was profound.

Once there, I was assessed and they took the plastic block off my head. The doctor wanted to see what movement I had and I rolled around a bit. He looked a little perturbed and told me, judging from the scan, that I shouldn't be able to move the way I was, but the hospital had a policy of looking at the man and not the scan. They'd observe me for a couple of days before deciding whether I needed any further operation, but right now maybe I wouldn't need one. My spirits were improving– maybe I wouldn't need to go under the knife again.

They gave me a standing scan on the following Wednesday and later that day the doctor came to me and said the fracture might be unstable. They'd decide on Friday whether or not to operate early the next week. That was bad news but I accepted it. I went to sleep that night fairly relaxed because Friday seemed a long time away.

I woke up on Thursday morning and the tea trolley came around. It was a highlight of my day – a good cuppa. Next was the bowl of cornflakes. I'd just dipped my spoon into the bowl when the nurse poked her head round the corner to ask if I had eaten yet. I said 'no', and knew what was coming next.

'Have you drunk anything yet?'

'No.'

'There has been a cancellation and they've decided to operate on you this morning.'

My stomach hit the floor and she took away my tea and cornflakes. With hindsight I'm glad it happened like that as I didn't have time to fret about my back being sliced open and metalwork placed inside. The alternative option was to risk spending the rest of my life with a stoop and I wasn't prepared to accept that. Next thing I was being prepared for theatre and was knocked out.

Gary Keogh and Amanda Eager from Rizla were due to visit me that morning. When they 'phoned from the car to speak to me the nurses told them I was in surgery. They immediately called Shelley to offer support but she didn't know anything about it. She was due to visit later in the day.

A rod was placed either side of my spine to fuse the bones because they were unstable. I was in the operating theatre from 10am and didn't get back to my bed until 10pm. Shelley kept calling the ward and by early evening was worried, but the nurses told her if anything had gone wrong they'd have heard about it.

I remember lying in recovery with pipes and drips everywhere. One of the first people I saw was the surgeon. I asked if everything was OK – he said 'yes'. He showed me an X-ray and, although spaced out, I was still lucid enough to think that if he was happy then that was a good thing.

A couple of days later they stood me up and made a plaster cast from the bottom of my waist to the top of my head. They waited for it to set and then cut it off me. This was the mould for making a hard plastic body cast that I'd have to wear for the next three months. It was cut into two halves and came right up to my chin and the back of my neck. If I wasn't in bed I had to wear it to make sure everything stayed in place. If I slipped over it would offer some protection as well.

It was extremely uncomfortable to wear. Even sitting down watching TV was tough because the chin support pushed my head up and I couldn't relax. I ended up cutting the front piece off just to get back some quality of life. It was a calculated risk on my part and the doctors weren't impressed next time I saw them.

I'd spent four weeks in hospital and the next time I went to see the doctor I knew I'd be working for Suzuki in 2006 and needed to know if I could ever ride a bike again. I asked him what my chances were and he said there should be no problems with riding a bike again in March. I instantly thought about racing again and whether retirement really was the right choice. It was. That didn't take long to decide. I was in such pain and had put my family through too much to contemplate competing again.

The lowest point in my recovery came in November. I'm a big fan of the Nottingham Goose Fair in October, bonfire night in November, and Christmas in December. They're family events and highlights of the year for the Reynolds household. I missed the Goose Fair but was home for bonfire night. I got up on 5 November just to watch the fireworks outside the window. Then I got back into bed. That was all I did that day. It made me think how people with terminal illness must feel, grabbing glimpses of normal life when they could. I was out of my bed for only five minutes in the whole day and I spent as much time looking at my family as the fireworks. I was incredibly lucky to have them beside me and looked forward to being able to be a husband and father again – not an invalid. Back in bed again I cried my eyes out.

The road to recovery was very difficult. It was going to be hard work to get back on my feet. But if there's one thing that doesn't scare me, it's hard work, and I clenched my teeth and told my body to heal as quickly as possible.

At the end of 2005 I retired while still sporting the number one plate. I retired while I was still the British Superbike Champion, which is what I always wanted to do, although under different circumstances. There was no planning or design – just like the crash itself, this was unexpected, a sudden end to my career. It was a massive contrast to two days before the crash, when I'd been excitedly telling my friends I'd be racing in 2006 and going to challenge to win the championship back.

The 2005 British Superbike Championship was won by Spain's Gregorio Lavilla and he really impressed me. He came new to the series, without knowing many of the circuits, and won on the first attempt. He's world-class and was a very hard rider to race against. He doesn't give an inch on track.

A couple of times in 2005 the podium didn't feature a British rider. That adds credibility to the series in my eyes. It's almost a mini World Championship, which is great for fans and spectators, as well as for the riders. There's proper value in winning the title.

There continues to be fantastic strength in depth in the British Superbike Championship and, although I'm not riding, I'm very proud to have secured a job that keeps me in the paddock. This may be the last chapter of my riding career but that won't stop me from staying in racing and going for more championships as a member of a team.

Chapter 20

NEW BEGINNINGS

While I was in hospital at Darent Valley, recovering from my Brands Hatch crash, Paul Denning, owner of the Rizla Suzuki team, came to see me. I told him I was retired. He said I should think about it and we'd speak later. He didn't quite know the full extent of my injuries and was giving me the benefit of the doubt, because it's very easy to make a snap decision when you're in hospital and hurting severely. A couple of days later he visited again and I told him I was still retired and he accepted it. He could see the pain I was in. In typical fashion though, Paul could see the positive side and told me he thought there might be a position with Suzuki if I was interested.

I was still in agony and desperate to be transferred to Nottingham to be near my family, but that registered with me. Although I'd just retired from riding, the carrot of continuing to work within the motorcycle industry was exactly what I needed. After nearly 20 years of racing as a professional, that was my world. It was everything I knew and loved – not so much a job but a calling. Without motorcycling I'd be like a fish out of water.

Initially my plan had been to take a year out of work and try my hand at different things. I could spend the time reviewing my options before deciding on a new career path. I knew I wanted to remain within motorcycling, but wasn't sure how. I had a lot of experience under my belt, and that had to count for something. I'd witnessed Niall Mackenzie and Rob McElnea make the transition to team management and that appealed. When Paul said there might be a job helping out the Rizla Suzuki race team, it was exactly what I wanted and my plans for a year out were cancelled immediately.

I felt very touched that Suzuki was prepared to stand by me. I've always tried to be loyal to my employers, and for Suzuki to reciprocate was incredible. To think they had faith and value in me helped me through the dark days in hospital. I didn't want to disappoint Suzuki and that gave me a new target to aim for. I've no doubt that Paul Denning had a lot of influence in tabling the proposal, and for that I owe him a massive debt of gratitude. It's as if he knew what the best medicine would be for me and he delivered it. In one fell swoop, all of the insecurities and worries I had about my future – how I was going to earn any money and what life held out for me – were washed aside. I had a new focus.

As I continued to heal through the winter of 2005/2006, the fact that I was retired and had a new career path in front of me sank home. I'd achieved everything I could in bike racing and was comfortable to retire. I'd suffered crashes, travelled the world, won races, been soundly beaten and paid my dues. I'd experienced the highs and lows and now it was time to move on to new life experiences. I knew I'd miss racing but it wasn't as difficult as I'd feared.

I met with Suzuki GB at its impressive offices in Milton Keynes to find out what they wanted me to do. I was invited to be Suzuki's Brand Ambassador.

The job is pretty broad. The first aspect is to attend British Superbike meetings as Suzuki's representative within the Rizla Suzuki squad. I'm there to help with any advice or knowledge I can provide. At first I wasn't sure how I could fit in to what's actually a tight, highly efficient team of professionals, but as the rounds have passed it has been easier for me to integrate. Perhaps I'm a little shy but I keep telling myself I've a lot of experience and information that can help the riders and the team. My confidence is growing and it's great to be part of the team.

At the first round at Brands Hatch I was in the garage on race day watching the monitors when the TV cut to a picture of Niall

Mackenzie and me. That rammed home to me how much experience we have between us. Together we've won six British Championships. I think the TV commentator said as much.

Sometimes I take a scooter to a particular corner and watch our riders go through and then provide feedback. Are they hitting their apexes, braking too late or early? Is the bike composed or fighting the rider? How do they compare with the competition? I can recognise the small details that may just help to cut a tenth of a second from lap times when you add it to the rider feedback. After listening to the rider at the end of a session I might be able to suggest solutions or ideas to the technicians. I developed the Rizla Suzuki GSX-R1000 from a new bike in 2002 and know the old girl pretty well.

I feel one of the most important aspects of my new job in the garage is to listen to and support the riders. As an ex-rider myself, I know what they're going through and can empathise more than most. I know how difficult it can be for a rider who's struggling and maybe looking for new direction. I try to model myself on Paul Denning. He was always supportive. No matter what the result, he'd look for the positive side. If Yuki had stepped on to the podium and I was off it, then before going to the celebrations Paul would wait for me to come into the garage and greet me, pat me on the back and make sure I was valued. Then he'd go to the podium. That sort of support was fantastic and really helped when you'd had a tough day or bad luck. The boss understood and worked with you. You might not have won but his actions spoke louder than words.

I do my best to have the same sort of approach to the riders in the Rizla Suzuki Superbike team. I don't know how useful I am in the grand scheme of things but I like to think I'm contributing.

Team management is a job I'd dearly love to develop into. I've experience of racing and teams but I'm still learning about management. I've had some of the best managers in the business working with me throughout my career and I hope to be able to use what I've learned from them. I also think I can add my own particular insights, so team management as a career path is one of the most exciting prospects for the future.

Perhaps one of the most enjoyable aspects of the job with Rizla Suzuki is delivering pillion rides at race weekends. There's something invigorating about putting a member of the media or public on the back of a tuned GSX-R1000 and giving them a couple of fast laps. Their smiles and laughter are enough reward in themselves.

As well as advising Rizla Suzuki, I've a few other duties for Suzuki that I enjoy. The title 'Brand Ambassador' can sound a little like a paid-for advertisement but it isn't – and I'm grateful for that. I didn't want to be a hanger-on, doing little and not sure of my role. All through my career I've worked hard and always tried to deliver the results asked of me and I decided to treat my new job with the same vigour. For example, if I'm not at race weekends or tests, I'll represent Suzuki at its dealer showrooms around the UK. That means I'm working more weekends than ever before – and the great thing is that I love it.

I thoroughly enjoy meeting fans and customers. They're the best in the world, I'm sure of that. I know why they like bikes and riding, and it's a thrill to answer their questions and share experiences with them. I also help when Suzuki is holding major events, whether for dealers or customers. I attended the Isle of Man TT in 2006 and hosted a conference for 160 authorised Suzuki dealers. It was awesome, although I was quite nervous about standing up and speaking in front of so many people.

I started my racing career on a Suzuki 80cc motocross bike when I was eight years old. I finished my racing career on a Rizla Suzuki GSX-R1000 with the number one plate in 2005 when I was 42 years old. Suzuki has made me feel part of its family and for that I'm so very grateful. I'll do my best to repay the firm many times over.

In addition to the Suzuki job, a couple of my old friends and sponsors have also asked me to work for them now I'm retired. Teknic, the leather manufacturer, continues to support me and I make a handful of appearances for the company through the year at various events and showrooms. The same is true of Arai, the helmet specialist that was with me for the last years of my career.

The Department of Transport's road safety arm – THINK! – also uses me to champion the campaign for safer road riding. This is something dear to my heart and I hope my words carry weight and help road riders to think before they go out for a ride. Today's congested roads aren't the best place for exploring the performance of a modern Superbike. If you want to go fast, you should go to a circuit and enjoy yourself legally and in comparative safety.

Audi continues to personally sponsor me and some of the experiences I've had are incredible. Early in 2006 Audi flew me to Finland to drive the new Q7 all-terrain car – it was brilliant driving and navigating through the snow and mountains. It's a cracking car and was very impressive off-road, although that didn't stop me from putting it in a ditch when I tried to help someone else who'd crashed.

Audi also let me test new cars and during the summer of 2006 I got the chance to drive the 420bhp RS4 and 450bhp Lamborghini-engined S8. I've told them they don't need to look far if they ever have a spare berth in a Le Mans car...

When I'm not working, which isn't often it seems, I spend time with Shelley and Ben. My family is the most important aspect of my life and I love them both more than they could ever guess. Taking Ben to school and spending days with Shelley are simple joys I never really had the time to do when I was racing.

I sold my motorhome after retiring from racing and recently bought a new caravan so that we can go away as a family on holiday. We enjoy visiting the east coast of England during the school holidays. Ben likes the donkey rides, but over the years the prices have risen and I'm seriously considering buying him his own donkey for the future. I'm sure it would be cheaper than £1 a go ten times a day for three weeks in a row.

As Ben is developing an interest in motocross, I've bought him a little Suzuki JR80 bike to start on. While I was at it I bought one for myself so we could ride round together. We have a real blast and Niall Mackenzie has given us some great tips about where to ride, because he's going through the same enthusiasm with his sons Tarran and Taylor.

I've always been a bike racing fan and that has been compounded now I'm no longer on track myself. If there's racing on TV I'm glued to it. This also allows me to have my opinion whenever sitting in the pub with my Rizla Suzuki team-mates the night before a race.

Perhaps one of the most common questions I'm asked is about MotoGP multiple champion Valentino Rossi. Is he the best ever? I think that he is, without a doubt. To win in the 125, 250, 500 and then MotoGP classes shows incredible talent. It's not just the fact that he's a winner but the manner in which he's successful that's almost as important. He has ridden the best bike and won and then jumped on to a much less competitive bike and still won. The Hondas are the best bikes in MotoGP but Rossi took a Yamaha, a bike struggling to get in the top ten, and won the World Championship at his first attempt. The rest of the Yamaha riders on the same machinery continued to struggle to get into the top ten. His enthusiasm and charisma are also something special. He has a special ability to connect with the race fans.

I also get asked if I think I could beat Valentino if I was riding the same machinery? I'd like to think I could give him a run for his money but, to be honest, at my very best I'd be happy to have recorded a lap time within a second of Rossi on the same bike. Valentino is a class act. He has feel, vision, bike control and PR skills, and there are very few who could ever dream to tread the path he walks on.

It's wonderful having these sorts of discussions in bars and around dinner tables with friends. That's something I could never do when I was competing because I'd be in my motorhome preparing for the next session or race. Nothing could distract me from the racing. I can now have a social drink instead of being teetotal. Don't get me wrong, I still consider myself a professional athlete and keep to the same healthy living routines, but a glass of red wine every now and then is refreshing.

And what of Ben Atkins? I can confidently tell you that if Ben hadn't supported my racing at the end of 1994 then my career would have stalled or completely ended. Our families are still best friends, and Ben and I think of ourselves as brothers.

Ben still loves racing. After I left Reve Racing he felt he had no choice but to disband his team. He has always said he could race with me but could never race against me as he always wanted me to win. Now I've retired, however, we've been talking and Ben's interest in racing is starting to reawaken. There's a chance we could work together again in the future and there's nothing I'd like more than for us to come together and challenge for titles again.

There's one more thing to say about Ben. If Rizla Suzuki hadn't offered me a ride for 2006, I'd still have had an option to race. I'm not talking about Virgin Yamaha, HM Plant Honda, Hawk Kawasaki or any of the other established teams. It would have been a different opportunity. Ben was prepared to resurrect Reve Racing just for me in 2006 and to go racing in British Superbikes to hunt an unprecedented fourth title.

The thought that he'd do that for me blows me away. I cannot find the words to explain how much that means. I'm grateful for his gesture but more than that I'm humbled by the fact I have a friend like Ben.

I'm also flying much more than ever before. It's my hobby and I can't get enough of it. I have both helicopter and fixed-wing aircraft licences. I favour fixed-wing aircraft, largely because I was rather put off helicopters when Steve Hislop was killed in one, and they're also very expensive.

I've bought myself a little plane instead. This is a secondhand fixed-wing plane, which cost about the same as a family saloon car. I've only recently peeled off the British Airways stickers as it was an old training craft of theirs. I asked Insignia, the firm that makes Rizla Suzuki's stickers, if it would make me some JR logos with the number one plate. I got them and was then embarrassed, thinking I was being a real egotistical maniac, but they do look good on the plane. It's my pride and joy so I think I can indulge myself a little without feeling too self-conscious.

I'm really happy with my life in 2006 and so delighted to still be within the world of motorcycling. Without doubt I count myself as one of the luckiest men alive to have worked, and continue to work, in the motorcycle industry. The people who are involved in motorcycling and racing tend to be the very best the human race has to offer. As a bike fan I'm privileged to count myself within their number.

My injuries are healing and, apart from setting off the odd alarm while going through airport security because of the metalwork stitched into my body, I'm enjoying life more than ever now. Looking at my crashes, you could argue that motorcycling nearly killed me, but I'd disagree. I think it saved me from a life of hard manual labour and struggling to make ends meet. I'm very grateful to have had the opportunities to race. Motorcycling gave me, and continues to give me, purpose in life.

For me this is the final chapter of the story of my riding career, but I also view it as the first chapter of the rest of my life. And I'm looking forward to those new chapters in the future with a big smile on my face.

CAREER HIGHLIGHTS

1986

Racing career for this former British Schoolboy Motocross Champion began late season at Cadwell Park riding a 250cc Velocette

1987

Started season racing in Classic events, aboard a 250cc Velocette, enjoying a first victory at Mallory Park. Later switched to riding a RD350 Yamaha, and then a 350TZ Yamaha as he totalled 37 victories in club race action in a hectic and highly successful campaign

1988

ACU Shell Oils British Championship

Senior Stock

Round Four – Mallory Park – 12 June	6th (Honda)
Round Six – Cadwell Park – 26 June	5th (Kawasaki)
Round Seven – Knockhill – 10 July	6th (Honda)
Round Ten – Cadwell Park – 31 July	4th (Kawasaki)
Round Eleven – Thruxton – 20 August	2nd (Kawasaki)
Round Twelve – Mallory Park – 4 September	5th (Kawasaki)
Round Fifteen – Brands Hatch – 23 October	5th (Kawasaki)

(end of season, eighth overall, 48 points)

350cc ACU Star Championship (riding Yamaha)

Carnaby	1st

CHAMPION

British Junior Championship
(Riding Yamaha)

Mallory Park	2nd

(ended season ninth overall)

Honda CBR Challenge

Snetterton	3rd
Mallory Park	3rd

(ended season ninth overall)

1989

Motor Cycle News/ACU British Championship
(Riding Kawasaki)

Supersport 400

Round One – Mallory Park – 21 May	3rd
Round Five – Cadwell Park – 30 July	1st
Round Six – Cadwell Park – 24 September	1st
Round Seven – Donington Park – 1 October	1st
Round Eight – Brands Hatch – 15 October	1st

(end of season, runner-up, 70 points)

Supersport 600

Round Two – Mallory Park – 21 May	5th
Round Four – Snetterton – 16 July	6th
Round Six – Cadwell Park – 24 September	6th
Round Seven – Donington Park – 1 October	4th

(end of season ninth overall, 24 points)

TT Formula 1

Round Two – Mallory Park – 21 May	7th

Shell Oils ACU Supercup
Supersport 600

Round Three – Thruxton – 20 August	3rd
Round Four – Mallory Park – 3 September	5th
Round Five – Brands Hatch – 17 September	1st

(end of season 4th overall, 24 points)

Shell Oils ACU Supercup
750cc TT Formula 1 (Riding Kawasaki)

Round three – Thruxton – 20 August	8th

Isle of Man TT races

Supersport 400	9th
Production 750	18th
TTF1	24th riding a 750cc Kawasaki

Non-championship

Prince of Pembrey race	1st

1990

Shell Supercup/ACU British Championship
(Riding Kawasaki)
Supersport 600

Round One – Snetterton – 20 May	1st
Round Two – Cadwell Park 24 June	2nd
Round Four – Knockhill – 8 July	3rd
Round Six – Mallory Park – 2 September	3rd
Round Seven – Donington Park	5th

(CHAMPION, 41 points)

750ccTTF1

Round Three – Pembrey – 1 July	7th
Round Four – Knockhill – 8 July	6th
Round Six – Mallory Park – 2 September	5th
Round Seven – Donington Park – 30 September	1st

(end of season, 6th, 25 points)

Motorcycle News Superbike Challenge
(end of season seventh overall)

F1 National Championship

Pembrey	1st

(end of season, runner-up)

Non-championship

Prince of Pembrey race	Winner

1991

Shell Supercup/ACU British Championship TTF1

(Riding Team Green Kawasaki)

Round One – Snetterton – 28 April	3rd
Round Two – Donington Park – 19 May	8th
Round Three – Brands Hatch – 16 June	3rd
Round Four – Cadwell Park – 30 June	3rd and 3rd
Round Five – Oulton Park – 18 August	4th and 4th
Round Six – Mallory Park – 8 September	4th and 3rd

(end of season third overall, 122 points

Motor Cycle News TT Superbike Challenge

Oulton Park	1st
Donington Park	1st
Brands Hatch	1st
Knockhill	1st and 1st

(end of season, third overall)

Diesel Jeans World Superbike Championship

(Riding Team Green Kawasaki as a 'wild-card' entry)

Round One – Donington Park – 1 April	10th and 12th

Non-championship

King of Donington – April Spring Cup	Winner

1992

Motor Cycle News 750cc Supercup/ACU British Championship

(Riding Team Green Kawasaki)

Round One – Donington Park – 24 May	dnf and dnf
Round Two – Mallory Park – 28 June	1st and 1st
Round Three – Snetterton – 12 July	1st and 1st
Round Four – Cadwell Park – 16 August	1st and dnf
Round Five – Oulton Park – 6 September	1st and 1st
Round Six – Brands Hatch – 20 September	1st and 1st

(CHAMPION, 180 points)

MCN TT Superbike Championship

Oulton Park	1st and 1st
Snetterton	1st and 1st
Knockhill	1st and 2nd
Mallory Park	1st and 1st
Scarborough	1st and 1st
Donington Park	1st and 1st
Cadwell Park	1st and 2nd
Mallory Park	1st and 1st

(CHAMPION with 329 points)

World Superbike Championship

Round One – Albacete – 5 April	Dnf and 8th
Round Two – Donington Park – 19 April	13th and 9th
Round Three – Hockenheim – 10 May	Dnf and 8th

Non-championship races

Mallory Race of Year	Winner
also setting first ever 100mph lap average at the circuit	
Snetterton Race of Aces	Winner
Brands Hatch International 'Shoot-out'	Winner

1993

World 500cc Championship

(Riding Padgett Harris Yamaha)

Round One – Eastern Creek, Australia – 28 March	dnf
Round Two – Shah Alam, Malaysia – 4 April	12th
Round Three – Suzuka, Japan – 18 April	dnf
Round Four – Jerez, Spain – 2 May	dnf
Round Five – Salzburgring, Austria – 16 May	14th
Round Six – Hockenheim, Germany – 13 June	17th
Round Seven – Dutch TT, Assen – 26 June	10th
Round Eight – Barcelona – 4 July	dns
Round Nine – Mugello, Italy – 18 July	dnf
Round Ten – Donington Park – 1 August	9th
Round Eleven – Brno, Czech Republic, 22 August	12th
Round Twelve – Misano, Italy – 5 September	11th
Round Thirteen – Laguna Seca, USA – 12 September	9th
Round Fourteen – Jarama, Spain – 26 September	9th

(end of season 15th overall, 42 points)

Also raced in Suzuka Eight Hours	19th

(Riding Honda VFR 750R)

1994

World 500cc Championship

(Riding Padgett Harris Yamaha)

Round One – Eastern Creek – 27 March	10th
Round Two – Shah Alam – 10 April	12th
Round Three – Suzuka – 24 April	12th
Round Four – Jerez – 8 May	10th
Round Five – Salzburgring – 22 May	10th
Round Six – Hockenheim – 12 June	10th
Round Seven – Dutch TT – 25 June	dnf
Round Eight – Mugello – 3 July	dnf
Round Nine – Le Mans, France – 17 July	dnf
Round Ten – Donington Park – 24 July	14th
Round Eleven – Brno – 21 August	12th
Round Twelve – Laguna Seca – 11 September	dnf
Round Thirteen – Buenos Aires, Argentina – 24 September	dnf
Round Fourteen – Barcelona – 9 October	11th

(end of season 14th overall, 43 points

1995

British Supercup TT Superbike
(Riding Reve Racing Kawasaki)

Round One – Donington Park – 17 April	3rd and 2nd

(ended season 12th overall – 22 points)

World Superbike Championship

Round One – Hockenheim – 7 May	17th and dnf
Round Two – Misano – 21 May	7th and 9th
Round Three – Donington Park – 28 May	7th and 11th
Round Four – Monza – 18 June	9th and 10th
Round Five – Albacete – 25 June	12th and 8th
Round Eight – Brands Hatch – 6 August	4th and 3rd
Round Nine – Sugo – 27 August	9th and 12th
Round Ten – Assen – 10 September	6th and 3rd
Round Eleven – Sentul – 15 October	9th and 9th
Round Twelve – Phillip Island – 29 October	5th and 7th

(end of season, tenth overall, 155 points)

1996

World Superbike Championship

(Riding Team Suzuki)

Round Three – Monza – 16 June	dnf and 7th
Round Four – Brno – 30 June	5th and 8th
Round Six – Brands Hatch – 4 August	7th and 8th
Round Seven – Sentul – 18 August	9th and 6th
Round Eight – Sugo – 25 August	14th and 12th
Round Nine – Assen – 8 September	13th and dnf
Round Ten – Albacete – 6 October	7th and 9th
Round Eleven – Phillip Island – 27 October	11th and 10th

(end of season 12th overall, 99 points)

Also raced Suzuka Eight Hours	10th

1997

Motor Cycle News British Superbike Championship

(Riding Reve Red Bull Ducati)

Round One – Donington Park – 13 April	2nd and dnf
Round Two – Oulton Park – 27 April	2nd and 1st
Round Three – Snetterton – 11 May	8th and dnf
Round Four – Brands Hatch Indy – 22 June	dnf and 1st
Round Five – Thruxton – 6 July	5th and 3rd
Round Six – Oulton Park – 20 July	2nd and 2nd
Round Ten – Brands Hatch GP – 14 September	2nd and 4th
Round Eleven – Donington Park – 28 September	2nd and 7th

(ended season 4th overall – 227 pts)

World Superbike Championship

(Riding Red Bull Ducati as a 'wild-card' entry)

Round Three – Donington Park – 4 May	9th and 11th
Round Twelve – Sentul – 12 October	7th and dnf

(end of season 21st= with 21 points)

1998

Motor Cycle News British Superbike Championship

(Riding Reve Red Bull Ducati)

Round One – Brands Hatch Indy – 29 March	9th and 10th
Round Two – Oulton Park – 26 April	dnf and dnf
Round Three – Thruxton – 4 May	12th and 9th
Round Four – Snetterton – 10 May	8th and 8th
Round Five – Donington Park – 21 June	8th and 6th
Round Six – Oulton Park – 19 July	4th and 5th
Round Seven – Knockhill – 9 August	3rd and 9th
Round Eight – Mallory Park – 16 August	2nd and 5th
Round Nine – Cadwell Park – 31 August	2nd and 6th
Round Ten – Silverstone – 6 September	4th and 4th
Round Eleven – Brands Hatch – 20 September	2nd and 1st
Round Twelve – Donington Park – 27 September	10th and 7th

(ended season fourth overall, 252 points)

World Superbike Championship

(Riding Reve Red Bull Ducati – as a 'wild-card' entry)

Round Nine – Brands Hatch – 2 August	dnf and 14th

1999

Motor Cycle News British Superbike Championship

(Riding Reve Red Bull Ducati)

Round One – Brands Hatch – 28 March	3rd and 4th
Round Two – Thruxton – 5 April	5th and dnf
Round Three – Oulton Park – 25 April	dnf and 3rd
Round Four – Snetterton – 9 May	1st and·2nd
Round Five – Donington Park – 31 May	dnf and 1st
Round Six – Silverstone – 20 June	2nd and 3rd
Round Seven – Oulton Park – 18 July	1st and 3rd
Round Eight – Knockhill – 8 August	5th and 1st
Round Nine – Mallory Park 15 August	6th and 1st
Round Ten – Cadwell Park – 30 August	3rd and 3rd
Round Eleven – Brands Hatch – 19 September	6th and 1st
Round Twelve – Donington Park – 26 September	3rd and dnf

(end of season 3rd overall, 357 points)

World Superbike Championship

(Riding Reve Red Bull Ducati as a 'wild-card' entry)

Round Three – Donington Park – 2 May	7th and 7th
Round Nine – Brands Hatch – 1 August	4th and 8th

(end of season 18th overall, 39 points)

2000

MB4U.com British Superbike Championship

(Riding Reve Red Bull Ducati)

Round One – Brands Hatch – 26 March	1st and 4th
Round Two – Donington Park – 9 April	1st and 2nd
Round Three – Thruxton – 24 April	4th and 3rd
Round Four – Oulton Park – 21 May	3rd and 1st
Round Five – Snetterton – 25 June	3rd and 1st
Round Six – Silverstone – 2 July	3rd and 5th
Round Seven – Oulton Park – 16 July	5th and 3rd
Round Eight – Knockhill – 13 August	5th and 4th
Round Nine – Cadwell Park – 28 August	3rd and 4th
Round Ten – Mallory Park – 17 September	3rd and 2nd
Round Eleven – Brands Hatch – 24 September	3rd and 3rd
Round Twelve – Donington Park – 8 October	2nd and 3rd

(end of season 3rd overall, 405 points)

World Superbike Championship

(Riding Reve Red Bull Ducati as a 'wild-card' entry)

Round Four – Donington Park – 14 May	10th and dnf
Round Six – Hockenheim – 4 June	dnf and dnf
Round Ten – Brands Hatch – 6 August	4th and dnf
Round Thirteen – Brands Hatch – 15 October	1st and 4th

(end of season 17th overall, 57 points)

(also raced in Ford Fiesta challenge, taking 11th place)

2001

British Superbike Championship

(Riding Reve Red Bull Ducati)

Round One – Donington Park – 1 April	1st and 1st
Round Two – Silverstone – 16 April	1st and 2nd
Round Three – Snetterton – 7 May	1st and 1st
Round Four – Oulton Park – 13 May	2nd and 2nd
Round Five – Brands Hatch – 17 June	2nd and dnf
Round Six – Thruxton – 1 July	4th and 1st
Round Seven – Oulton Park – 22 July	2nd and 2nd
Round Eight – Knockhill – 12 August	1st and 1st
Round Nine – Cadwell Park – 27 August	3rd and 2nd
Round Ten – Brands Hatch – 2 September	2nd and 1st
Round Eleven – Mallory Park – 16 September	1st and 5th
Round Twelve – Rockingham – 30 September	3rd and 2nd
Round Thirteen – Donington Park – 14 October	1st and 1st

(CHAMPION with 536 points)

World Superbike Championship

(Riding Reve Red Bull Ducati as 'wild-card' entry)

Round Six – Donington Park – 27 May	dnf and 5th
Round Ten – Brands Hatch – 29 July	dnf and 7th

(end of season 24th=, 20 points)

2002

Motor Cycle News British Superbike Championship

(Riding Rizla Suzuki)

Round One – Silverstone – 1 April	4th and 2nd
Round Two – Brands Hatch – 14 April	2nd and 3rd
Round Three – Donington Park – 28 April	Dnf
Round Four – Oulton Park – 5 May	5th and 5th
Round Five – Snetterton – 3 June	2nd and dnf
Round Six – Brands Hatch – 16 June	1st and 4th
Round Seven – Rockingham – 23 June	6th and dnf
Round Eight – Knockhill – 7 July	5th and 4th
Round Nine – Thruxton – 11 August	4th and dnf
Round Ten – Cadwell Park – 25 August	4th and 4th
Round Eleven – Oulton Park – 1 September	8th and 2nd
Round Twelve – Mallory Park – 14 September	Dnf and 7th
Round Thirteen – Donington Park – 29 September	2nd and 6th

(end of season sixth overall, 283.5 points)

2003

British Superbike Championship

(Riding Rizla Suzuki)

Round One – Silverstone – 30 March	Dns – injured in practice
Round Two – Snetterton – 13 April	3rd and 3rd
Round Three – Thruxton – 20 April	12th and dnf
Round Four – Oulton Park – 5 May	8th and 2nd
Round Five – Knockhill – 18 May	3rd and 2nd
Round Six – Brands Hatch – 22 June	2nd and 1st
Round Seven – Rockingham – 6 July	5th and 5th
Round Eight – Mondello Park – 20 July	1st and 1st
Round Nine – Oulton Park – 10 August	dnf and 2nd
Round Ten – Cadwell Park – 25 August	2nd and 2nd
Round Eleven – Brands Hatch – 14 September	1st and 2nd
Round Twelve – Donington Park – 28 September	3rd and 2nd

End of Season – Runner-up with 358 points

World Superbike Championship

Round six – Silverstone – 15 June	6th and 10th
Round nine – Brands Hatch – 27 July	dnf and 2nd
Round ten – Assen – 7 September	dnf and 10th

2004

British Superbike Championship

(Riding Rizla Suzuki)

Round One – Silverstone – 28 March	3rd and 1st
Round Two – Brands Hatch – 12 April	1st and 3rd
Round Three – Snetterton – 25 April	2nd and 1st
Round Four – Oulton Park – 3 May	2nd and 2nd
Round Five – Mondello Park – 22 May	2nd and 2nd
Round Six – Thruxton – 6 June	2nd and dnf
Round Seven – Brands Hatch – 19 June	1st and 7th
Round Eight – Knockhill – 2 July	4th and 3rd
Round Nine – Mallory Park – 17 July	1st and 2nd
Round Ten – Croft – 15 August	5th and 3rd
Round Eleven – Cadwell Park – 30 August	dnf and 8th
Round Twelve – Oulton Park – 11 September	1st and 1st
Round Thirteen – Donington Park – 18 September	3rd and 6th

CHAMPION with 446 points

2005

Bennetts British Superbike Championship

(Riding Rizla Suzuki)

Round One – Brands Hatch – 28 March	9th and 9th
Round Two – Thruxton – 10 April	14th and dnf
Round Three – Mallory Park – 24 April	dnf
Round Four – Oulton Park – 2 May	dns
Round Five – Mondello Park – 15 May	dns
Round Six – Croft – 5 June	dnf and 12th
Round Seven – Knockhill – 26 June	7th and 6th
Round Eight – Snetterton – 10 July	3rd and 4th
Round Nine – Silverstone – 21 August	3rd and dnf
Round Ten – Cadwell Park – 29 August	12th and 8th
Round Eleven – Oulton Park – 11 September	3rd and 3rd
Round Twelve – Donington Park – 25 September	5th and dnf
Round Thirteen – Brands Hatch – 9 October	dns
	– injured in practice

(end of season – ninth overall, 139 points)

INDEX